E.U Bouzique

The History of Christianity

Vol. II

E.U Bouzique

The History of Christianity
Vol. II

ISBN/EAN: 9783744659123

Printed in Europe, USA, Canada, Australia, Japan

Cover: Foto ©ninafisch / pixelio.de

More available books at **www.hansebooks.com**

THE HISTORY OF CHRISTIANITY.

THE

HISTORY OF CHRISTIANITY.

BY

E. U. BOUZIQUE,

A RETIRED MEMBER OF THE FRENCH LEGISLATURE AND THE FRENCH BAR,
AUTHOR OF "LES SATIRES DE JUVENAL TRADUITES EN VERS FRANCAIS;" "THEATRE ET SOUVENIRS," ETC.

TRANSLATED FROM THE FRENCH ORIGINAL WITH THE CONCURRENCE OF THE AUTHOR,

BY

JOHN R. BEARD, D.D.

"And ye shall know the truth and the truth shall make you free."—
JOHN viii. 32.

VOLUME II.

WILLIAMS & NORGATE, LONDON & EDINBURGH.
MDCCCLXXV.

CONTENTS OF VOLUME II.

Book the Second.

THE IMPERIAL CHURCH.
(325-891.)

CHAPTER I.

FROM THE COUNCIL OF NICE TO THE COUNCIL OF CHALCEDON.
(325-451.)

PAGE

SUMMARY—Erection of Churches—Recall of the Eusebians—Deposition of Eustathius—Trial of Athanasius—Council of Tyre—Athanasius at Trèves—Marcellus of Ancyra—Death of Arius—Baptism and Death of Constantine—Return of Athanasius—Constantius favourable to the Eusebians—Council of Antioch, called of the Dedication—Athanasius at Rome—Councils of Sardis and of Philopopolis—Athanasius Restored—Photinus of Sirmium—Council of Milan—Athanasius in Flight—Council of Sirmium—Councils of Rimini and Seleucia—Semi-Arians Persecuted—Pure Arians—Macedonians or Pneumatomachs—Julian, Emperor—Restoration of Hellenism—Reappearance of Athanasius—Fresh Expulsion—Death of Julian—Return of Athanasius—Valentinian and Valens Emperors—Basil of Cæsarea—Philosophers Persecuted—Ambrosius of Milan—Apollinaris—Theodosius Emperor—Œcumenical Council of Constantinople—Laws against Dissidents and Idolaters—Priscillianists in Spain—Maximian Emperor—Jovinian, Bonosus, The Collyridians—Massacre of Thessalonica—Destruction of the Pagan Temples—Valentinian II.—Eugenius—Death of Theodosius—Pagano-Christian Fusion—Augustin Opposed to Manicheans and the Donatists—Origenists Persecuted—John Chrysostom at Constantinople, his Exile, and Death

P.

—The Pelagians and Semi-Pelagians—Invasion of the Barbarians—Capture and Sack of Rome—The Jews Driven from Alexandria—Murder of Hypatia—The Vandals in Africa—Nestorius—Œcumenical Council of Ephesus—Eutyches—Council of Ephesus, called the Robber Council—Œcumenical Council of Chalcedon— Canon Rejected by the Bishop of Rome—Capital Punishments against Idolatry — Progress of Christianity — Government of the Church — Ecclesiastical Orders — Monkism—Discipline—Doctrine—New Beliefs : Invocation of Saints ; Images ; Relics ; Pilgrimages—New Rites : Assemblies, Solemn Festivals, Fasts, Baptism, Limbo of Infants, Eucharist—Agapae Suppressed—Celibacy—Divers Superstitions . . . .

CHAPTER II.

FROM THE COUNCIL OF CHALCEDON TO THE SCHISM OF PHOTIUS.

(451-891.)

SUMMARY—Reaction against the Council of Chalcedon— Timothy Elurus—Peter the Fuller—The Henoticon of Zeno—Justinian Proscribes Hellenism and Dissent— Neoplatonism at Athens—Closing of the Schools of Philosophy—The Eutychians and James Baraeus—The Barbarians in the West—Attila—Fall of the Western Empire—Odoacer—Theodoric—The Goths—The Franks —The Anglo-Saxons—The Vandals—Belisarius—Narses —The Origenists—The Three Chapters—Vigilius at Constantinople—Œcumenical Council of Constantinople (the Second)—The Incorrupticoles—Disasters in the East— The Lombards in Italy—Precarious Situation of the Popes of Rome — Monotheism — The Ecthesis of Heraclius—The Type of Constans—Œcumenical Council of Constantinople (the Third)—The Quini-Sextus—The Suevi—The Visigoths and the Burgundians abjure Arianism—The Church of the Franks—Invasion of Provence, of Burgundy, of Aquitania—Charles Martel—The Abassides—Conversion of the Belgians, of the Anglo-Saxons, of the Saxons and other Germans—Mohamed and Islamism—Abubeker—Omar—Othman—Ali—The Ommiades— The Moslems in Persia, in Syria, in Palestine, in Egypt, in Africa, in Mauritania, in Spain, in Septimania— Worship of Images — Leo the Isaurian — Constantine Copronymus — Council of Iconoclasts — Irene — Œcumenical Council of Nice (the Second)—Opposition of the Franks—Charlemagne—Michael the Stammerer—Theophilus—Theodora—The New Manicheans or Paulicians—Kalifs of Bagdad—Almamon—Courses of the Saracens in Italy—Martyrs of Cordova—Felix of Urgel—Gothescalk—The Real Presence—Commencements of the Greco-Latin Schism—Procession of the Holy Spirit—Conversion of the Bulgarians—Encyclic of Photius—His Deposition—Œcumenical Council of Constantinople according to the Latins (the Fourth)—Photius Restored—Œcumenical Council of Constantinople according to the Greeks (the Fourth)—End of Photius—His Spirit Remains Behind—Domination of the Popes in the West—Ignorance, Riches, and Corruption of the Latin Clergy—Monkism—Benedictines—The Descent of Jesus to Hell—State of Souls—Superstitions—Mary—Peter—Purgatory—New Festivals—New Rites . . . 95

CHAPTER III.

Apocryphal Books, Fables, and Legends.

Summary—Divers Apocryphal Writings—Lives of Saints—Creed of Athanasius—False Decretals—Dionysius the Areopagite—Saint Mary's Resurrection—Legend of the Assumption — John — Peter and Paul — Fables—Discoveries and Transferences of Relics—The True Cross—The Body of Stephen—The Head of John the Baptist—Mark at Venice — James at Compostella — Ceaseless Miracles 190

Book the Third.

THE CHURCH OF THE MIDDLE AGES.

CHAPTER I.

From the Schism of Photius to the End of the Crusades. (891-1291.)

Summary—The Successors of Charles the Bald to the Empire—Dependence of the Popes—Their Bad Characters—Theodora and her Two Daughters—The Othos—Crescentius—Sylvester II.—The Approaching End of the World—Conversion of the Hungarians—Henry the Third (the

Black)—Leo the IX.—Berenger—The Normans in Italy —Greco-Latin Schism—Michael Cerularius—Henry IV. —Rules for the Election of the Popes—Gregory VII.— Celibacy of the Clergy—Investitures—Struggle of the Priesthood and the Empire—The Countess Matilda— Abjection of Henry IV.—Rodolph of Suabia—Henry Vanquished, Excommunicated, and Deposed—The Anti-Pope Guibert—Pretensions of Gregory VII.—Dictatus Papae—Death of Gregory VII.—Urban II.—Revolt of Conrad—The Crusades—The Saracens Driven from Sicily —Capture of Toledo—The Cid—Fatimite Kalifs—Seldjukides Turks—Capture of Jerusalem—Revolt of the Young Henry—Death of Henry IV.—William the Red— Disagreements of Henry V. with the See of Rome— Agreement on Investitures—First General Council of the Lateran (the Ninth Œcumenical of the Latins)—Innocent II. and Anacletus—Bernard, Abbot of Clairvaux—Second General Council of the Lateran (Tenth)—Arnold of Brescia—Abelard—Gilbert de la Poree—Conrad—Louis the Younger—Frederick Barbarossa—Alexander III.— Thomas a Becket—Third General Council of the Lateran (Eleventh)—Election of Popes—Saladin—Philip Augustus—Richard Cœur de Lion—Innocent III.—Philip of Suabia and Otto of Saxony—John Lackland—Latin Empire of Constantinople—Manicheans—Peter de Bruys —Henry—Vaudois—Crusades against the Albigenses— Fourth General Council of Lateran (Twelfth)—Begging Monks—Inquisition—Frederick II.—War of the Pope and the Emperor—First General Council of Lyons (Thirteenth) — Louis IX.—The Tartars — Charles of Anjou, King of Sicily—Conradin—Death of Louis IX. —Second General Council of Lyons (Fourteenth)—Reunion of the Greeks—Conclave—Begging Monks—Rodolph of Hapsburg—Sicilian Vespers—Loss of Palestine —End of the Crusades 219

Book the Second.

THE IMPERIAL CHURCH.

(325-891.)

CHAPTER I.

FROM THE COUNCIL OF NICE TO THE COUNCIL OF CHALCEDON.

(325-451.)

SUMMARY :—Erection of Churches—Recall of the Eusebians—Deposition of Eustathius—Trial of Athanasius—Council of Tyre—Athanasius at Treves—Marcellus of Ancyra—Death of Arius—Baptism and Death of Constantine—Return of Athanasius—Constantius favourable to the Eusebians—Council of Antioch, called of the Dedication—Athanasius in Rome—Councils of Sardis and Philippopolis—Athanasius restored —Photinus of Sirmium—Council of Milan—Athanasius in flight— Council of Sirmium — Councils of Rimini and Seleucia — Semi-Arians persecuted—Pure Arians—Macedonians or Pneumatomachs— Julian Emperor—Restoration of Hellenism—Reappearance of Athanasius—Fresh Expulsion—Death of Julian—Return of Athanasius— Valentinian and Valens emperors—Basil of Cesarea—Philosophers persecuted—Ambrosius of Milan—Apollinaris—Theodosius emperor —Œcumenical Council of Constantinople—Laws against Dissidents and Idolaters—Priscillianists in Spain—Maximian Emperor—Jovinian, Bonosus, the Collyridians—Massacre of Thessalonica—Destruction of the Pagan Temples—Valentinian II.—Eugenius—Death of Theodosius —Pagans—Christian Fusion—Augustin opposed to the Manicheans and the Donatists— Origenists Persecuted—John Chrysostom at Constantinople ; his Exile and Death—The Pelagians and Semi-Pelagians —Incursion of the Barbarians—Capture and Sack of Rome—The Jews driven from Alexandria—Murder of Hypatia—The Vandals in Africa —Nestorius—Œcumenical Council of Ephesus—Eutyches—Council of Ephesus, called the Robber Council—Œcumenical Council of Chalcedon—Canon rejected by the Bishop of Rome—Capital Punishment against Idolatry — Progress of Christianity — Government of the Church—Ecclesiastical Orders — Monkism — Discipline—Doctrines— New Beliefs: Invocation of Saints ; Images ; Relics ; Pilgrimages— New Rites : Assemblies ; Solemn Festivals ; Fasts ; Limbo of Infants ; Eucharist—Agapæ suppressed—Celibacy—Divers Superstitions.

IN the foregoing Book we have seen the twelve apostles announce the gospel to the Jews of Palestine, and Paul, breaking off from the Hebrew tradition, lay among the Gentiles the foundation of a church open to all men; we have seen introduced into that church, in the following generations, dogmas borrowed from the oriental religions and the

Greek philosophy; institutions having their origin in India, rites or usages imitated from the Hellenic mysteries. We have spoken of the earliest debates occasioned by Christo-theism and the divine triplicity which takes the place of the unity of the God of Israel. But the Council of Nice was far from putting an end to the disputations. The empire will be long agitated by the enigmas of the trinity and the twofold nature of Jesus, enigmas which will be finally settled by the authority of the prince rather than solved by the inspiration of the Holy Spirit.

Meanwhile Constantine does not cease to bestow his favours on the Christian religion, of which he calls himself the external bishop. The holy sepulchre had been long buried under a heap of ruins covered by a temple consecrated to Venus. The emperor demolished the profane image and levelled the whole spot. "There," says Eusebius, "there offers itself to the eye that sepulchre which may be verit-ably called the Holy of Holies" (the historian does not report by what signs its existence was ascertained). A church is built on the ground with a thoroughly regal munificence.

The aged Helena, the emperor's mother, proceeds to Palestine, where she builds two churches, one at Bethlehem, near the cavern where Jesus was said to have been born; the other on the Mount of Olives in memory of the ascen-sion. Christian temples equally rise in the principal cities of the empire; all of them are liberally endowed by Con-stantine.

He goes to Rome to celebrate the twentieth year of his reign (326). It is his last journey to that city. His pre-dilection for the new religion had rendered him odious in the eyes of the Roman people and Senate, of which a very large majority was still addicted to idolatry; they were profuse in words injurious to his person. Then Constantine forms the resolution of founding on the shores of the Bosphorus a new city, which will become the rival of the ancient capital of the empire (330). Already Diocletian and Galerius, by their residence in Nicomedia, had in some sort transferred the seat of Government into those regions there they were near at hand to resist the attempts of the barbarians on the Danube and on the Euphrates. The spot where stood ancient Byzantium is chosen by Constantine for the city which was to bear his name and that of New Rome. The worship of idols is interdicted there. Statues of brass are taken from the provinces to ornament the profane places of the new city; in the public squares, in the circus, in the imperial palace, may be seen the statue of Pythian Apollo, those of the Muses of the Helicon; the tripods of Delphi, Pan dedicated after the war of the Medes. The emperor at the same time applies himself to destroy the superstitions of the Gentiles. The vestibules of divers temples are despoiled; their gates are carried away and the edifice laid bare. The idols, brought forth from their privacy, are given up to the public gaze and stript of their ornaments; they are dashed to pieces or burned in the presence of the crowd. At Aphachus a temple of Venus is destroyed, in Cilicia a temple in honour of Æsculapius. The measure of the Nile which was formerly kept in the temple of Serapis was carried into the Church of Alexandria. Most of these facts, however, date only from the last years of Constantine and take place only in the Greek and oriental regions where the Christians exist in great number. Nothing of the kind is presented in the provinces of the west.

The example of the emperor contributes greatly to the increase of the numbers of the disciples of Jesus; but as yet no law restricts the liberty of the ancient religion. The worship of the Jews, pure of idolatry, also experiences the imperial good will. The patriarchs and the elders, who are at the head of the synagogues, are exempted from all personal and civil charges (330). Constantine endeavours to reduce the different sects of Christianity to unity. We have said what he did for the Donatists. The governors of the provinces receive orders to dissipate and destroy the other dissidents. A communication is addressed to the Novatians, the Valentinians, the Marcionites, the Paulianists, and the Cataphrygians, to exhort them to conform to the official worship. They are informed that their meeting-houses will be interdicted, their oratories given up to the Imperial Church, their other edifices publicly sold; they are besides forbidden to assemble anywhere else. The Arians are not yet considered as dissidents; they continue to communicate with the consubstantialists. Both in the eyes of the emperor are members of the universal church. There is even reason to think that the constitution of which we have just spoken, was drawn up under the inspiration of the Eusebians, then restored to favour.

Constantine appears always to have preserved in this regard the opinion which he expressed in his letter to Alexander and Arius. The theories for or against consubstantionalism appeared to him not matters of faith, but philosophical speculations and sophistical subtleties. If, in the Council of Nice, he acted powerfully for the Athanasians, he did so on account of his dissatisfaction with Eusebius of Nicomedia. When once his decision was taken he resolved to cause every one to accept it. A decree to that effect was issued with his concurrence. Resistance seemed to him rebellion. But the futility attaching to the question inclined him to welcome acts of submission without insisting on the form or the terms. This disposition of the emperor was profited by in order to obtain the recall of the exiles. The Eusebians had numerous friends at Court. Arius returned the first (328). In the profession of faith which he sent he declares that he believes in the Father, the Son, and the Holy Spirit, as is taught by the Scriptures and the universal church, and in that he says nothing new, but he carefully avoids stating that the son is consubstantial and begotten from all eternity, as was maintained by his adversaries. Nevertheless, the emperor is contented with the declaration, and limits himself to not yet permitting him to live in Alexandria, for fear lest his presence should excite fresh troubles. Some time after, Eusebius and Theognis, after having given the appearance of an adhesion, are also recalled from exile, and re-established in their sees. Eusebius, who recovers the favour of the prince, ceaselessly strives to ruin the credit of his antagonists, while feigning to be submissive to the official doctrine. From thence

Constantine seems to have acted under the direction of the Eusebians. Without searching for the intimate thought of each, he requires of all a spirit of toleration, and shows himself inflexible toward whosoever works favourably for discord or sedition. By ably playing this game they succeed in making him unfavourable to the consubstantialists.

The Eusebians first direct their attacks on Eustathius, Bishop of Antioch. He was one of the most ardent contradictors of the doctrine of Arius. He had vigorously used his influence against Patrophilus of Scythopolis, Paulinus of Tyre, Eusebius of Cesarea, and others. He accused Eusebius of Cesarea of not holding the consubstantial doctrine. He, on his side, charged Eustathius with professing the dogma of Sabellius; this was the charge that was ordinarily made against consubstantialists, and it was not easy to reply to it. A grave sedition having sprung up in Antioch, Eustathius, on whom rested heavy suspicions, is banished into Thrace or Illyrium, and remains an exile until his decease. In his place they elect Eulalius, who does not rule long, then Eusebius, who refuses, then Euphronius, who dies the following year, and finally Flaculus. These different bishops were all Eusebians; but a portion of the people and of the clergy, attached to the cause of Eustathius, separates from their communion. There results a local schism which is prolonged to the end of the fourth century. The Eusebians also depose and banish Asclepas, Bishop of Gaza, and Eutropius, Bishop of Adrianople. This party dominates over all the East, Egypt excepted. Athanasius, then Bishop of Alexandria, was a young man, eloquent, zealous, full of knowledge, and of an inflexible character. A simple deacon at the time of the Council of Nice, he accompanied thither Alexander, his bishop, and showed himself the most able adversary of Arius. He may be regarded, if not as the creator of consubstantialism, at least as its introducer into the Christian religion. During more than forty years he has defended it with the devotedness of a father, the skill of a subtle dialectician, and the obstinacy of a convinced sectary. The Eusebians, despairing of obtaining from him any concession, put themselves in open war with him. They skilfully work to his disadvantage the enmities which he drew on himself from the Meletians, whose schism still subsists, notwithstanding the decision of the Council of Nice, and the death of Meletius. Athanasius appears not to have employed in this affair all the conciliation desirable. The Meletians make loud complaints against him and the bishops of his way of thinking, imputing to him acts of violence, and even murders. The emperor had written on the matter to Athanasius, who, on his part, reproached the Meletians with illegitimate promotions of priests, unsoundness of doctrine, and seditions against the orthodox.

The Meletians present to the emperor different complaints against Athanasius; they accuse him of having levied tribute in Egypt, under pretext of purchasing linen coats for the priests of Alexandria, and of having sent the profit of the transaction to a certain Philumanes who aspired to the sovereign power. They at the same time denounce the priest Marcarius as culpable of breaking a sacred vase. Athanasius, ordered to Constantinople, justifies himself, and returns into Egypt with a letter from the emperor full of eulogy for the bishop and of blame for the Meletians.

The latter renewed their accusations, and first of all, that which concerns the sacred vase (333 A.D.). The circumstances that gave occasion to it are these. There existed, in a village of Mareotis, a certain Ischyras, who, ordained priest by Colluthus, had been reduced to the condition of a layman by the Council of Alexandria, which was presided over by Osius. That man did not the less continue to usurp the sacerdotal functions in attempting to draw to himself the inhabitants of his village. Athanasius sent the priest Macarius to seek him out. Macarius, according to the version of the Athanasians, found Ischyras ill in his bed, and contented himself with enjoining on his father not to permit him to intrude again into the functions of the priesthood. The Meletians affirm, on the contrary, that Macarius, entering with violence while Ischyras was at the altar, broke the chalice, overturned the table, burned the sacred books, beat down the pulpit, and destroyed the Church to its foundations.

To this accusation they add another against the bishop of Alexandria. Arsenius, a Meletian bishop of Hipsala in the Thebaid, had secretly retired into a monastery, under the influence of the enemies of Athanasius, according to some, in order to avoid bad treatment, according to others. This sudden disappearance excited suspicion of a murder. The Meletians charge Athanasius with it, who, they say, had cut off the right hand of Arsenius to make use of it in witchcraft. They carry into all places a withered hand, to excite the public indignation against him whom they accuse. The emperor convokes a council at Cesarea to take cognizance of the affair. But Athanasius, in justifying himself with him, succeeds in getting the assembly countermanded. The Bishop of Alexandria then enjoys tranquillity for some time, during which he applies himself to the task of maintaining and spreading his dogma of the consubstantial trinity. The opinion of the monks having great weight with the multitude, the Arians asserted that the celebrated Antony favoured their doctrine. On the invitation of Athanasius and other Egyptian bishops, Antony descends from his mountain and repairs to Alexandria, where he publicly speaks against the Arians, whom he treats as heretics and precursors of Anti-Christ. He is welcomed everywhere by great crowds. On his departure, he is conducted by a concourse of people; the bishop accompanies him to the gates of the city.

Convinced that Egypt will escape from them as long as Athanasius governs the Church, the Eusebians, employing every resource, impel the Meletians to reproduce their anterior accusations. Constantine, fatigued with so many complaints, convokes a council at Tyre, for the purpose of deciding on all things and terminating the troubles. Count Dionysius represents the emperor in it. A military force is put at the disposal of the Eusebians. Athanasius brings with him forty-nine Egyptian bishops. An effort is made to reproduce before the assembly the deeds already imputed to the bishop of Alexandria, specially those of the breaking of the chalice and the murder of Arsenius; but the accusations fail. Arsenius himself made his appearance and covered the enemies of Athanasius with confusion. Proofs failing as to the breaking of the vase, a commission is charged to make inquiry in Mareotis; six of the principal Eusebians compose it, namely Theognis, Maris, Theodore, Macedonius, Ursacius, and Valens. Athanasius seeing that everything is going on according to the wishes of his enemies, quits the city of Tyre to proceed to the emperor. Then the council draws up a decree which deposes him and forbids his entrance into Alexandria for fear he should excite troubles and tumults. By the same act, the Meletians are admitted to the communion, and each of them recovers his rank in the clergy. Letters are addressed to the emperor and to all the bishops to inform them of what has been resolved on, and to exhort them to have no more communication with Athanasius. While these things are going on, Constantine invites the council to betake itself to Jerusalem to dedicate the monument which he has had raised on Mount Calvary. The bishops repair thither, and the new temple is consecrated with the concurrence of the heads of all the churches and an innumerable multitude which had come together from different provinces. This dedication took place in honour of the thirtieth year of Constantine's reign, ten years after the council of Nice.

Arius and his partisans profit by the occasion to effect their restoration. Furnished with a letter from the emperor, they present themselves to the council by whom they are admitted without difficulty. Synodal letters make it known in all places that the Arians have been received into the bosom of the universal Church. Meanwhile Athanasius had carried his complaints before the emperor by entreating him to send for the bishops of Constantinople in order that he might justify himself in his presence. Constantine, who at first refused to hear him, at last yielded to his urgency. He writes to the bishops, and treating them as authors of trouble and suppressors of the truth, he enjoins on them to come promptly to defend their acts. Frightened at such a message, the Eusebians are not eager to go together to Constantinople: at first only some of the principal betake themselves thither. When they are before the emperor, instead of speaking of the breaking of the chalice or the death of Arsenius, they put forward a new accusation against Athanasius. He has, they say, threatened to prevent the transport of corn which is every year made from Alexandria to Constantinople. Athanasius, putting forward decided contradictions, maintains that such a thought could never have entered the head of a man poor and destitute of authority. Eusebius of Nicomedia declares that Athanasius is rich, powerful, and capable of everything. Constantine, flying into a passion, will listen to Athanasius no longer, and banishes him to Treves in Gaul. Nevertheless, despite the decree of deposition passed at Tyre, he does not permit the election of another bishop of Alexandria, and by a kind of compensation he also banishes John, head of the Meletian party, although the council has admitted him to the communion of the church, and re-established him in his episcopal functions. In his exile, Athanasius is well received by Maximin, bishop of Treves, and honourably treated by Constantine the younger, who resides in the metropolis of northern Gaul. While the bishops are united at Constantinople, a book by Marcellus of Ancyra, a partisan of Athanasius, is brought before them. The work has for its object to refute the author of a writing in favour of the Arians. Marcellus, in the ardour of discussion, had not been able to guard himself against an opinion which was heterodox in the eyes of all trinitarians. He, like Paul of Samosata, went so far as to declare that Christ was simply a man. Required to retract and to burn his book, he refuses, asserting doubtless, as he did afterwards, that his meaning was misunderstood. On this refusal he is deposed by the bishops who call Basil to the episcopate of Ancyra. From this decision the Eusebians drew a double profit; they dealt a blow on a friend of Athanasius, and at the same time proved that they did not deny the deity of Christ, as they were reproached with doing by the Athanasians. After being received by the Council of Jerusalem, Arius went to Alexandria to be admitted into the Church of that city. But the people had refused to communicate with him, and a sedition threatened to break out. Arius is recalled to Constantinople, where the emperor authorises him to present himself to the Church. Bishop Alexander resists, the Eusebians declare that the next day they will conduct Arius to the temple, and compel his admission, despite opposition. In effect the next day Arius comes forth from the imperial palace escorted by the Eusebians, and directs his steps toward the church. But on the road he is suddenly taken ill and is forced to go aside to ease himself. There his bowels burst out with an effusion of blood, and soon he ceases to live. Such an end under such circumstances receives different interpretations; some see in it an effect of divine punishment; others speak of poison. The death of Arius changes nothing in the state of things. The people of Alexandria in vain demand the return of Athanasius; in vain Antony writes several letters to the Emperor. Constantine imposes silence on the Alexandrines; in his reply to the hermit, he puts forward the sentence of the Council, saying that if some of the judges might have yielded to hate or to favour, it is not credible that so great a number of bishops acted from such motives. Athanasius, he adds, is a proud spirit, dealer in discord. In 337 the emperor, being sick and feeling his end near, determines to ask for baptism. He is admitted as a catechist at Helenopolis, then repairing to the neighbourhood of Nicomedia, he there receives baptism in presence of the bishops, and partakes of what are called the sacred mysteries (of the Communion). He was baptised by Eusebius of Nicomedia.

Then Constantine takes measures for transmitting the empire to his three sons, no one of whom is near his person. At each of the ten years of his thirty years' reign he had nominated them Cæsars; at the first, Constantine, the eldest of the three, was put at the head of the western provinces. At the second the oriental regions were decreed to Constantius. Constans, the youngest, was declared Cæsar at the third decennium. After the death of the aged emperor, his states are divided among them as his paternal heritage; Constantine has Gaul, Spain, Brittany; Constantius receives Italy, Africa, and Illyrium; Constans guards the provinces of the east. Constantine left also a brother, Jules Constantius, and two nephews, Jules Dalmatius, and Claude

Hannibalian, children of a brother who had died before him. Dalmatius had received from his uncle the title of Cæsar, with Thrace, Macedonia, and Achaia ; Hannibalian, under the title of king, governed Armenia, Pontus, and Cappadocia. Shortly after Constantine's death these three princes are massacred by the soldiers on a secret order from Constantius as is presumed. Jules Constantius had two sons, Gallus and Julian, who was afterwards emperor. Both of them were spared, Gallus on account of his bad health, Julian by reason of his youth. The three emperors recall those who are in banishment. Athanasius leaves Treves, furnished with a letter from Constantine the younger for the people of Alexandria (338). He passes through Constantinople, finds Constantius at Cæsarea in Cappadocia, and traverses Syria to make his way into Egypt. He is received by the Alexandrines with great joy ; his return had even been preceded by a reaction in which excesses were committed which are imputed to Athanasius. The Eusebians endeavour to prejudice Constantius against him, but without much success during the life of Constantine the younger ; Constantius does not wish to commit himself with his brother in connection with religious quarrels.

Alexander, bishop of Constantinople, having died in the year 339, the city is divided into two camps on the choice of his successor. Paul is elected by the partisans of Consubstantialism. But Constantius, who was absent, on his return convenes a council which annuls that election, and chooses Eusebius of Nicomedia ; the new bishop openly saps the doctrine of the Council of Nice; these disputes shake the whole of the East. Constantine the younger is killed by soldiers while he is preparing to attack his brother Constans; the latter remains alone at the head of the Western provinces (340).

Then the Eusebians have an open field before them. Till then, under the Emperors, as in the lifetime of their father, they had in appearance held the creed of the Council of Nice. But after the death of Constantine the younger, assured of the favour of Constans, they no longer keep terms with the Athanasians. In the year 341, on occasion of the dedication of the Church of Antioch, whose foundations his father had laid, Constans got together in that city ninety-seven bishops of the East, Eusebians for the most part; not one Western bishop comes to the Council; Constans attends in person, and confirms the resolutions passed. First the accusations against Athanasius are revived. To the ancient charges which had caused him to be deposed at Tyre new reproaches are added, to the effect that despite his deposition, he resumed possession of his see, contrary to the laws of the Church; that a great number of persons had perished in the tumult excited at his return, and that he himself had committed cruelties and acts of violence against many others. Gregory of Cappadocia is appointed his successor, and he is conducted into Egypt by the prefect Philager and the eunuch Arsacius.

Afterwards the Council occupies itself with the abrogation of Consubstantialism. In their synodal letter, the Fathers begin by saying that they have never been followers of Arius. Members of the Episcopate, how could they tread in the steps of a mere priest? But after due examination they approve his doctrine; then they give their profession of belief in these terms:—

"We have from the beginning learnt to believe in one sole God the creator and preserver of all things sensible and intelligible, and in his own only son, subsisting before all ages and co-existent with the Father by whom he was begotten; by whom all things visible and invisible were made; who in these latter days came down from heaven, according to the Father's will, took flesh of the virgin Mary, and, after fulfilling all the will of his Father, suffered death, rose again, went back into heaven; who sits at the right hand of the Father; who will come to judge the living and the dead; who remains King and God through all ages. We also believe in the Holy Spirit, and, if there is need to add it, we believe also in the resurrection of the flesh and everlasting life."

In this formula no mention is made of the substance of the Father and of the Son, nor of the terms omoousian (of the same substance) or omoiousian (of similar substance); every expression which is not admitted by one or the other of the two parties is advisedly omitted ; but to omit the word omoiousian, after the Council of Nice, was evidently to refuse that qualification to the Son. At the same time the Council publishes another exposition of belief, said to have been composed by Lucian the martyr, and written by his own hand. In this it is indeed affirmed that the Son was begotten before all ages, that he is changeless, the perfect image of the deity, of the substance, the power, the will, and the glory of the Father ; but it is not said that he is co-eternal and consubstantial. The Eusebians circulate it in order to weaken the doctrine of Nice, and, under the name of Lucian, to support their own opinion that the Son is similar in substance to the Father—an opinion which, to please the Emperor, they did not put forth in the Exposition of the Council. The Athanasians, on their part, deny the authenticity of the letter attributed to Lucian, and maintain that it is the fraudulent product of the Antioch Fathers ; cautious people remain in doubt. However, in the public formula bearing the name of the Council, the Eusebians henceforth had a creed to put in opposition to that of their adversaries. But while disallowing the authority of the Nicene Fathers, those of Antioch opened the way to new contests, and gave to others a right to abrogate their own decisions. If Eusebius of Nicomedia had survived a certain time, he might perhaps have succeeded in maintaining the Antioch symbol ; his death, which took place the following year (342) contributed to occasion in his party divisions which the consubstantialists turned to their own account.

Independently of its decrees in the matter of belief, the Council of Antioch had also published on discipline twenty-five canons which were generally received. However, Gregory of Cappadocia, supported by public force, puts himself in possession of the see of Alexandria, and, as his adversaries assert, commits all sorts of violence against the Athanasians, especially against the clergy, monks, and virgins.

These accusations of abuse of power and of ill-usage are reciprocal between the two parties ; they hurl them the one at the other. Making allowance for exaggeration, we cannot deny acts of intolerance on the part of the majority of the bishops. The spirit of persecution seems to have passed from the Gentiles to the Christians; the latter frequently run both against dissidents and against Hellenism, to the same excesses as were formerly endured by the new religion. The Eusebians, possessors of the sees of Constantinople, Antioch, and Alexandria are masters throughout the East. But Athanasius, foreseeing the storm, had, before that of Antioch, got together a council in Alexandria, composed of a hundred bishops of Egypt, the Thebaid, Libya, and the Pentapolis; a synodal letter had been addressed in his favour to all bishops, and specially to Julius, bishop of Rome (337-352), constrained to flee at the time of the intrusion of Gregory. Athanasius sends from the place of his retreat a circular to the bishops of his communion, to inform them of the facts and to exhort them to sustain the common cause. A short time after he embarks secretly for Italy. Julius gives him a distinguished welcome in Rome. About the same time there arrive in that city other bishops, equally driven from their sees by the Eusebians, among others Marcellus of Ancyra, Lucian of Andrianopolis, Aesculapius of Gaza, and Paul of Constantinople. Down till now the West had remained a stranger to all these divisions; few Latins had been present in the Council of Nice, but its doctrine was generally received in the Western provinces. The majority of the bishops of those regions, not understanding the questions controverted among the Orientals, saw no reason for returning to the first decisions. If the Fathers of Nice had decided in favour of Arius, their opinion would have been equally admitted in the West, who would have upheld it with no less firmness. In the midst of these sophistical debates the wisest step would have been to cling to the first solution, whatever it was; the ignorance of the West had in the actual circumstances less inconveniences than the subtlety of the Orientals. This state of mind on the part of the Latins naturally led Athanasius and his party to seek among them for refuge and aid. Julius writes to the Orientals complaining of what had been done in Antioch without his participation, and instructs them to send some of their party to explain matters before a council which he was about to convene in Rome. The bishops of the East, in their reply, express their astonishment at the pretensions of Julius; without denying the illustrious character of the Roman Church, they, with a certain irony, recall the fact that its first doctors came from the East; and that their residing in cities less imposing did not make them inferior to him, if they surpassed him in virtue, knowledge, and wisdom. On the day indicated by Julius there assemble in Rome some fifty bishops, by whom Marcellus of Ancyra and the others are justified and received into communion. A synodal letter is sent to the Eusebians, but it does not reach the East till after the death of Eusebius of Nicomedia. At the news of that event, Paul returns to resume the see of Constantinople. The Arians on their side ordain Macedonius in another church. Something like a civil war arises. Constans, hastening from Antioch, where he still remains, drives away Paul again, without confirming the election of Macedonius. Athanasius continues to reside at Rome. Julius, in agreement with him and other bishops, persuades Constans that the assembling of an Œcumenical council is necessary for putting an end to the troubles. The emperor comes to an understanding with his brother, and they convoke a council at Sardica in Illyrium, on the confines of the two empires (347). One hundred and seventy bishops assemble there, both Greeks and Latins, but the Greeks demand, to join themselves to their colleagues, that those should separate from Athanasius, Marcellus, and others, whom the Eastern Councils had already condemned. On the refusal of the Westerns, the Eastern bishops quit Sardica and retire to Philippopolis in Thrace, a city under the dominion of Constans. By this withdrawal the council, losing the quality of œcumenical, which it had been wished it should bear, divides into two parts, one consisting of Latins at Sardica, the other of Greeks at Philippopolis. The Assembly of Sardica acknowledges the innocence of Athanasius by whom it is led, of

Marcellus, of Æsculapius, and other exiles, while forcibly reproaching those who pronounced their condemnation. It then deposes Theodorus of Heraclea, Narcissus of Neroniades, Acasius of Cæsarea, Stephen of Antioch, Ursatius of Singidon, Valens of Mursa, Menophantes of Ephesus, George of Laodicea. Nothing was determined as to belief in this Latin council, the fathers holding to the symbol of Nice. But they drew up on discipline several canons, whose authenticity was afterwards contested, especially that which authorised appeals to the See of Rome, on the part of the bishops condemned in the council of their province. Such a prerogative has always been denied to that See by the Eastern Churches and even by the Church of Africa, as contrary to the sixth canon of Nice and the second of the Œcumenical Council of Constantinople (381). The bishops of the East, on their part, assembled at Philippopolis, seventy-three in number, anathematise and depose Julius of Rome, Hosius, Protegencs of Sardis, Gaudentius, Maximin of Treves, Athanasius, Marcellus, Paul, and Asclepas. They address to all the churches an encyclical letter, forcibly incriminating the last four, they complain that the Westerns presented themselves at Sardica as their defenders and not as their judges, and pretended to have jurisdiction over oriental bishops; they end with an exposition of belief in which the word consubstantial is not found. The fathers of Philippopolis take measures moreover against both different Eastern bishops who are opposed to them and the re-establishment of those who were restored at Sardica. Thus the East and the West were divided in church communion. Nearly all the Western bishops hold to the Council of Nice. The contrary opinion prevails in the oriental regions, although it was combatted by Paul and Athanasius, and specially by an incredible number of monks.

Each of the two emperors protecting the belief which predominates in his provinces, the decisions of the fathers of Sardica remain a dead letter in the East, as do those of the fathers of Philippopolis in the West. The Western bishops request through the Emperor Constans the re-establishment of Paul at Constantinople and that of Athanasius at Alexandria; the letter of that prince even threatens to restore them by force; it is no merit on the part of the Episcopate that war does not break out between the two brothers. But Constantius, whose spirit is not bellicose, prefers mildness toward the Consubstantialists. The exiled priests and deacons are set at liberty; all persecution against the Athanasians is suspended. On hearing these things the multitude of Alexandria rises and murders Bishop George through resentment or in the hope of thus facilitating the return of Athanasius. Constantius writes thrice to the latter, bidding him return to his native land without fear (349). At last the bishop puts himself on his journey. At Antioch he has an interview with the emperor, who gives him letters for the inhabitants of Alexandria. Most of the bishops of Syria welcome him warmly. Those of Palestine, assembled in Jerusalem, give him a synodal letter for the Egyptian disciples. Athanasius, on his arrival, deposes the Arian priests and bishop of that country. It is even said that he had done the same in other provinces which were not dependent on him. Paul of Constantinople, Marcellus of Ancyra, Lucian of Adrianople, Æsculapius of Gaza obtain, like him, permission to return into their churches. Ursatius and Valens, whose dioceses make part of the Western empire, write letters of repentance to Athanasius as well as to the bishop of Rome who consent to admit them into their communion. But at the death of Constans, they return to the Arians, saying that their retractation had been extorted by violence (351).

In effect that death changes the entire state of things. The bishops who had been restored are exiled afresh. Marcellus is expelled from Ancyra; Lucian dies in prison; Paul, banished to Cucusa in Armenia, soon dies there, not without suspicion of violence. Macedonius resumes possession of the See of Constantinople. The Arians renew their accusations against Athanasius, but the emperor, then at war with the usurper Magnentius, writes to that bishop to give him confidence, doubtless from fear of raising religious troubles in the grave circumstances of the moment.

In the midst of these discussions, occasioned by the Greek and Oriental philosophy, a voice was raised among the bishops to restore to honour the doctrine of Jesus and the apostles on the divine nature. Photinus, a native of Galatia and a former disciple of Marcellus of Ancyra, having, owing to his merit, been called to the bishopric of Sirmium, metropolis of Illyria, soon spread abroad doctrines which, without doubt, he had learnt from his master, but which he maintained with more consistency and firmness. He recognised only one God who had created all things by his word; he denied the generation of the son before the ages, and maintained that the existence of Christ began in Mary's womb. These opinions were heterodox in the eyes of all the Trinitarians, whether Arians or Athanasians, Photinus found himself condemned by both. But his eloquence and good character having procured him the favour of the people, he had succeeded in maintaining himself in his See down to the war against Magnentius. Then the emperor came to Sirmium to await the issue of battle. Photinus, far from concealing his opinions, does not hesitate to publish them still more openly; hence great scandal and great tumult. Constans irritated, convokes at Sirmium a council of Eastern bishops with some Western ones. Photinus is deposed as professing the dogmas of Sabellius and of Paul of Samosata. Exiled by the emperor, he nevertheless continues to advance his opinions.

The defeat of Magnentius, followed by his death, finally leaves Constans full liberty to act against the Consubstantialists (353). The Arians denounce to him Athanasius as having tried to raise civil war between the two brothers, and as having by letters put himself into communication with the usurper Magnentius. The emperor assembles a council at Milan (355). The Eastern bishops repair thither in small number, but there were present nearly 300 Westerns. The Arians have the direction; all means are employed to oblige the western bishops to commune with them, and to subscribe to the condemnation of Athanasius. Some resist and are sent into exile. The greater number, yielding to terror, submit to the will of the prince. The

Arians have full power in the empire. Threats, fines, banishment, are employed against those who refuse to condemn Athanasius. After having been severe on a great number of others, Constans endeavours to seduce Liberius, Bishop of Rome (352-366). The latter repels emissaries, and rejects presents. Taken before the emperor, he withstands all urgency. He is banished to Berea in Thrace, and a person named Felix, who tries to keep in with the two opinions, is placed in the see of Rome. At the same time the governors of Egypt receive orders to seize Athanasius at any cost (356). He escapes from the soldiers who come to seize him, and takes refuge in the desert, where he is looked for in vain. George, elected by the Arians, is put into possession of the see of Alexandria. Throughout Egypt the Athanasian bishops are driven away, and the churches put into the hands of their antagonists. Severity is used toward the monks, all of whom remain attached to the Council of Nice. The persecution makes itself felt not less at Constantinople under the direction of Macedonius. It even reaches the Novatians, who, notwithstanding their schism, do not the less combat the Arian doctrines. Among the bishops exiled on account of their Consubstantialism, some remain always firm; others, beaten down by the hardness of the penalty, yield at last, and come to an understanding with Arianism. In 357 the bishops, assembled again at Sirmium, publish another formula, in which the words substance and consubstantial are designedly omitted because, it is said, they are not found in Scripture, and because those things are above human knowledge. Afterwards it is declared that the Father is greater than the Son in honour, in dignity, in glory, in majesty; that the Son is subject to the Father, who alone is without beginning, invisible, impassable, immortal. Hosius, more than a hundred years old, had been detained at Sirmium during a year. By bad treatment he is brought to commune with Ursatius and Valens, and to subscribe the new formula, without yielding so as to condemn Athanasius. He dies shortly after, protesting, it is said, against the violence that had been put upon him. Liberius, overcome by two years of exile, finally consents to all that is demanded of him ; he subscribes the formula of Sirmium, as well as the condemnation of Athanasius, and solicits friendship and communion with the Arians. In 358 he re-enters Rome, when he becomes governor in common with Felix ; but the latter is soon constrained to retire, and dies far from the capital. Henceforward Arianism is the official religion. Everything seems to correspond to the desires of its partizans. Then division arises in the midst of them, and they separate into several sects. Ætius, deacon of the church of Antioch, resuming the primitive opinion of Arius, publishes openly that the Son is derived from nothing, and that he is unlike the Father. Seconded by Eudoxus, who has passed from the see of Constantinople to that of Antioch, he founds the sect of the pure and true Arians, and who are accordingly called Anomeans (not similar). The other Arians (or the Eusebians), who are the more numerous, then receive the name of Semi-Arians. Basil, Bishop of Ancyra is their principal doctor. Most of them differ from the Athanasians only in not admitting Consubstantialism, however different opinions spring up in their bosom.

These dissensions give rise to a desire for a new council ; but the difficulty of bringing together in the same place the Eastern and the Western bishops, leads to the holding of two distinct assemblies. The westerns are convened at Rimini (Armenium), and the easterns at Seleucia, in Isauria. Whilst deliberations proceed as to the places where the two councils shall be held, the Bishops of Gaul, who do not understand the difficulties which have to be solved, write to Hilary of Poictiers, exiled in Phrygia, and ask him to explain to them exactly what is the belief of the Easterns on the divinity of the Son of God, and what is the meaning of so many expositions of belief issued by them since the Council of Nice. In reply Hilary sends them his *Treatise on Synods*, which he had just composed on the occasion. The bishops of the western provinces assemble at Rimini. Out of about four hundred, eighty hold for Arianism ; they, the interpreters of the imperial will, request the Council to adhere to the last formula of Sirmium. The other Fathers refuse, saying that they are not come to subscribe this new symbol, that of Nice satisfying them, but to pronounce anathema on the enemies of the latter. The Arians, resolved to maintain the belief of Sirmium, the Council condemns as heretics Ursatius, Valens, Germinius, Auxentius, Caius, and Demophilus. It then sends to Constance twenty deputies, with letters explanatory of its resolution. At first, the emperor refuses to receive the envoys, and under different pretexts creates delay, while writing to the Fathers to expect his answer at Rimini. The delegates, however, desire to return. Matters come to the point that the bishops, with few exceptions, consent, being weary of war, to report the sentence rendered against Ursatius and the rest, and to give their assent to the formulary of Sirmium.

On their part the Eastern bishops meet together in Seleucia to the number of 600; they sit in the presence of Leonas, questor of the palace. In that assembly only some bishops are in favour of Consubstantialism, of which there is scarcely any question. The rest divide into two principal parts; that of the Anomeans or pure Arians, and that of the Semi-Arians. The first, which has for its head Acatius of Cesarea, comprises about 40 bishops; Basil of Ancyra is at the head of the second. The Acatians openly attack the Council of Nice, whose decisions they wish to abrogate, in order to decide afresh on all the questions. The rest criticise the decisions of that Council only in the word consubstantial, which, by reason of its obscurity, seems suspicious and dangerous to a great number of persons. After many contests and debates Leonas at last breaks up the assembly and refuses to be present at fresh sittings, declaring that he was sent to take part in a synod which was in concord, and not a meeting of dissentients, and that without him they might go and prate at their ease in the Church. Acatius and his partisans, strengthened by this reply, abstain from the Council. The Semi-Arians assemble and depose Acatius, Eudoxus, George, Patrophelus, and several others of the same opinion. They send to Constantinople, whither the Emperor has returned, ten of their body to give him an account of their decision. But the Acatians have got the start of them, and on their arrival the Semi-Arians find Constans predisposed in favour of their adversaries. To defeat these manœuvres, they put into his hand a document that had emanated from the Acatians, and filled with blasphemies against the Son in the trinitarian point of view. Ætius, acknowledging himself its author is juridically condemned and then banished by Constans.

Meanwhile the deputies of the Council of Rimini, at the head of whom are Uratius and Valens, bring the resolutions adopted by that Council. The Acatians hasten to join them and to accept their formula in which the words consubstantial and similar in substance are not found. The deputies of the Semi-Arians, on the contrary, protest that the word substance ought not to be rejected. But the Emperor commands the bishops to consent to the formula of Rimini, and after a long conference with the Semi-Arians, he obtains their adhesion. The Acatians, having regained favour by their prompt acceptance of this formula, gather together at Constantinople a Council of fifty bishops (360), with a view of destroying what was done at Seleucia. The first act of this assembly is to confirm the creed of Rimini; it then deposes Aetius from the diaconate, in order to please the Emperor; finally it condemns the adversaries of the Acatians, not for an error of doctrine, but under the supposed pretext of breaches of discipline and morals. Among the bishops thus deposed was Macedonius of Constantinople, who had incurred disgrace with the Emperor, and Basil of Ancyra, who was regarded as the head of the Semi-Arians. The imperial authority confirms its decisions and banishes the condemned bishops; Eudoxus of Antioch is promoted to the see of Constantinople. At Cyzicum Eleusius is replaced by Eunomius, disciple of Aetius. But Eunomius, not being able to conceal the pure Arianism which he professes like his master, is soon denounced to the Emperor and deposed by his own party, who finds itself obliged to sacrifice him. He then separates from the other Arians, and forming a distinct sect, he retires into Cappadocia, his native land, where he ordains bishops and priests notwithstanding his own deposition. The Council of Constantinople having sent all over the empire the formula of Rimini, with the Emperor's command to banish those who refused to subscribe to it, a real persecution of the Churches ensues. Nearly all the bishops yield to the times, and resign themselves to giving their signature. Nevertheless the persecution seems not to have reached the bishops of Gaul, who were protected by Julian, proclaimed Augustus at Paris in the year 360. Euzoius, one of the first disciples of Arius, is instituted bishop of Antioch by order of Constans (361). The pure Arians or Acatians assemble in that city in small numbers. Deserting the formula of Rimini, they proclaim their own doctrine, that is, that the Son is unlike the father in substance and in will, and that he was formed from nothing. The partisans of Aetius in Antioch adhere to that opinion which their head had published the first after Arius. The new dissidents receive the names of Anomeens (ἀνομοιος unlike) and of exoncontians (ἐξ οὐκ ὄντων out of nothing, of what is not). Among these controversies in regard to the Father and the Son it was natural that the question should arise what is the Holy Spirit? on whose nature the Council of Nice had said nothing. What was to be thought and said of this third person of the trinity? Was he, like the Son, either consubstantial or like the Father? Was he their equal or their inferior? created or increate? On these points it seemed likely that each party would profess an opinion analogous to that which it held as to the Father and as to the Son. Thus the pure Arians would depart least from the antitrinitarian party ; the Semi-Arians would consult Origen and Plato ; the Consubstantialists would tend to a veritable assimilation of the Holy Spirit to the two other members of the Trinity.

It was after the Council of Constantinople of the year 360 that the question of the Holy Spirit began to be publicly put. Macedonius, deposed by that council, maintains himself in regard to the Son, in the Semi-Arianism which proceeds from Origen and the ancient fathers, and in regard to the Holy Spirit, he publishes an opinion drawn from the same sources. He was the first to declare that the Holy Spirit is a divine force spread through the universe, and not a person distinct from the Father and the Son, that he is their minister, and was created as the angels who nevertheless are much inferior to him. This opinion is followed by Eleusius and the other Semi-Arians who are thenceforward designated under the name of Macedonians. It reckons many adherents in Constantinople, as well as in Thrace, Bithynia, the Hellespont and the neighbouring provinces. They are also called pneumatomachs (assailants of the Spirit). The partisans of Consubstantionalism in their turn embrace on the Holy Spirit a doctrine conformed to that which they profess on the Father, and the Son. They make of the third person of the Trinity a person consubstantial with the two others. Basil, called the great, makes a distinction in his struggle against the pneumatomachs. The death of Constans, which took place in 361, brings an unexpected return in religious affairs. Hellenism regains authority in the person of Julian who attempts to revive it with the help of the neo-Platonic philosophy.

This philosophy, as we have seen, was not at first hostile to Christianity. Ammonius passed for a disciple of the Gospel. Plotinus limited himself to combatting the doctrines of Gnosticism. His successors showed themselves less well disposed. Porphyry engages against the Christian religion in a struggle which prolongs itself, in a more or less active state, until the close of the schools of philosophy. Assyrian by birth, he had at an early day removed into Hellenic lands. After studying under Longinus at Athens, he in 254 comes to Rome, where he is the most faithful disciple of Plotinus. On the death of the latter he takes the direction of the Neo-Platonician school, which contained a great number of learners. He then retires into Sicily and writes against the Christians a work in fifteen books, the popularity of which is immense. Several Fathers combatted the work; the Christian emperor took pains to suppress it afterwards; at present there remain of it only divers fragments preserved in the refutations of the fathers. Porphyry dies under the reign of Diocletian. After the example of Plotinus he has recourse to the allegorical interpretation in order to defend the Hellenic myths; but in the fragments which still subsist we do not see reasons to think that he conceived an entire system for the explanation of mythology. Porphyry is free from the superstition and theurgy of the popular worship; he keeps his feet on the ground of philosophy. With him religion consists in the practice of virtue and good works. None the less he makes himself the defender of the Hellenic civilisation and the ardent adversary of the new religion. He knew Hebrew and was familiar with the Jewish and Chaldean doctrines. The Old Testament is specially the object of his attacks; it is by sapping that basis that he attempts to overthrow Christianity which rests on it.

The hostility of Porphyry is the less easily explained at first because at that epoch metaphysical doctrines were pretty nearly the same on both sides. The conceptions of Origen, then received without dispute, in the trinitarian church, come from Platonism. The Christian Trinity, not yet completed, tends to confound itself with that of the neo-platonicians. The point of divergence between the two systems lies in this that, according to Porphyry the Christians mingle the Greek philosophy with foreign fables; while the neo-platonicians endeavour to innoculate it with Hellenism, in order to reform it and maintain with it the Greco-Roman civilisation. At the time when Porphyry flourished (270-304) Christianity underwent rapid extension; it was predominant in the ancient provinces of the Greek empire. The danger which ancient society ran was apparent to all eyes. Of course the philosophers tried to save it, and with it the philosophy which was connected with it by intimate bonds. Hellenism had not yet ceased to be the religion of princes. Diocletian and Galerius had even commenced in Porphyry's last years, their sanguinary persecution of the new worship.

At a later day the scene changes, the emperors themselves proclaim the victory of the persecuted by ceasing to assail them. Constantine puts Christianity on the throne.

The civil power withdraws its support from the ancient religion, and begins to take against it measures which end in a final interdiction of it. Who will sustain the struggle in its favour ? The priests of Polytheism are scattered without any bond among them, without a common organisation. The emperor, who was the chief of that worship, has put himself at the head of its enemies. Philosophy, the belief of enlightened men among the Gentiles, feels itself threatened and called upon to take in hand the cause of Hellenism. The philosopher becomes a priest and receives initiation. He carries to the temple his enthusiasm and gives himself up to the practices of the ancient worship which he attempts to revive and to purify by an allegorical interpretation.

Jamblicus, a disciple and successor of Porphyry, lived in the first third of the fourth century. He is the first Alexandrine who left pure speculation to yield himself to theurgy. He unites the neo-platonician mysticism with the popular superstitions, and supports himself on the authority of the books of Hermes. In his treatise on *Mysteries*, he distinguishes different orders of intelligence — gods, devils, heroes, and souls, all of whom emanate from the supreme unity ; he describes in detail the different classes of angels ; he believes in divine apparitions and determines their conditions. Divination in his eyes is an intimate communication with the divine being ; it is born of contemplation and enthusiasm. Theurgy, the only worship that pleases the gods, consists in the practice of certain mysterious acts, in virtue of certain symbols which draw to us the divine substances. It is a science which has nothing in common with physical nature. All religious ceremonies have a sense and an object. Nevertheless Jamblicus rejects the worship of idols as vain superstition ; he equally condemns the operations of magic.

This new direction of the school of Alexandria continues after his death. Among its numerous disciples, Edesius, his successor, is distinguished. He becomes the master of Eusebius of Myndes and of Priscus of Molossia, both of whom reject magic and theurgy ; as well as of Maximus of Ephesus and of Chrysanthes of Sardis who admit them.

The two last are priests convinced of the truth of the myths and the mysteries, as well as the efficacy of the practices. They have for disciples Eunapius of Sardis and the Emperor Julian. At the same time lived Sallust, who was consul in the year 363, and who is regarded as the author of the treatise *on the Gods and the World*, a complete system of mythological interpretation. Julian, born in 332, was not more than eight years old when his father Julius Constantius is killed in a revolt of soldiers, in which he himself runs the same danger of his life as Gallus his elder brother. Both of them are banished to Marcellum not far from Cesarea in Cappadocia. Constantius having grown milder in his feeling in regard to them, Gallus goes into Ionia and frequents the schools of Ephesus. Julian, now a young man, is instructed in literature in Constantinople. He goes to the Basilica where the schools are, accompanied by his tutor and very simply attired. His remarkable progress gaining for him popular favour, the emperor feels umbrage and sends him to Nicomedia, with an express prohibition to attend the school of the Sophist Libanius, who observed the worship of the Gentiles. Julian purchases of the Sophists orations and reads them with ardour. The elevation of Gallus to the rank of Cæsar procures for his young brother a little more liberty in his actions (351). He sees at Pergamus Edesius, then the most illustrious of the neo-platonicians, receives from him lessons in philosophy, and puts himself into connection with two of his disciples, Eusebius and Chrysanthes. He is then drawn to Ephesus by the reputation of Maximus, who gives himself up to all the operations of theurgy. That philosopher, aided by Chrysanthes, initiates Julian into the secrets of their mysterious science. The emperor informed of the fact, Julian, to turn away suspicions, has his head shaved and affects the exterior of the monastic life ; he even discharges the functions of reader in the Church of Nicomedia. None the less does he continue in secrecy the studies of which he is fond. At the bloody death of his brother he becomes suspected, and guards are put round his person (354). He is sent to Como, near Milan, which he quits, after a short residence there, to go into Greece for the cultivation of his mind. There he wears the costume of the philosophers, and does not cease to render secret worship to the divinities of Hellenism. He obtains initiation into the mysteries of Eleusis. Recalled by the emperor into Italy, he leaves Athens with regret, placing himself under the protection of Minerva (355). At Milan he is made to lay aside the beard and the cloak of philosophy. Constantius proclaims him Cæsar, gives him in marriage his sister Helena, and sends him to combat the barbarians that infest Gaul. Julian, after several victories, drives them entirely out of the territory of the empire. During his stay in Gaul he does not cease to worship in the shades the Hellenic gods. His nights are divided into three parts, one for sleep, the other for public business, the last for the muses. He rises in the middle of the night, and before applying to his work, addresses a prayer to Mercury (Hermes) whom certain theological doctrines, says Ammeanus Marcellinus, represent as the primary thought of the universe, the principle of all intelligence. In the year 360, Julian is declared emperor by the army. Civil war is about to break out when the death of Constantius leaves his competitor in possession of the whole empire. Then being free, Julian openly professes polytheism, he takes the title of Supreme Pontiff, and by precise and formal decrees, orders the temples to be opened there, where they have been closed, and victims to be immolated to the gods. He sends for the bishops that are divided in opinion, as well as the heads of the different sects, and mildly intimates to them that they are to put an end to the discords, and that each shall observe his religion freely and without fear. He remains firm on this point in the thought that the dissensions of the Christians increasing with their liberty, there will be no reason in future to fear at all a people united in the same sentiments. "He knew by experience," says Ammianus, ' that most Christians are worse than wild beasts in regard to one another."

Under the favour of this liberty the banished return from exile, among others, Meletius of Antioch, Hilary of

Poictiers, Eusebius of Verceil, Lucifer of Cagliari, partizans of consubstantialism. The two last, who had been banished into the Thebaid, remain sometime in Egypt and in Syria before returning into their dioceses. Among the Arians, Aetius is recalled and loaded with favours, because he had been a friend of Cæsar Gallus. The unitarian Photinus equally returns to his church; Julian congratulates him on not believing in the deity of Jesus Christ. But the new decrees profit, specially the consubstantialists, who were persecuted under Constans. The emperor does not limit himself to the recall of the exiles; he also redresses certain vexations of one party against another; thus Eleusius of Cyzicum is compelled to rebuild the Church of the Novatians which he had beaten down. No rigour is any longer exercised against the Donatists in the African provinces; they recover their churches and see the bishops return who had been banished by the Emperor Constantius.

Julian, without persecuting the Christians, does not consider himself bound in regard to them to any except the duties of strict justice. His favours are reserved for others. He suppresses the pensions, gifts, and privileges which Constantine and his sons had granted to the ministers of the new religion. He gives a preference to the Gentiles for public offices; he even goes so far as to forbid the Christians to teach grammar and rhetoric. We have less reason for throwing on him divers excesses which accompany every re-action. Certain governors went further than the prince could wish, popular passions were for the Christians occasions of evils which sometimes they drew on themselves by their imprudence; we ought not to consider as martyrs men legally condemned for having thrown down altars, overturned idols, or committed some other violent act of religious intolerance.

While guarding himself against injustice, Julian does not the less take an active part in the struggle of the two religions. He openly discharges the functions of supreme Pontiff. He repairs the losses which the old worship had suffered under his predecessors. The temples are restored, those which had been demolished rise again. The height of the Nile is reported in the temple of Serapis. He reestablishes the honours and the salaries of the priests of Hellenism. The philosophers surround him ; he leads a philosophic life in their midst. Maximus is welcomed into his court with the greatest honours. Priscus comes in his turn ; but Chrysanthes persists in not quitting his province. Not satisfied with reinstating the sacrifices, the divinations, and the divers practices of the ancient religion, Julian does his best to introduce into it a moral and philosophical reform. He requires of the priests that they shall give an example of gravity and purity of life, that living truly good men, they abstain from all that is vile and shameful. The study of serious history and sound philosophy is recommended to them, as well as the singing of hymns, frequent prayers, charity toward strangers and the poor, whom Julian orders to be supported in imitation of the Jews and the Christians. He proposes to imitate some of the institutions in use among the latter, to introduce into the temples of the Gentiles the furniture and the order seen in the churches, steps, pulpits, readers and teachers, to set forth and explain the doctrines of Hellenism, prayers on certain days and at certain hours. His religion was also to have monasteries for such men and women as should wish to give themselves up to philosophy, houses for the reception of foreigners and the indigent. He bestows funds to contribute to the cost of these various establishments. But Julian does not find in most of his fellow religionists the zeal and enthusiasm with which he himself is animated ; the multitude understands nothing of the philosophic interpretations given to the ancient worship ; the others live in a kind of religious indifference which is little fit for struggling against the ardent proselytism of the Christians. In the midst of his cares on behalf of public worship, the emperor does not lose from view the public interests in general. He is specially desirous of resuming the war against the Persians, to avenge the continual reverses which the Romans had suffered under the reign of Constans. With this design he betakes himself to Antioch in July 392, and remains there until the spring of the following year, attending to the preparations for a new expedition. Differently from other cities of Syria, where Polytheism had resumed its ascendancy, Antioch, a Greek city, counted a great number of Christians. Julian repels them by his superstitious practices; railing breaks forth on all sides; people laugh at his exterior, his numerous sacrifices, his theurgic operations. He on his part contracts an aversion for the city, and to revenge himself writes the Misopogon (Beard or Philosophy Hater) a biting satire on the inhabitants of Antioch.

At the same time, Artemius, ex-governor of Egypt, suffers capital punishment. The citizens of Alexandria, according to Ammianus, allege against him overwhelming accusations; the Christians make him into a martyr. At the news of his death, the Alexandrines, who had believed in his return, rise against George, the Arian bishop, of whom they had had reason to complain under the preceding reign. The Gentiles reproach him principally for menaces uttered against the magnificent temple of Serapis. The agitated multitude seized him and tore him in pieces, without any one's coming to his defence, for he was not less odious to the Athanasians than to the polytheists. Julian, indignant, at first resolves to punish the murderers; but overcome by his circle, he restricts himself to protesting in an edict, threatening with death whoever in future should be guilty of any crime against justice and the laws. Athanasius, fearing George's power, had till then remained in the place of his exile. The death of his adversary allows him to return, after seven years of absence. He makes a solemn entry into Alexandria. His partizans drive the Arians from all the churches; they, on their part, reduced to assembling in private houses, choose for their bishop a priest, Lucius by name. In order to deliberate on the affairs of religion, Alexander convokes at Alexandria a not numerous council, at which are present Eusebius of Verceil and two deacons sent by Lucifer, who was then at Antioch. In this assembly it is decided that the lapsed who should return to the faith should be pardoned, with this distinction, however, that if they had been among the leaders or promoters of Arianism, they should be deprived of their reli-

II.   C

gious functions, and reduced to the state of laymen, while if they had only yielded to necessity and violence, they should be restored to their ministry; but both should be admitted only on condition that they should abjure the Arian dogmas, and condemn those who say that the Holy Spirit is a creature, as well as all the other dissidents, old and new.

This resolution was formed with a view to pacification. To reply to the scruples of those who were disinclined to use the words substance and hypostasis, which are not found in Scripture, the council goes so far as to say that it is not proper to employ them in speaking of God, unless you have to refute the Sabellians. Doubtless the necessity was felt of union among Christians with a view to a new struggle with Polytheism. According to Gregory Naziance, Athanasius, on his return, applies himself to the task of pacifying men's minds, of bringing back his adversaries, of solacing the oppressed without distinction of sect, and of reuniting those who had wandered from the right path. He preaches freely, and does honour to the doctrine of the consubstantial Trinity. "At the same time, he gives laws to the world at large, and attracts all spirits. He sends letters to these, calls those to his side, instructs some who come to him of their own accord; all he tries to inspire with an ardent love of the law, which seems to him sufficient of itself to bring men to God."

Lucifer shows a disposition much less conciliatory. He had gone to Antioch in order to bring about the reunion of those who held for consubstantialism; his rigidity produced a contrary effect. He does not pardon Meletius, who returns from exile, his former relations with the Arians instead of grouping every one around that bishop, he ordains another Paulinus. This step revives the schism between the Meletians and the Eustathians. Eusebius of Verceil disapproves the new ordination; Lucifer in his turn, rejecting the decisions of the Council of Alexandria refuses to receive the lapsed, and separates from those who do not act as he does, that is from the generality of the Churches. A new schism, similar to those of the Novatian and the Donatists is the result. His followers, few in number, receive the name of Luciferians; they are found principally in Spain and Sardinia. However, Athanasius does not remain long in Alexandria. The pagans complain to Julian of his conduct, and characterise him as a disturber of the public peace, as the most dangerous enemy of their religion. The Emperor expels him, saying in his letter that Athanasius, banished by several decrees, ought not to have re-entered his house until he was recalled by another decree, and that in formerly allowing the exiled Galileans to return into their country, he did not authorise them to take possession of their churches. The Christians of Alexandria write to him in favour of Athanasius; the Emperor replies to them that they should agree one with another if they wish to persist in their superstition, but they were not to ask for that bishop. "There are," he adds, "a great number of his disciples, among whom they may choose one to explain the scriptures to them; as to Athanasius, he is a cunning person, a poor creature, who, mixing himself up with everything, has already run the risk of his life. He banishes Athanasius for fear he should again disturb the public peace. Athanasius is compelled to hide himself until the Emperor's death. In the spring of 363 Julian enters on his expedition against the Persians. Before setting out, he gave an order for rebuilding the Temple of Jerusalem in order to procure for the Jews the means of immolating victims, and perhaps also to falsify the prophecies according to which that temple was never to be reconstructed; but the death of the Emperor, which took place shortly after, caused the work to be given up, and no one has attempted it since. In regard to the prodigies to which the discontinuance has been ascribed, they never existed except in the credulous spirit of men of the period, both Christians and Gentiles.

The Emperor perishes in Persia, struck by an unknown hand. When he was brought into his tent "he pronounced," says Ammianus, "a discourse imprinted with a thoroughly philosophic resignation," then, after making his will and reproving those who wept around him, he had a conversation on the nature of the soul with the philosophers Maximus and Priscus, who had followed him in his expedition. He was thirty-one years of age (26th June 363).

Whatever opinion we may form of the attempt of Julian to restore Hellenism, we cannot deny his entire good faith. He was led to it by a philosophic and religious fervour which is explained at once by his education, his youth, and the nature of his genius. His adversaries themselves bear testimony to the purity of his morals, as well as the mildness of his character. He carefully cultivated all the virtues taught by philosophy. His talents as a writer, a statesman, and a general promised one of the greatest princes that have thrown lustre on the Roman Empire. Jovian, whom the army elected in his place, makes a discreditable peace, and hastens to regain Antioch. He restores to the Churches the liberalities suppressed by Julian. The bishops, mute for some time, soon renew the disputable questions on doctrine. Each party tries to gain over the Emperor. Jovian, calling them back to concord, declares that he shall trouble no one on account of his creed, whatever it is, but that he shall honour most those who shall study to re-establish peace in the Church. He shows favour to Athanasius who, on Julian's death, hastens to return to Alexandria. Jovian dying in Bithynia (10th Feb. 364), Valentinian is proclaimed by the army. The new emperor associates with himself in power his brother Valens, to whom he assigns the East as his share, reserving the West for himself. From the commencement of their reign several laws are passed in favour of Christianity. They forbid the pagans to practise nightly sacrifices and magical ceremonies, while permitting them to worship the gods according to ancient usages, but without additions.

The two princes separate in 365. Valentinian resides in Milan, Valens in Constantinople. The former holds with the West for consubstantialism, while tolerating the opposite opinion. The latter, in the East, favours the Arians and persecutes their adversaries. The Macedonians or Semi-Arians, assembling at Lampsacus, confirm the doctrine of

the Council of Antioch of the dedication, condemn that of
Rimini, and approve the deposition of the bishops of the
party of Acatius and Eudoxus. The civil war, raised by
Procopius, suspends the revenge of the latter and gives for
some time the upper hand to the Semi-Arians. The dogma
of Macedonius on the Holy Spirit, little known before, is
then brought into greater prominence; it is held in honour
specially on the borders of the Hellespont. After the death
of Procopius, Valens, whom Eudoxus of Constantinople has
gained over, pronounces for the pure Arians, and gives
them the churches of their antagonists. The Semi-Arian
bishops are exiled, all the adherents to Consubstantialism,
comprising the Novatians, are driven from the capital. The
Macedonians then determine to recur to Valentinian and
Liberius of Rome, rather than to communicate with
Eudoxus and Valens. They send three deputies into Italy.
These cannot have an interview with Valentinian, who
is carrying on war in Gaul; but Liberius, after receiving
their written adhesion to the Nicene creed, admits them to
his communion and gives them letters for the Consubstantialists in the East. On the return of these deputies it is
agreed by common accord to assemble at Tarsus to confirm
the creed of Nice and to effect the definitive union of the
Macedonians. This assembly is interdicted by an order
from Valens.

A short time afterwards that prince commands the governors to drive away the bishops, who, deposed under Constance, resumed possession of their churches in the time of
Julian. Then the prefect of Egypt prepares to dispossess
Athanasius. The disciples of his Communion interpose,
asserting that he was not restored but persecuted by Julian;
that it was Jovian who gave him back his see. The people
rise in insurrection and the governor pretends to yield.
Some days after, he suddenly, during the night, makes his
way into the church where Athanasius dwells. Fruitless
searches are made, foreseeing the attempt the bishop had the
previous evening withdrawn into his father's sepulchre; there
he conceals himself during four months. At the end of
that time Valens recalls him, whether from fear of some

movement or in order not to commit himself with Valentinian and the Westerns to whom the bishop of Alexandria might have appealed, as he had done under the reign of Constance and Constans. Notwithstanding the persecution which rages in other places, Athanasius governs his church in peace until the time of his death.

Eudoxus of Constantinople, having died in the year 370, the Arians appoint Demophilus his successor. Evagrius is nominated by the Consubstantialists ; but he is sent into exile by the emperor, and the Arians take occasion to vex their adversaries. A war against the Persians takes Valens to Antioch. In traversing Asia Minor he persecutes all that are not Arian. Basil, then priest and shortly after bishop of Cesarea in Cappadocia, opposes him, and succeeds in preserving the Consubstantialist Church of the country. At Antioch Meletius and his church are exposed to the imperial rigours ; Paulinus is not disquieted doubtless because of the small number of his adherents.

About the same time a great number of philosophers are given up to capital punishment. Some of them, cherishing a chimerical hope, had had recourse to divination in order to learn who would be Valens' successor. Their wishes incline to a Pagan named Theodore, a man of distinction. In the magical operation, a ring mysteriously prepared, having, it is said, indicated the first four letters of his name. They persuade themselves that Theodore will soon be the master of the empire. Valens seeing in this an attempt at high treason secures Theodore and his fellow magicians ; one perishes by the sword, the others by fire ; the most illustrious philosophers are given into the hands of executioners, among others Maximus, the teacher and friend of Julian. All who wear the philosopher's cloak whether they are philosophers or not, suffer cruelties. However the persecution continues against the Christians who do not hold the official belief. They are harrassed with deposition and exile. The pure Arians are put into the possession of the churches. Egypt had remained in peace during the life of Athanasius. After his death things took a different course (373). Peter, his successor, is expelled by the Arians who are supported by the civil power. Lucius returns to Alexandria. The partisans of Consubstantialism in that city are persecuted. Peter retires to Rome. Basil of Cappadocia is exposed to threats of all kinds. Valens himself repairs to Cesarea and endeavours to get him to communicate with the Arians. From respect for his knowledge and virtue he dares not remove him from his church; but he divides Cappadocia into two provines; Cesarea remains the metropolis of the first; Tyana is put at the head of the second. Basil, as a consequence of this division, creates several new bishoprics, one, among others, in the town of Sasima, situated on the confines of the two provinces. He calls to the government of that church his friend Gregory Naziance; but the opposition of the metropolitan of Tyana prevents the installation of the new bishop.

While these things are taking place in the east the western church remains exempt from troubles. Valentinian leaves full liberty to all the sects. The bishops are maintained in their functions without regard to religious opinions. The greater number, who had adhered under compulsion to the Council of Rimini, eagerly return to the Council of Nice. Milan, where the emperor resides, has for the head of its church Auxentius, ordained by the Arians, and partisan of the Council of Rimini. Eusebius of Verceil, and specially Hilary of Poictiers, take up the defence of Consubstantialism against him. Valentinian, who is satisfied with the profession of the creed of Auxentius, orders Hilary to quit the city. The latter, after publishing a writing against Auxentius, returns to Poictiers where he remains till his death (367).

Liberius having died in 366, the election of his successor occasions a schism in Rome. One party chooses Damasus, priest of the Roman Church (366-84). Ursinus, a deacon of the same church, is elected by another party. Civil war bursts out. The prefect, unable to restore peace, is compelled to retire into a suburb. Fighting takes place in a church; thirty-seven persons are killed. Ammianus explains the animosity of the competitors by the brilliant advantages which, in that city, attach to the Episcopal dignity.

"Those who obtain it," he says, "are enriched by the oblations of matrons, and appear in public carried on chariots, and splendidly attired; the profusion of their festivities surpasses that of royal tables." Accordingly an illustrious Pagan of that day repeated that he was ready to become a Christian, provided they would make him bishop of Rome. Damasus wins the emperor to his side, but this does not put an end to the schism. Ursinus, driven away in 366, returns to Rome the following year. He is again expelled shortly after, and banished into Gaul. He is permitted to leave Gaul in 371, but on condition that he does not return either to Rome or into the suburban districts.

Auxentius of Milan dies in 374. The Consubstantialists and the Arians are divided in regard to the election of his successor. A sedition breaks out which threatens universal confusion. Ambrosius, governor of the province, interposes in order to maintain peace. While he is addressing the two parties in the Church, all the people, by a spontaneous movement, choose him himself for bishop. He long resists, flees away, and conceals himself. An order from the emperor forces him to yield. He becomes one of the most illustrious chiefs of the Church. Valentinian, in dying, leaves two sons, issue of different mothers (375). Gratian, the elder, had been associated in the empire as early as the year 367. Valentinian, the younger, is named Augustus by the army immediately after the death of his father, although scarcely four years old. In his share of the empire, he has Italy, Illyrium, and Africa; Gratian guards for him Gaul, Spain, and Brittany. By the death of his brother Valens remains more free in his opposition to consubstantialism. The monks, zealous partisans of that dogma, are drawn from their cells and compelled to carry arms. About the same time Apollinaris, bishop of Laodicea, publishes a doctrine which is qualified as heterodox. He was a learned man who had been the friend of Athanasius and Basil. When the Emperor Julian forbade the disciples of Jesus to study profane letters, Apollinaris, to supply the place of the poems of ancient Greece, composed a number of works in verse on biblical subjects. He also showed himself one of the great adversaries of Arianism. But in opposing it, he fell into another opinion which is not less condemned by the Consubstantialist Church. He asserts that Jesus was not endowed with a human soul, the deity absorbing in him the intelligence (nous) which exists in other men ; he had only a sensitive soul. To Apollinaris other errors are attributed which seem consequences deduced by his adversaries rather than his personal opinions. He had a large number of disciples. But his system which seemed likely to prevail in the East, ended by falling gradually into discredit. After a reign of thirteen years, Valens perished, a victim of his imprudence in introducing the Goths into the Roman provinces. These people dwelt beyond the Danube, where they commanded several nations. The Huns, suddenly falling on their country, compel them to pass over the river. The Goths entreated Valens to receive them, promising him to serve them against his enemies. The emperor consents, and establishes them in Thrace. Under the influence of Ulphila, their bishop, they embrace Arianism, which prevailed in those countries. But they did not long remain quiet. Far from rendering to Valens the services which they had promised, they rise in revolt in 377, pillage Thrace, and threaten Constantinople. Valens hurries to repel them. He is conquered, and perishes miserably. His two nephews remain possessed of the whole empire. By reason of the brother's immaturity, Gratian alone exercises authority. Disapproving of the rigour of his uncle, he leaves everyone liberty in religious opinions. The exiles are recalled ; all the sects remain free to hold assemblies, except the Manicheans, the Photinians (Unitarians), and the Eunomians. None the less, Gratian himself remains a Consubstantialist ; he is the first emperor that refused the dignity of supreme pontiff of Roman Polytheism. The law passed in favour of the exiles allows Meletius to return to Antioch. The schism between his church and that of Paulinus subsisted still. The two parties, in order to put an end to it, agree that the bishop who died first should not have a successor. Six of the principal priests, Flavian among the others, take an oath not to accept the Episcopate before each other's death. Under Valens the Arians occupy all the churches of the East, except that of Jerusalem. The Macedonians, persecuted by them, approached the Consubstantialists, as we have said. But liberty being restored to the various Trinitarian sects, some Macedonian bishops resume their churches, and assembling at Antioch in Caria, agree to return to their primitive opinion. Meanwhile the situation of the empire, assailed on all sides by the barbarians, induces Gratian to associate with the sovereign power Theodosius, a Spaniard, to whom he assigns the provinces which Valens had governed; the West continues to obey Valentinian's two sons. After some success obtained by the barbarians, Theodosius received instruction, and was baptised by the Bishop of Thessalonica, a partisan, like himself, of Consubstantialism (380). In his neophytic fervour, he orders the Nicene creed to be received in all the provinces of his dominions. Demophilus, Arian bishop of Constantinople, refusing to submit, is expelled from his See. The Consubstantialists are replaced in possession of the churches of that city, which they have not occupied for forty years. Dispersed under Valens, they had, after his death, invited Gregory Naziance, who, without having the title of bishop, had succeeded, by his zeal and eloquence, in gathering a flock around him. A schism soon came to threaten them, as a consequence of the enterprises of Maximus, who had been a cynic philosopher. Without Gregory's knowledge, he had got himself consecrated bishop of Constantinople, an irregular ordination doubtless, but one which does not cease to trouble the Church of the Consubstantialists. Theodosius forms the resolution of convoking an œcumenical council to confirm in the East the Council of Nice, to appease dissidences, and to choose a bishop for Constantinople. In the year 381, one hundred and fifty oriental bishops assemble in the last-mentioned city. The emperor had summoned to that council the Macedonians or Semi-Arians, in the hope of effecting a re-union. They come in number thirty-six, mostly from the shores of the Hellespont; Eleusius of Cyzicum is at their head. In spite of the urgency of the other bishops, who remind them of the deputation to Liberius, and the long continuance of one and the same communion, they reject Consubstantialism and withdraw. The council annuls the ordination of Maximus, and following the emperor's desire, names Gregory Naziance to the episcopate of Constantinople.

The death of Meletius, which then takes place, appears to furnish an opportunity for terminating the schism of Antioch by recognising Paulinus as sole bishop. But as he is favoured by the Westerns, a kind of spirit of rivalry induces the Fathers to choose Flavian to take the place of Meletius.

Gregory of Naziance, whose election is contested by several, resigns his functions; Nectarius succeeds him. The council then passes several laws touching belief and discipline.

Its first canon confirms and corroborates the doctrine of Nice on the consubstantiality and eternity of the son. It anathematises the opinion of the Macedonians and the Eunomians, who, denying the deity of the Holy Spirit, maintain that he was created by the Son, that he is of another substance and his inferior. At the same time it condemns all the sects of Arianism—the Eudoxians, the Anomeans, the Semi-Arians, as well as the Sabellians, the followers of Marcellus of Ancyra and of Photinus, and finally the Apollinarists. The second canon, regulating the hierarchy, enjoins on the bishops not to meddle with churches lying out of their dioceses, and not to mix and confound the churches. The same canon, in acknowledging in provincial councils, according to ancient right, all authority for ecclesiastical affairs, implicitly abrogates the faculty of appealing to the Bishop of Rome, which, it was asserted, had been conceded by the Council of Sardica, a faculty which the Greek Church has never acknowledged. The third canon decrees that the Bishop of Constantinople shall have the prerogative of honour after the Bishop of Rome since Constantinople is the new Rome. This is the first foundation of the power of the bishops of this latter city. The bishopric of Byzantium depended at first on that of Heraclea, metropolis of Thrace. When Byzantium had been transformed into Constantinople, numerous privileges were accorded by the emperors to that new capital. The decision of the council is a sequel of their kindness toward it. The only question was a prerogative of honour ; at a later day there will be added a jurisdiction which, extending ceaselessly, will become the source of constant rivalry between Rome and Constantinople, and finally of the schism which will divide the Greek and Latin churches.

The seventh canon determines the manner of receiving dissidents who return to the official church. The Arians the Macedonians, the Sabbatarians, the Novatians, the Quartodecimans, and the Appollinarists are required only to renounce all heresy ; after which they receive unction as a sign of the gift of the Holy Spirit. On the contrary, the Eunomians, who had received baptism by a single immersion, the Montanists or Phrygians, the Sabellians, and all other dissidents, especially those who came from Galatia are admitted only with the formalities prescribed for the Pagans themselves. The council, in confirming the symbol of Nice, make some additions thereto, principally in what concerns the incarnation of the Holy Spirit, on account of the dissidence of the Apollinarists, the Macedonians, and others, which had been pronounced since the first œcumenical council.

The symbol of Constantinople, as ordinarily read in the trinitarian churches, is conceived in these terms :

"We believe in one sole God, the Father Almighty creator of heaven and of earth, of all things visible and invisible ; and in one sole Lord Jesus Christ, the sole Son of God, and begotten by the Father, before all ages ; God of God, light of light, true God of true God, begotten and not made, consubstantial with the Father, by whom all things were made ; who for us men, and for our salvation, descended from heaven, and was incarnated by the Holy Spirit and the Virgin Mary, and became man. He was crucified for us under Pontius Pilate ; he suffered and was buried. The third day he rose from the dead, according to the Scriptures. He ascended into heaven, he sat down at the right hand of the Father; he will come in glory to judge the living and the dead; his reign will never end. We believe in the Holy Spirit, the Lord and Vivifier, who proceeds from the Father, who is worshipped and glorified with the Father and the Son, who spake by the prophets. We believe in one holy church, Catholic and apostolic. We confess one baptism for the remission of sins. We expect the resurrection of the dead, and the life of the future age." A law of the 3d July 381, called forth by the council, directs that all the churches shall be placed under the bishops who adhere to that symbol, and that the rest shall be driven away as heretics. Theodosius had already issued several decrees against the dissident sects, and in particular, against the Manicheans, whom he had forbidden, under whatsoever name they might disguise themselves, to hold meetings, and to make gifts the one to the other, whether by hand or by will. In the year 382 he publishes a new law, which inflicts death on them, and appoints inquisitors to seek them out. This is the first appearance of officers who in later times play so dreadful a part in the annals of the Roman Church. In regard to the Pagans, a law dated December 380 forbids them to offer sacrifices by night or by day, under pain of proscription. But the interdiction does not go beyond sacrifices; their temples remain open, and they may meet in them freely. However, the decrees of Theodosius for the restoration of the churches to the Consubstantialists are not executed without serious disorders. The Arians, all powerful in many cities, withstand the imperial commands. The prince is disquieted, and seeks qualifications. To open the way to some conciliation, he brings together at Constantinople the bishops of the principal trinitarian sects. Nectarius is at the head of the Consubstantialists, Demophilus of the Arians, Eunomius of the Eunomians, Eleusius of the Macedonians. Theodosius welcomes them all; but little time is needed to show him the futility of discussion. He then requires every sect to give him its profession of faith in writing, and after a true or pretended examination of these documents, he pronounces in favour of the Consubstantialists. He no longer satisfies himself with driving the dissidents from their churches but he forbids the Arians, the Macedonians, and the Apollinarists to assemble whether in private houses, or even in the country, and to ordain bishops, under pain of confiscation of the houses of assembly, and banishment of the doctors and ministers. The Novatians, who believe in Consubstantialism, preserve the liberty of meeting together These different laws concerned only the Eastern empire. The Council of Constantinople was well received as œcumenical in all the Western provinces; but Arianism having almost entirely disappeared from those regions, the emperors who governed them had no measures to take against it.

Valentinian II. limits himself to issuing in 383 a decree against the Christians who become idolators, Jews, or Manicheans.

Gratian, on his side, passes several laws which tend to the ruin of polytheism. He confiscates the lands of the temples, the revenues appropriated to the expenses of sacrifices and pontiffs, the pensions of the Vestals, whose privileges he suppresses; he even hands over to the public treasury the legacies made to the temples, the pontiffs, and the vestals. Under the reign of that prince, a person named Mark, a native of Memphis, introduces into Spain a doctrine which seems to have had much relationship with that of the Manicheans. Priscillian, a noble and wealthy man, is imbued therewith, and tries to spread the notions in the Spanish provinces. He draws over to himself several bishops, among others Instantius and Salvian. With one common accord they begin to form a sect whose members receive the name of Priscillianists. A council held at Saragossa condemns that sect, and specially bishops Instantius and Salvian, as well as the laymen Priscillian and Elpidius Shortly after the two former, in order to strengthen the party, ordain Priscillian as bishop of Avila. These sectaries are brought before the secular judges by Idacius, bishop of Merida, and by Ithacus, bishop of Sassuba, charged with pursuing the execution of the decrees of the council of Saragossa. A rescript from Gratian banishes the Priscillianists not from the churches and the cities only, but also from all the countries. They dare not defend themselves at law; their bishops yield of themselves; fear disperses the others. Instantius, Salvian, and Priscillian go to Rome to justify themselves in the eyes of Damasus (368), who refuses to receive them. At Milan, where Ambrose is not less opposed to them, they gain the master of the offices, and obtain from Gratian a rescript which commands their restoration to their Sees. Instantius and Priscillian (Salvian had died in Rome), return without opposition; and having obtained the favour of the pro-consul, they bring Ithacus before him as a disturber of the Christian population; Ithacus flees in all haste into Gaul. The insurrection of Maximus and the death of Gratian soon change the face of things (383). Ithacus denounces Priscillian and his sect to the new emperor, whose power extends over Gaul, Spain, and Brittany. By an order from that prince they are conducted to Bordeaux to undergo trial by a council. There Instantius is declared unworthy of the Episcopate; but Priscillian, without replying to the bishops, appeals to the emperor. All the accused appear at Treves before him. Idacus and Ithacus urge condemnation. Martin of Tours, who is in the neighbourhood, attempts to make them desist; he entreats Maximus not to shed blood; it is a thing unheard of, he says, for the cause of the church to be subjected to a secular judge. At first the emperor accedes to his request; but after the departure of Martin, he yields to the urgency of other bishops, and orders the accused to be condemned to death. Priscillian and six of his adherents undergo capital punishment; Instantius is banished into the Island of Syline; several others are equally sent into exile. Priscillian's death serves only to strengthen the sect who regard him as a martyr. The bodies of those who had been punished are sent into Spain and buried with great pomp. Ithacus obtains from the emperor an order for tribunes to be sent to seek out the Priscillianists and punish them with death and confiscation of their property. Public execration attaches to the persecutors. In the sequel Ithacus is deposed ; Idacus of his own accord renounces the Episcopate. Meanwhile Theodosius had acknowledged Maximus in the quality of Augustus. On the intercession of Ambrosius, Maximus gives up his intention of marching into Italy against Valentinian II. The young prince was under the direction of Justina, his mother, who was in favour of Arianism. At the commencement of the year 386 she gets a law published which allows partisans of the Council of Rimini to form assemblies, and appoints the penalty of death against those who shall attempt to oppose it. Ambrose finds himself exposed to the imperial persecutions. Nevertheless it is found necessary to have recourse to him again. He is again sent to Maximus to confirm the peace and to ask for the body of Gratian ; but the bishop of Milan returns without any success, Maximus passes the Alps and seizes Italy and Africa (387). Valentinian II. and his mother place themselves under the protection of Theodosius, who takes in hand the cause of the young prince, while condemning his inclination in favour of Arianism. They, with common accord, address to the prefect of the Italian Pretorium a law which revokes the favours granted under the influence of Justina, and orders the Arians to be driven out of all the cities (388). The troops of Maximus are twice beaten in Pannonia. He himself is surprised in Aquilea and put to death. A rumour having spread in Constantinople that a reverse had been suffered by Theodosius, the Arians arose and set fire to the house of bishop Nectarius. This sedition promptly put down furnishes to the prince an occasion for revoking the orders that he had given in their favour. Eunomius is banished from Constantinople, and dies shortly after.

After passing the winter at Milan, Theodosius goes to Rome, from which he drives the Manicheans, who were there in great number (389). A council assembled at the same time condemns different dogmas that were asserted by an ex-monk named Jovinian. The principal heads of that doctrine are these: those who have received baptism with full faith cannot be ever overcome by the devil ; all those who have preserved the grace of baptism will obtain the same reward in heaven; virgins have merit only by their works—any more than widows and wives; there is no greater merit in abstaining from food than in making use of it with thanksgiving. He also asserted that Mary remained a virgin after her giving birth to Jesus; Jesus had a fantastical body, as is held by the Manicheans. Some time after, a council at Chalcedon condemns Bonosus, bishop of Sardica, who published that Mary did not remain a virgin after the birth of Jesus, but that she had other children; he maintained also that Jesus was a mere man. This opinion of Bonosus on Jesus and Mary, was nothing else than that of the apostles and the apostolic men. We have seen how Christotheism had succeeded in gaining predominance. In regard to Mary, the idea of her superhuman nature, which a very small sect professed at the time of the Council of Nice, continued to make its way, and divided men's minds in certain regions. A sect spread abroad in Arabia, and whose adherents were called antidicomarianites, held the opinion of Bonosus on the mother of Christ. At the same time, and in the same country, there existed sectaries of a totally opposite opinion. They make Mary a goddess, whom they honour as queen of heaven, while offering to her cakes (collyrides), whence they received the name of Collyridians. This sect, proceeding from Thrace and upper Scythia, extended itself into the Arabian provinces. It was, perhaps, the same as that of the Mariamites of which we have spoken previously. Women specially were eager to adopt its beliefs. They decorate a chariot, on which is a square seat, covered by cloths at a certain time of the year; during several days, they offer a loaf consecrated to Mary, and each one takes a portion of it. This worship of which women are the priestesses, does not perpetuate itself in the same form; but the tendency of the semi-pagan populations to create a feminine divinity, does not receive less satisfaction; before a century is passed, the apotheosis of Mary commences in the official church. Theodosius, returning to Milan, sojourns there during two years. In that interval, as the sequel of a sedition, he orders the massacre of Thessalonica, in which perish seven thousand victims. Ambrose forbids him entrance into the church during eight years, and before receiving him, subjects him to public penance. Theodosius, leaving the young Valentinian in Italy, returns to Constantinople (391). Up to this time, he had satisfied himself with interdicting sacrifices on the part of the pagans, and with withdrawing from their worship imperial favours, without closing their temples or restraining their religious liberty. But at last persecutions begin. Hellenism is outlawed. In virtue of imperial rescripts, the bishops actively work for its ruin, especially in the oriental princes. Theophilus, bishop of Alexandria, openly attacks the ancient religion. He urges the demolition of the temples, in making their superstitions a laughing stock. His acts call forth sedition. The heathen rush to arms; sanguinary conflicts take place in the streets. The pagans, withdrawing into the temple of Serapis, as into a fortress, fall thence on their adversaries. At their head is a philosopher named Olympus, who excites them to die rather than abandon the laws of their ancestors. Reference is made to the emperor; he commands the temples to be beaten down as being the cause of the sedition. The Gentiles are astounded. Many of them flee into different places. The temple of Serapis is abandoned; Olympus retires into Italy. The Christians break the image of Serapis into pieces; the temple is demolished, and two churches rise on its ground. The other temples of Egypt are afterwards beaten down. The bishops preside over the work of destruction. A law published in the year 391, addressed to the governors of Egypt, forbids all sacrificing, walking round the temples, visiting them, rendering any service to the gods. But despite the zeal of Theodosius, some celebrated temples are protected in the East by the resistance of the population; some remain standing in Arabia, in Palestine, in Phenicia, in Syria. In the west, the ancient worship is still full of strength. The emperors had indeed made two laws against it, one dated 27th Feb. 391, addressed to the prefect of Rome, which forbids all persons to immolate victims, to visit the temples, to worship the idols; the other the 11th of May following, sent to the prefect of the pretorium of Italy and Illyrium, by which the Christians who return to paganism are characterised as infamous. But after the departure of Theodosius for Constantinople, Valentinian II. is too weak to withstand the power of the Gentiles. There are many senators, as well as others, that defy the law, for instance, Symmachus, consul that same 391st year. The most dangerous of all is Arbogastes, a Frank by nation, who, placed at the head of armies, overrules or despises the will of the young emperor. While that prince was in Gaul, a letter from the senate requests of him the restoration of the privileges taken by Gratian from the temples of the idols. A positive refusal is the reply of Valentinian II.; he remains unshaken by the urgency of the Gentiles who surround his person. Argobastes caused him to be strangled at Vienne (392), and proclaims as emperor a literary man named Eugenius, who believes in Auruspices and astrologers. Argobastes intends to exercise the power himself under the name of this new prince. Theodosius prepares to wage war in the west without ceasing to take steps against the idolatry and the dissidents of the oriental regions. A law of November 392, interdicts sacrifices to idols under pain of high treason, and publishes confiscations or heavy fines for simple offerings or acts of homage; penalties are declared against the judges and magistrates who shall not denounce or punish the guilty. Two other laws of that same year decree confiscations and fines for ordaining priests in the dissident sects, and banishment against such as trouble the people by discussing official dogmas. At the same time, the dissidents ruin their cause themselves by their divisions. The Arians dispute whether God could be called a Father before the birth of the Son. Others reject the trinal form of baptism in order to give it in the name of the death of Jesus Christ. A priest named Ærius forms the sect of the Ærians, who assimilate the bishop and the priest, repel prayers for the dead, as well as fasts and the observance of days. But Arianism, divided and persecuted, finds an asylum in the barbarous nations. The emperor Eugenius seeks a support in the ancient religion, which is very powerful in Italy, and in the western lands; the liberty of their worship is restored to the Gentiles; the idols again stand on their pedestals; the altar of victory is re-established in Rome; their revenues are restored to the temples; the image of Hercules surmounts a military standard. Theodosius passes the Alps in 394. After an alternative of successes and reverses, he finally remains conqueror owing to the defection of a part of the troops of Eugenius, who is given up and slain. Arbogastes flees into the mountains and puts himself to death. The conqueror associates with himself his two sons in the empire. The East is given to Arcadius, the West to Honorius, who repairs to Italy. In vain does the emperor try to bring the senators of Rome over to the Christian faith. To the exhortation which he addresses to them, they reply that they cannot renounce a religion under which their city has subsisted for 1200 years, to adopt another in which they are required to believe without reasoning. The princes discharge the public treasury from the cost of the sacrifices and the other pagan ceremonies. Then the sacrifices cease; the festivals fall into neglect, the priests that serve the idols no longer officiate, and their temples are abandoned. Theodosius dies at Milan at the commencement of the year 395. But his death makes no change in the measures taken against the idolators and the dissidents. Acadius prosecutes the destruction of the temples in the East. A law of the year 397 commands them to be demolished even in the rural districts. In the West, where idolatry is stronger, Honorius seems in attacking it, to respect certain susceptibilities. If he prohibits sacrifices and the old superstitions, he at the same time spares the ornaments which decorate the monuments and the public places, that is the statues which are found there. Instead of beating the temples down, he orders that they be turned into churches. These measures do not seem to have been carried into effect instantaneously and in a general manner. In 407, a new law requires that the idols and the altars be destroyed, and the temples applied to some other purpose, interdicting also all pagan solemnities.

The laws passed against the ancient worship make few martyrs. The Pagans had not a faith sufficiently vivid to dare death. They yield to force while keeping their beliefs in the bottom of their hearts. It is more easy to demolish temples than to destroy superstitions. A great number of persons doubtless end by approaching the new worship; but all these conversions, more or less voluntary, are not without danger to Christianity. The new pupils have not put off the old man ; in entering the church they bring with them their superstitious ideas and the imitation of the Pagan rites. A kind of assimilation takes place between the two religions, and toward assimilation Christian teachers lean in order to attract the multitude of the Gentiles, being drawn away by the tendencies of the populations. The mixture becomes sensible from the time of Theodosius ; it will end in becoming a veritable Pagano-Christian fusion. With equal zeal the two emperors pursue the extinction of the dissident sects. In the three first years of his reign Arcadius publishes several laws against them, either in general or in particular against the Eunomians and the Apollinarists. Their ministers are driven from the cities, and their assemblies are forbidden even in rural districts under pain of death and loss of goods. The two last sects do not exist in the West, which has little taste for the subtleties of oriental trinitarians ; but the Priscillianists maintain themselves in Spain and the Manicheans spread into different regions. In Africa the system of the Donatists still divides the church into two parts ; they count then more than 400 bishops. A schism which takes place in their bosom facilitates attacks upon them. Moreover, they find a formidable antagonist in the person of Augustin. The great doctor, imbued at first with Manichean ideas became converted at Milan, and received baptism at the hands of Ambrosius. Ordained priest at Hippo in 391 and bishop in 395, he vigorously attacks his old fellow religionists, as well as the Donatists. In 398 a law of Honorius decrees capital punishment against the last, whose acts of violence were redoubled on the occasion of a war kindled by Gildon, a petty king of Mauritania. In 407 and 408 the same emperor puts forth rigorous laws against both the Manicheans and the Priscillianists. The doctrines of the Arians, and specially those of the semi-

Arians, came, we have said, from Origen, who was followed by all the fathers anterior to the Council of Nice. The decisions published against Arianism fell then indirectly on the celebrated doctor of the third century. But as yet no one thought of his being himself brought to book. His authority is so great in the early days of the Arian discussions, that Athanasius ably invokes its aid in favour of his opinions. Basil and Gregory also interpret in a favourable manner the passages of his works appealed to by the Arians; other fathers of the fourth century are not less well disposed toward Origen. But he is attacked by many. The Arians, in profiting by his decisions, necessarily draw upon him the hostility of their adversaries. Nevertheless the critics have little injured his reputation. More detrimental has been the excessive admiration of some of his partisans. Not satisfied with accepting his sound doctrines, it espouses hazardous opinions which he drew from Platonism, and set forth not as articles of belief, but as simple speculations; his allegorical interpretations are thus transformed into dogmatic assertions. Accordingly there are about the end of the fourth century two kinds of Origenists. These, who are called orthodox, admit only those of his doctrines which are received by the official Church; those, who are accounted heterodox, accept as truths a certain number of his hypothetical opinions. The latter are found chiefly in the monasteries of Egypt. The points of Origen's doctrine which are controverted at that time are the following. The Son cannot see the Father, nor the Spirit the Son; the soul, on account of its sins, has been put into the body as into a prison: the devil and his angels will one day repent and will reign in heaven with the saints; Adam and Eve received only after their sin human bodies which the Scripture calls "coats of skins" (Gen. iii. 21). The flesh will not rise; human beings will have no sex in heaven; the earthly paradise is to be understood allegorically; the waters which Scripture says are above the heavens, are the angels; those which it puts below the earth are devils; man by his sin has ceased to be the image of God. These questions agitated by the monks were spread abroad. Disagreements proceeded from them between John, bishop of Jerusalem, and Epiphanes, bishop of Salamis. Minds dividing, some took part for John, others for Epiphanes. Rufinus, priest of Aquilea was an Origenist ; Jerome combatted Rufinus and John of Jerusalem. Theophilus of Alexandria, whose jurisdiction extended over the Egyptian monks, had till then, despite the urgency of Epiphanes and Jerome, abstained from declaring himself against Origen. Dissensions which arise in the monasteries, and the animosity which he censures against certain monks, determine him at last to take his part. The most simple of the monks, literally interpreting diverse passages of the Old Testament, represented God under a human form ; whence they were called anthropomorphites. The more instructed, in order to bring them to ideas less unworthy of the Deity, put under their eyes the allegorical explanations of Origen. The others, infatuated with their opinion, denominate their brethren Origenists, a name which they take unfavourably. Theophilus tries to draw out of their error those poor anthropomorphitic monks. But they, hastening in crowds to Alexandria, accuse him of Origenism and utter threats of death against him. The bishop, in order to calm them, declares himself not less than they an enemy of Origen's books, and promises to condemn their doctrines. Matters might perhaps have remained there if Theophilus had not been carried further by a personal resentment. Among the monks who combatted anthropomorphism, there were at Scetis four celebrated for their zeal and who were called the *great brothers* ; they were believed to be favourable to Origen's opinions. Theophilus, irritated with them without a very legitimate reason, convenes a council in which it is ordained that whoever shall approve Origen's works shall be expelled from the church. A synodal letter is addressed to all the bishops, in which Origen is principally accused with having declared that the kingdom of Christ will come to an end ; that the devil will be saved by his merits, like all reasonable creatures ; that bodies will not rise entirely incorruptible, and that finally they will be annihilated ; and that the Son of God should not be prayed to.

The bishop moreover excommunicates by name three of the great brothers without their being summoned. Furnished with an order from the Prefect of Egypt, he in the night falls with soldiers on the monasteries, drives away the inhabitants, pillages and burns the cells. The great brothers, fleeing into Palestine, settle with eighty monks at Scythopolis. Theophilus writes against them to the bishops of the countries where they are. They finally repair to Constantinople (401).

Jean, surnamed Chrysostom (golden-mouthed), had been bishop of that city for about three years. The firmness of his character, his eloquence and his virtue had gained him the love of the people; but he had incurred animadversion as much from a part of the clergy, whose morals he had reformed, as from great people for whose vices he had no indulgence. The monks go and cast themselves at his feet begging him to intercede for them with their bishop. Chrysostom, without admitting them to communion, allows them to worship in the Church, and writes to Theophilus according to their desire. But a rumour having reached Alexandria that the fugitives had partaken of the holy mysteries, the bishop sends five monks charged to denounce their doctrines. The great brothers, after having anathematised every bad opinion, present to Chrysostom and to the emperor petitions containing divers accusations against Theophilus and his deputies. The Bishop of Constantinople having in vain exhorted the parties to reconciliatiôn, ends by occupying himself with the affair no longer. The envoys of Theophilus are put in prison under the presumption of calumny, awaiting the arrival of their chief who had been sent for by the emperor. Meanwhile, the Bishop of Alexandria had attached to his cause Epiphanes, Bishop of Salamis in Cyprus, a man held in high consideration generally, and of great simplicity of character. The latter, having got together the bishops of his island in Synod, gets a canon passed which interdicts the reading of Origen's books; at the same time he writes to Chrysostom to induce him to adopt a similar measure. When Theophilus is called to Constantinople, Epiphanes, at his instigation, goes thither the first, carrying with him the acts of his council. He refuses to see the bishop of Constantinople unless he condemns Origen and drives away the great brothers and their monks. He is even ready to carry things further; but a remonstrance made to him by Chrysostom changes his resolutions, and determines him to return to Cyprus ; he dies on shipboard before reaching the island.

Theophilus finally disembarks at Constantinople, followed by a great number of Egyptian bishops. He abstains from communicating with Chrysostom, and puts himself into relations with all the enemies that he might have whether among the clergy that he has reformed or among the high personages whom his censures have not spared. The empress is among the latter ; she urges Theophilus to call a synod in order to depose John. Forty-five bishops, of whom thirty-six are from Egypt, assemble under the presidency of the bishop of Alexandria, in the village Chene, near Chalcedon (403). A part of the clergy of Constantinople lay before them articles against Chrysostom, filled with futile or calumnious accusations. Forty-four bishops come from different provinces to Constantinople, protest against the conduct of Theophilus, and summon him to clear himself of charges brought against him. Chrysostom declares that he will present himself before any council that does not contain Theophilus and the three bishops who are his enemies. None the less does the assembly at Chene continue its proceedings ; Chrysostom pronounces before the people sermons in which he warmly assails his adversaries and the empress herself, whom he designates under the names of Jezabel and Herodias. Condemned in his absence, he appeals to an Œcumenical Council. The emperor sends him beyond the Bosphorus, whence popular irritation compels his immediate re-call ; Chrysostom returns in triumph amidst the acclamations of the multitude. Fear of the people's movements disperses the Council of Chene. Theophilus flees to Alexandria, but after being reconciled with two of the great brothers (the others were dead), and having admitted them to his communion. In the Council of Chene the question of the

Origenists did not come up; the affair fell to sleep in the East; Theophilus himself has no longer difficulty to read the writings of Origen.

This quarrel had its reverberations in the Western Church. Translations by Rufinus and Jerome had just made Origen known to the Latins. Rufinus even saw himself condemned by Anastasius, Bishop of Rome (390-402), who, after the decision of Theophilus against Origen, had, by a similar sentence, interdicted the reading of the works of that Alexandrine doctor (Origen). In a letter written, the year following, to the Bishop of Jerusalem, Anastasius avows that before the translation of Rufinus he did not know who Origen was or what he had said. This declaration proves how little the works of the Greek Fathers, those true founders of the Trinitarian Church, were then read and known in the West. However Chrysostom does not long remain in peace in Constantinople. He is still pursued by the enmity of the empress. A new council is brought together in which John is deposed, for the sole reason that after his first condemnation he put himself again into possession of his seat without having been restored by any synodal authority. He is banished to Cucusa in Armenia and thence to Arabissa, a city situated a little more to the north. Finally, in the year 407, he is taken to Pytionte, a desert place near the shores of the Pontus Euxinus. He dies on his way to Cumana. A great number of the inhabitants of Constantinople refuse to enter into relations with his successor, and hold meetings apart; they receive the name of Johnites. On its part the Church of Rome abstains from all communication with the East, so long as the memory of Chrysostom has not been re-established. The Emperor Arcadius dies sometime from this date (408), leaving for successor his son, Theodosius II. or the younger, who is not more than eight years of age. While the Oriental Church is troubled by discussions on Origen, or rather by the passions of the bishop and the court, that of the West sees arise in its bosom a dissidence which is more or less directly connected with the doctrines of that Father.

Pelagius, a simple lay monk, born in Brittany, had long lived in Rome, where he was renowned for his knowledge and his virtues. Rufinus, on his return from Syria, communicates to him certain opinions on grace and freewill which were already current in the East. They were taught by Theodore of Mopsuesta; but they passed unseen in countries where other doctrines pre-occupied men's minds. Pelagius begins to sow them in the year 400 with certain precautions, and afterwards offers them more openly by means of his disciples. They spread from neighbour to neighbour. Celestius, the most celebrated of the disciples of Pelagius, speaks freely against original sin, belief in which was then spreading. Both quit Rome in 409 to pass into Africa; thence Pelagius proceeds to Palestine where he makes a long stay. Celestius wishing to be ordained priest at Carthage, his opinions are laid before the bishops. He is brought before a not very numerous council, condemned and deprived of the communion of the Church, he appeals to the Bishop of Rome; and nearly at the same time, without following up his appeal, he repairs to Ephesus.

The following were his maxims, which the Council condemned:—Adam was created mortal; his death was not the consequence of his sin; that sin injured no one but himself, and not the human race; children are born in the same state as Adam before his sin; Adam's sin is not the cause of men's death, nor is the resurrection of Christ the cause of the general resurrection; the law can save as well as the gospel; there existed men without sin even before the coming of Jesus Christ; infants possess the life eternal without being baptised. Augustin had not been present in that Council of Carthage, but he soon set himself to combatting the Pelagians both by his preaching and by his writings. He maintains the doctrine of original sin and the necessity of baptism for children; he affirms that the law, howsoever good and holy in itself, cannot save us, if the grace of the Holy Spirit does not give us strength to work out our salvation.

Pelagius sends from Palestine to Carthage a book in

which his doctrine is exposed:—God in giving man free will has given him power to turn his will toward either good and evil ; it is by this natural gift that the philosophers have practised virtue, and that so many saints appeared in the world before Jesus Christ ; sin comes solely from the will and not from any vice of nature ; it is by a consequence of his free will that Adam was expelled from Paradise ; every one may acquire spiritual riches ; the commands of God do not surpass our strength ; otherwise, could he, who is so just and so good, punish us? Zealous defenders support the cause of Pelagius in the East, among others Theodore of Mopsuesta, who publishes five books in support of those opinions ; they are equally approved by a council assembled at Diospolis in the year 415. At Carthage, on the contrary, a council held the following year anathematises in a general manner those who profess the doctrine against grace. At the request of the bishops of Africa, Innocent of Rome (402-417) condemns also the opinions of Pelagius. Celestius returns to Rome in the year 417 on the pretext of supporting his anterior appeal. He presents to Zozimus, then bishop (417-18) a confession of faith, in which he declares that he professes what he has drawn from the apostles and the prophets without pretending to decide anything as the author of dogma. The baptism of children is necessary, he says, "because it is written that the kingdom of heaven can be given only to the baptised ; but the transmission of an original sin does not form a part of Christian doctrine ; sin is introduced by the will and not by nature." At the same time Pelagius sends from Jerusalem a letter containing a similar profession of faith, with an able justification. Zozimus, convinced of the purity of their doctrine, writes in their favour to the bishops of Africa. But the Emperor Honorius, deciding like the Council of Carthage, and by decree banishing Pelagius, Celestius, and their adherents, the bishop of Rome retraces his steps and condemns them in his turn. A full council, containing more than two hundred bishops from all Africa and even from Spain, meets at Carthage in 418 ; its soul is Augustin. There they decide against the Pelagians that Adam was not created mortal, but became such by his sin ; that newly-born children bring with them an original sin derived from Adam, and ought to be baptised for the remission of sins ; that without baptism infants cannot enter into the kingdom of heaven, which is everlasting life; that the grace of God which justifies us by Jesus Christ, serves not only for the remission of committed sins, but also to aid us so that we commit sins no more ; that the same grace opens to us a knowledge of God's commands, and leads us to love and to be able for what is required of us ; that the grace of justification is necessary for us to accomplish God's injunctions. The bishops who refuse to subscribe to the decisions given against the doctrine of Pelagius are driven from Italy in virtue of imperial laws. Eighteen of them, obstinate in their resistance, justify themselves by a profession of faith analogous to those of Pelagius and Celestius. In the number of these opponents is Julian of Eclane, who afterwards becomes the principal defender of Pelagianism. Down to 431 the Pelagians cease not to ask for a universal council. They address themselves to the Eastern bishops, alleging that they are unjustly persecuted by the Westerns. Some of their deputies are thrown on Constantinople and Ephesus. In 421 a council, presided over by the bishop of Antioch, condemns Pelagius, who is expelled from the sacred places of Jerusalem. From that event nothing more is known of Pelagius. Augustin continues to his death, which takes place in 430, to write against the Pelagians, and to handle the questions of grace, free will, and predestination.

A great number of persons, from the time of the celebrated doctor, consider that he went too far and allowed himself to be drawn into a kind of fatalism. A reaction took place even among the adversaries of Pelagius. This movement makes its appearance in Gaul about the year 430, and specially in the neighbourhood of Marseilles. Near that place there lived in a monastery, of which he was the founder, John Cassian, an old Eastern monk whom Chrysostom had ordained a deacon. In his " Conferences on the Fathers," he puts forth a doctrine intermediate between Pelagius and Augustin, a doctrine held by Oriental Christians, who had always maintained the same sentiments. His partisans, who are designated under the name of Marsellians, Gaulish, Semi-Pelagians, confess that every man perished in Adam ; that no one could be delivered by his free will alone, nor had the power of persevering in righteousness. But they think that prevenient grace is not necessary for the production of the first movements of repentance ; that man is susceptible of faith and of good desires by his own proper strength, just as he can withstand the influences of grace and not yield to its inspirations ; that it may be gained by our prayers or lost by our neglect. They maintain that the doctrine of predestination relaxes the energy of saints and takes from sinners the care of rising into virtue ; that all virtue is annihilated if God's decree must go before man's will. This opinion is embraced and defended by Faustus, bishop of Riez; Vincent, abbot of Lerins ; Gennadius, priest of Marseilles ; Honoratus, bishop of Marseilles ; Hilary, bishop of Arles. It has for contradictors in the fifth century Prosper of Aquitaine ; Celestin, bishop of Rome (422-34) ; Germain of Auxerre ; Loup of Troyes ; John Maxentius ; Fulgens, bishop of Ruspa in Africa ; Cesarius of Arles ; and different councils. We here remind the reader of the fact that the primitive Church knew nothing of original sin. This opinion seems to have been introduced to give a reason of the custom of baptising children, a custom imitated from Hellenism about the end of the Second Century, and which was blamed by Tertullian. In regard to the omniscience and foreknowledge of God, to grace and predestination, placed alongside of conscience and man's free will, it is one of those questions on which the human mind cannot attain absolute truth ; oscillating now on this side, now on that, it at last settles between the two extremes, in a sort of middle term which is indeterminate.

During these discussions the Western empire was a prey to the barbarians. About the year 406 the Vandals, the Alains, the Quades, the Sarmatians, the Gepidae, the Heruli, the Saxons, and the Germans ravaged with impunity the regions of Gaul. After the death of Stilico (401) the Visigoths fall upon Italy, under the leadership of Alaric. In 409 they lay siege to Rome. The greatest part of the people was still idolatrous in heart ; despite the Imperial laws, the pagans, with the Senate at their head, offer public sacrifices in the Capitol and in the other temples with a view to turn aside the woes that are ready to fall on the city. This once it gets off by paying the price of impunity. The Romans, by Alaric's order, raise to the empire Attalus, prefect of the city, who favours the ancient religion. The following year Attalus is deposed by Alaric, after having entered into an agreement with Honorius. The truce being broken, Rome is besieged afresh by the barbarous chief, who captures it (24th Aug. 410), and gives it up for plunder during three days. Then he devastates Campania and dies at Cosentia, when he was arranging for passing into Sicily. Ataulphus, his successor, in 412 penetrates into Gaul, establishes himself between the Rhone and the Pyrenees, and thence passes into Spain ; about the same time the Burgundians found a state in the countries bordering on the Rhone ; the two are Arians. The Vandals had passed over the Pyrenees in the year 409, and after them the Alains and Suevi ; these peoples divided Spain among them ; some were still idolators, others professed Arianism.

These invasions furnish the Gentiles with occasion for declaiming against the Christian religion, which they accuse of the public calamities. "The Roman power," they say, "ceases not to decrease since this superstition appeared among us. The protecting gods of the empire withdrew in the degree in which their worship was neglected, and the Christians themselves have not more than we been defended by their new god." These complaints leave an impression on many minds, and it is to refute them that Augustin composes his great work, " On the City of God." Meanwhile, the episcopacy is no longer satisfied with the ruin of Hellenism and heresy ; the civil power is an object of its enterprises. The Bishops of Rome and of Alexandria, among others, effect an absolute dominion. In the second of those cities, the Governor Orestes had ceaselessly to struggle against Cyril, who, three years before, had succeeded Theophilus, his uncle. One Sunday the governor publicly flogged one of the dependents of the bishop, for having excited a tumult in the theatre where the Jews were assembled. Cyril, throwing the blame on the latter, utters great threats against them. The irritation increases on both sides, and in the night there breaks out between the Jews and the Christians a sanguinary conflict in which the latter get the worst of it. The next day, the bishop, at the head of the multitude, seizes the synagogues, drives the Jews out of the city, and gives up their goods to pillage. Orestes informs the emperor, to whom Cyril writes to justify his party. Shortly after the governor is attacked by five hundred monks, who insult and stone him, and would have put him to death, had not his defence been undertaken by the people. Orestes gives up to punishment a monk who has struck him; the bishop transfers the corpse into a church to make relics of it.

Cyril's animosity does not stop there. There existed in Alexandria an illustrious woman named Hypatia, daughter of the philosopher Theos. Surpassing in knowledge all the men of the time, she taught in the Platonic school the diverse branches of philosophical science; from all sides pupils gathered around her. The confidence and the authority which she had gained permitted her sometimes to approach the magistrates. Her exquisite modesty conciliated for her universal respect and veneration. But envy was only the more irritated; a story gets abroad among the Christians that in her conversations with Orestes she opposes obstacles to the reconciliation of the governor and the bishop. Men, conducted by a leader named Peter, lay in wait for her on her way to her own home, drag her from her carriage, hurry her into a church, where she is stripped naked and killed by blows from broken pots; then her body is torn in pieces and burnt bit by bit. This crime, which is cast on the bishop, covers him with infamy —both him and his church. It does not appear that the governor gave himself the trouble of punishing the murder of this illustrious woman any more than he did to punish the expulsion of the Jews and the pillage of their property. It may be believed that Cyril's zeal did not lack imitators, and that both Jews and Gentiles were more than once exposed to excesses of the same nature. Accordingly, some years later (423), Theodore the Younger is obliged to issue several laws to prevent them in future; it is forbidden to plunder the Jews, and to take away their synagogues, while they are interdicted to build new ones; equally is the exercise of violence against them and against idolators prohibited; nor are they to be robbed of anything on pain of four-fold restitution. By way of compensation, the emperor renews the decrees of his predecessors against dissidents and against the Gentiles, yet while for the last reducing to banishment with loss of property the penalty of death decreed against such as offered sacrifices to the idols. Honorius, the emperor of the west, dies this same year 423, leaving the greater part of his estates in the hands of the barbarians, and the remainder under the incessant fear of invasion. He is succeeded in 425 by Valentinian III., son of his sister Placidia. The first care of the new emperor is to confirm the privileges of the Church, and to renew the laws against the heretics by ordering their banishment from the cities, as well as the authors or followers of schisms. At the same time, Boniface, Count of Africa, dissatisfied with the court, invites the Vandals into that province. The barbarians enter it in 428, under the leadership of Genseric, defeat the Romans, subject the country, and introduce into it the Arianism which they had already carried into Spanish lands. After the consolidation of his power by the capture of Carthage (439), Genseric persecutes the adherents to Consubstantialism; he exiles their bishops and clergy, seizes their churches, and reduces them to meet here and there for the celebration of their worship. In 440 the Vandals pass into Sicily, ravage it, and persecute the bishops that are not of their communion. Meanwhile, new discussions arise in the Oriental Church. The deity of Christ and the Consubstantial Trinity being established and recognised by the laws of the empire, it is next asked what in the incarnation is the relation of the divine and the human natures; are they separate or mixed? does not the one absorb the other? For questions of this nature there existed no solution whether in Platonism or the sacred scripture. If you consider them in themselves, you end in inextricable enigmas, in which, however, Hellenic sophistry liked to indulge. The promotion of Nestorius to the bishopric of Constantinople soon produces disagreements (428). The new bishop was a man full of zeal. Six weeks after his installation he obtains from Theodosius II. a law against all dissidents. They are required to restore the churches which they have taken from the Consubstantialists, and not to ordain new clerks. The Arians, the Macedonians, the Apollinarists are forbidden to have churches in any city, and the Novatians are forbidden to innovate. The Eunomians, the Valentinians, the Montanists, the Priscillians, the Phrygians, the Marcionites, the Borborians, the Messalians, the Euchites, the Donatists, the Audians, the Hydroparastates, the Ascrodugists, the Photinians, the Paulians, the Marcellines are deprived of meeting together for prayer in common in any place whatever; the Manicheans cannot even sojourn in cities.

The enumeration contained in this law proves that the ancient heresies still had partisans more or less numerous; but the Manicheans, in ceaseless progression, tended to absorb all the other oriental sects. Despite his zeal for orthodoxy, Nestorius was soon led to publish an opinion which seems heterodox to the majority; so difficult is it to walk straight on the perilous path of the trinity and the incarnation! During the two first centuries, we have said Mary was called mother of Jesus, mother of the Messiah. When at the beginning of the third century the opinion of the Deity of Christ began to establish itself, the usage was introduced by little and little of designating Mary under the title of mother of God, in order to affirm that deity against its opponents; an assertion which in the thought of the Christotheists, did not imply that she was not also the mother of the man, but solely that her son was at once mar and God. In the sequel, in the midst of the discussions with the partisans of Paul of Samosata, Sabellius, Arius, and Photinus, the deity of Christ tends ceaselessly to prevail over his humanity, which for more than once is threatened with being accounted fantastic. The expression of mother of God applied to Mary then appears to some improper, since, according to the official opinion, her son is at the same time God and man, and dangerous since it seems to say that he is only God and not man also. The expression of mother of Christ seems to them then more suitable as a designation of the mother of the God-man.

This last opinion was professed by Nestorius. As early as the first months of his episcopate at Constantinople, he begins to openly preach that Mary ought not to be called mother of God, since she did not give birth to God, but to a man with whom was united the Word of the Father. It is to be remarked that he did not the less believe, as his contradictors, that that union took place at the instant of the conception. His sermons collected and diffused at a distance shake many minds, especially among the Egyptian monks. Cyril, bishop of Alexandria, combats the doctrine of Nestorius in a letter addressed to those monks. There results between the two bishops an exchange of letters in which the question is discussed. Both of them write to Celestin, bishop of Rome. A strong opposition is formed in Constantinople against the bishop who persecutes the opposers; Theodosius inclines in his favour. To John, bishop of Antioch, his friend who seeks to bring him back, Nestorius replies that he has found the church divided, these calling Mary mother of God, those mother of a man, and that to reunite them, he employs the term mother of Christ, which comprises both natures. Celestin assembles in Rome a Council in which the Nestorian doctrine is condemned (430). He informs of the fact the bishops of Constantinople and Alexandria as well as those of the great sees of the east. The execution of that decree is entrusted to Cyril. The latter collects at Alexandria all the bishops of Egypt, and in their name writes to Nestorius that he means within ten days to anathematise the propositions he has advanced. The letter terminates with twelve anathemas against those propositions. Before the letter reaches Constantinople, an imperial rescript convokes an œcumenical Council at Ephesus for Pentecost in the year 431 ; this was a step solicited by both parties. Divers writings are published on both sides before the meeting of the council. Nestorius, attacking Cyril's twelve anathemas, proposes twelve others in reply. John of Antioch gives it as his opinion equally that Cyril has gone too far in his twelve anathemas, and has struck upon the error of Apollinaris ; he causes a reply to be made by the two most learned bishops of his province, Andrew of Samosata and Theodoret of Cyr. The piece produced by the former, composed in the name of the Orientals, is approved by the Council ; that of Theodoret, given in his own name, spreads into Phenicia and the neighbouring lands.

Nestorius soon betakes himself to Ephesus, followed by a prodigious multitude. Cyril arrives at the time indicated. John of Antioch and the eastern bishops make some delay. After waiting a fortnight Cyril and those of his party meet together in Council to the number of one hundred and fifty-eight. Nestorius and sixty-eight other bishops protest against this assembly, as well as Candidian, who is charged by the emperor to keep good order. Cyril and his associates pay no attention to them, and pronounce on Nestorius a sentence which deposes him and cuts him off from every ecclesiastical assembly. The bishop of Constantinople and Candidian refer to Theodosius. Cyril on his side sends him a synodal letter.

John of Antioch arrives five days after with the other oriental bishops. He holds a council of forty-two bishops in which Cyril and Memnon, bishop of Ephesus, are deposed as authors of disorder, and moreover, Cyril on account of his twelve anathemas which are declared heretical ; the bishops seduced by them are excommunicated until they give their assent to the sentence and re-unite with the Council of John of Antioch. On the report of Candidian an imperial rescript annuls what has been done contrary to Nestorius. Meanwhile the legates of the bishop of Rome arrive at Ephesus. They put themselves in relations with

Cyril, and approve the decision taken against the bishop of Constantinople. They then annul in the Council the acts of John of Antioch and his associates, who are sundered from ecclesiastical communion so long as they do not repent. The emperor Theodosius sends Count John to Ephesus to make himself acquainted with the real state of things. John puts under supervision Nestorius, Cyril, and Memnon, and makes vain efforts to conciliate the other bishops. The emperor orders to Chalcedon eight deputies of each of the two factions, without succeeding in bringing them into agreement. Finally he resolves to maintain the deposition of Nestorius, whom he sends into his former monastery near Antioch, and to consider as not having taken place what had been done by the bishops of John's party, or against them. Maximian is called to the episcopate of Constantinople. John of Antioch and his party who do not acknowledge the new bishop, meet at Tarsus where they depose Cyril a second time, and with him the seven bishops that ordained Maximian. Hostilities are prolonged on both sides. Finally, after many useless attempts, John of Antioch and Cyril come to an understanding nearly two years later. Nestorius remains deposed ; Maximian is maintained ; Cyril extenuates and explains what John of Antioch and his friends find reprehensible in his twelve anathemas.

The most ardent bishops of the two factions none the less continue to work for or against. The old partisans of John of Antioch refuse to commune with him ; those of Cyril oblige him in some way to justify himself. The Emperor enjoins on all the bishops to commune with John. Fifteen in the East and six in Europe condemn them for having refused to subscribe to the condemnation of Nestorius. Theodoret, while acknowledging that Cyril has retracted what was reprehensible in his twelve anathemas, none the less persists in believing that the doctrine of Nestorius has been ill understood ; but a desire for peace makes him enter into communion with John of Antioch. In 435 a law forbids the partisans of Nestorius to assemble under pain of the confiscation of their property. The former bishop of Constantinople (Nestorius) is, the year following, transferred into the desert in Egypt, and successively into several other places. At last he dies, overwhelmed with age and infirmities. The opinions of Nestorius had numerous followers in Cilicia. He passed for having been the disciple of Theodore of Mopsuesta, who himself received instruction under Diodorus of Tarsus. After the condemnation of their leader, the Nestorians take pains to spread the works of the two last bishops, both of whom died in the communion of the Church; they make it a support for their own sentiments. Some persons take occasion to speak against Theodore of Mopsuesta, to whom they impute opinions still more offensive than those of Nestorius. But a Council assembled at Antioch puts an end to these discussions, declaring that one may disapprove the sentiments of the ancients without anathematising them, and that to condemn deceased Fathers would be to open the way to every kind of confusion. Theodosius II. in 448 issues a command to drive from their churches the Nestorians who are bishops or clerks, to excommunicate those who are laics, and to burn the books whose doctrine does not agree with that of Ephesus. Several bishops are expelled in virtue of this law. We shall see Nestorianism rise again hereafter and maintain itself, but with some modifications of doctrine.

While Nestorius is undergoing persecution there arises among his antagonists a heresy the very opposite of his own. This new dissidence has for its author Eutyches, an old priest and abbot of a monastery of three hundred monks at Constantinople, one of the most zealous adversaries of Nestorius. In his excessive affirmation of the deity of Christ he is led, in some sort, to deny his human nature. According to him, the two natures existed long before their union in Jesus; but when that union took effect, it formed but one nature, in which the Word prevailed; the body that came from Mary, although of human nature, was nevertheless consubstantial with the Virgin.

When the existence of this opinion got known, Flavian, bishop of Constantinople, in 448 convened a council of thirty bishops, by which Eutyches was deposed and excommunicated for having fallen into the error of Apollinaris and Valentinian. But the condemned finds a powerful protector at Court in the person of the eunuch Chrysaphes, a particular enemy of the bishop. By his means Eutyches obtains a revision of the acts of the council. Dioscorus, bishop of Alexandria, at the instigation of Chrysaphes, and the empress Eudoxia, who wishes to annoy Pulcheria, his sister-in-law, induces Theodosius II. to convoke an œcumenical council at Ephesus for the examination of that question. The bishops who have condemned Eutyches are to be present, not as judges but as parties. Leo, bishop of Rome (440-461), sends legates with instructions favourable to the opinion of Flavian. The council meets under the presidence of Dioscorus, who directs all things (449). The judgment of the Council of Constantinople is corrected, and the Eutyches' profession of faith is approved. They depose Flavian and Eusebius of Dorylia (the accuser of Eutyches) for having altered the faith of the Council of Nice, as well as that of the first Council of Ephesus, and scandalised all the churches by the condemnation of Eutyches. Other bishops are also deposed on the charge of Nestorianism, among others Theodoret of Cyr and Ibas of Edessa, both absent and not summoned. The Church of Alexandria had already anathematised Theodoret as a Nestorian. Ibas of Edessa had in 448 been acquitted of an accusation of the same kind made against him for having in a letter to a Persian named Maris, charged with Apollinarism the anathemas of Cyril and bestowed praises on Theodore of Mopsuesta. The Roman legatees in vain oppose the resolutions of the assembly presided over by Dioscorus; and different bishops who also wish to resist, are constrained by violence to subscribe. This council afterwards received the title of the *Brigands of Ephesus*. Flavian is exiled into Lydia, where he dies after some days in consequence of the ill-treatment he suffered at the hands of Dioscorus and the monks. After the dissolution of the Council, Dioscorus and the Egyptian bishops go so far as to excommunicate Leo, bishop of Rome. Some months after, Leo convenes a council in which the acts of that of Ephesus are condemned unanimously. He then importunes Theodosius by means of Valentinian III. to convoke in Italy all the bishops of the world. But the Eastern Emperor persists in maintaining the judgment of the Council of Ephesus and the condemnation of Flavian, whose doctrine he confounds with that of Nestorius. The death of Theodosius II. changes the state of things (29th July 450). Marcion, elevated to the empire by Pulcheria, whom he marries, is eager to condemn the followers of Apollinaris and of Eutyches. Anatolius, the new bishop of Constantinople, assembles there a council which pronounces anathema on Eutyches, Nestorius, and their adherents. The body of Flavian is brought back to Constantinople; the bishops exiled for the same cause are recalled. At the command of the Emperor an œcumenical council meets at Chalcedon in October 451. Three hundred and sixty bishops and nineteen of the first officers of the empire sit in it. Different accusations are brought against Dioscorus, as much for his conduct in the last Council of Ephesus as on account of his doctrines and his acts of violence. As he refuses to appear he is condemned and deposed in his absence. Juvenal of Jerusalem and four other bishops, who presided over the Council of Ephesus with Dioscorus, are also declared to deserve deposition; but they are restored afterwards, when they have subscribed to the decisions of the Council. The affairs of Theodoret of Cyr and of Ibas of Edessa come in their turn. The first, whom Leo of Rome had admitted to his communion, notwithstanding the sentence of the Second Council of Ephesus, is introduced, in virtue of an imperial order, as accuser of Dioscorus. At his entrance the bishops of Egypt, Illyrium, Palestine, vociferate against him; he is supported by the Orientals. Having pronounced anathema on Nestorius he is restored to his seat. In regard to Ibas, part of his first trial and of an epistle from the clergy of Edessa, as well as his letter to Moris the Persian having been read, he is declared orthodox. He is restored on condition of anathematising Nestorius and Eutyches. But questions touching persons were not the most difficult to solve. Great is the embarrassment when the council addressed itself to the definition of doctrine. A first attempt was rejected. Finding it impossible to come to an understanding in the general assembly, they name a commission of twenty-two members charged to prepare a new statement. This commission reports to the council a definition which after confirming the belief of the œcumenical councils of Nice and Constantinople expresses itself in regard to the incarnation thus:—

"Following in the footsteps of the holy Fathers, we declare with one voice, that we ought to confess one sole and the same Jesus Christ, who is perfect in deity, and perfect in humanity, truly God, and truly man, composed of a reasonable soul, and of a body, consubstantial with the Father as to the deity, and consubstantial with us as to the humanity, and in everything resembling us except sin; begotten of the Father before the ages according to the deity, and in later times, born of the Virgin Mary, mother of God, according to the humanity, for us and for our salvation; one sole and the same Jesus Christ, unique son, Lord in two natures, without confusion, without change, without division, without separation, without the union removing the difference of the natures; on the contrary, the idioms of each are preserved and concur in one sole person, and one sole hypostasis; in such a way that he is not divided or separated into two persons, but is one sole and the same unique son, God Word, our Lord Jesus Christ. The council forbids each and all to think or to teach differently under pain to bishops and clerks of being deposed, to monks and to laics of being anathematised." This kind of conundrum is welcomed with transport by the Fathers, who seem quite happy at having a formula that they are not obliged to understand, but the terms of which guarantee them from accusations of heresy, either in one sense or in another.

The council then regulates certain particular affairs, among others the difference which existed between the bishops of Antioch and those of Jerusalem, in consequence of the pretensions of the latter to the supremacy not only over Palestine, but also Phenicia and Arabia. These pretensions were put forward for Palestine in the first days after the Council of Nice despite the seventh canon of that council, which, according to ancient custom, ascribed the right of metropolitan to the bishop of Cesarea. Cyril, bishop of Jerusalem, had contested the supremacy of Acacius of Cesarea, in taking his stand on Jerusalem's being an apostolic see : thence there had arisen between them enmities as a consequence of which Cyril had been deposed and re-established several times. The same spirit perpetuated itself in his successors. Juvenal, bishop of Jerusalem under Theodosius the younger, proud of the high distinction enjoyed by his church, as in some way mother of all the others, and supported by the imperial favour, aims to withdraw from the jurisdiction of Cesarea, and even to rise to the first rank among the bishops. At the time of the first council of Ephesus in 431, he tries to get for himself the primacy over all Palestine, by producing forged documents. But Cyril, president of the council, opposes it and writes to the bishop of Rome to induce him also to condemn the attempt. Juvenal, far from considering himself beaten, carries matters still farther ; he declares himself patriarch of the three Palestines, and desires ever to extend his jurisdiction over Phenicia and Arabia, which depend on the see of Antioch. We do not see that the bishop of Cesarea opposed the pretensions of Juvenal at tha time ; but they are contradicted by Maximus, bishop o Antioch, for the provinces connected with him. Ther arises a difference which the emperor submits to the decisioı of the Council of Chalcedon. The two bishops present compromise which gives to the bishop of Antioch the tw Phenicias and Arabia, and to the bishop of Jerusalem th three Palestines. This agreement is approved by all th Fathers. The bishop of Jerusalem in restoring Arabia an Phenicia, remains confirmed in all Palestine and in the ran of Patriarch. The Council of Chalcedon then establishe twenty-eight canons, twenty-seven of which are generall admitted, while the twenty-eighth has been constantly r pelled by the Church of Rome. The last is conceived i these terms :

"The Fathers have been right in granting to the see ancient Rome its privileges, because it was the ruling city and, for the same reason, the one hundred and fifty bishoj (of the Œcumenical Council of Constantinople), judged that new Rome, which is honoured with the empire and the senate, ought to have the same advantages in the ecclesiastical order, and to be second after it, in such a way that the metropolitans of the dioceses of Pontus, of Thrace, and of the provinces of Asia, and the bishops of the dioceses which are among the barbarians are ordained by the see of Constantinople, on the report which will be made to it of the canonical elections. It is well understood that each metropolitan of these dioceses shall ordain the co-provincial bishops according to the canons."

The arrangements form, as you see, a sensible progress in the authority of the bishop of Constantinople. The Œcumenical Council of the year 381 accorded to it only a prerogative of honour, without any jurisdiction. That of Chalcedon subjects to its authority the dioceses of the provinces of Pontus, of Asia, and of Thrace. But what would still more disquiet the bishop of Rome was the ground on which his increase of power was founded. According to the canon ancient Rome obtained its privileges only in the character of reigning city; whence it is inferred that Constantinople, the second capital, ought to have the same advantages after it. Now, at this time, nearly all the provinces of the west were invaded by the barbarians; the Western Empire existed but in name. Rome and some countries of Italy and Gaul were the sole regions where the Roman power still prevailed. It was even easy to foresee that soon they in their turn would fall under the yoke of the foreigners. What then would befall the bishop of Rome, if, as the canon said, his privileges had not been primitively conceded, except because he sat in the capital of the empire? When Rome lost the title would it not fall to Constantinople, which would have become the capital of the Roman world? Accordingly, the legates of the bishop of Rome strongly opposed this arrangement; none the less the canon was maintained. In their Synodal letter the Fathers of the council inform Leo that they have authorised the ancient custom of the Church of Constantinople to ordain the metropolitans of the dioceses of Asia, Pontus, and Thrace, and confirmed

the canon of the Œcumenical Council of Constantinople
which granted to the bishop of that city the prerogative
of honour after the See of Rome. In this, they say,
they have deferred to the desire of the emperor, the
senate, and the whole imperial city, and they pray the
Bishop of Rome to honour their judgment by his suffrage.
The emperor, the empress, the bishop of Constantinople wrote
to him equally to obtain from him the approbation of the
new canon; but all these efforts remain without effect;
Leo refuses to make any recognition in the matter. " The
city of Constantinople," he says in his reply, " has its
advantages, but they are only temporal; it is a royal city
and cannot become an apostolic city. The privileges established
by the canons cannot be trenched on; nor the
authority of so many metropolitans be wounded; Alexandria
ought not to lose the second rank, nor Antioch the
third. During the sixty years nearly that this enterprise i
put up with, the bishops of Constantinople have never sen
to Rome the pretended canon." Leo declares then that h
will never consent to such pretensions and that if the
Bishop of Constantinople persists in them, he will sunde
him from the peace of the universal church. Nevertheles
affairs do not the less follow their course without th
Bishop of Rome's executing his menace of ex-communica
tion, which doubtless was held in little respect. The othe
decisions of the Council of Chalcedon are received withou
difficulty in the West. But it is not the same in orient
lands. Egypt and Palestine refuse to obey. In vain doe
the emperor publish rigorous edicts to corroborate the synod
edicts. At Alexandria it is not without difficulty th
Proterius, the new bishop, is installed. The partisans (
Dioscorus attack the magistrates and disperse the troop
Reinforcements promptly arrive; but the multitude is n
easily restrained. A veritable insurrection breaks out i
Palestine. Juvenal, Bishop of Jerusalem, finds, on h
return, the monks and the people ill disposed in regard
himself. Even his life is threatened. He flees to Consta
tinople. The schismatics elect another in his place
those who adhere to the decisions of the council are pers

cuted. The schism is kept up during eighteen months, at the end of which the imperial authority succeeds in expelling the intrusive bishop and restoring Juvenal to the See.

The refusal made by Leo to approve the canon relative to the Bishop of Constantinople had given rise to the statement that he separated himself from the Council of Chalcedon. On the demand of the emperor he writes in 453 to the bishops who made part of it, that he adheres to all that was decided touching the faith ; but at the same time he protests that he observes the canons of Nice, and that he resists ambition, whatever council it may allege in its favour, as he has already done by his opposition to the enterprises of the Bishop of Constantinople. Marcion, in the time when he proscribes the heresy of Eutyches, also promulgates a law against the worship of the idolators. This law, under the penalty of death with confiscation of property, forbids the opening of temples that have been long closed, the ornamentation of their doors with festoons, the making libations and immolating victims. This law is a proof of the persistence of the ancient religion. The principal dogmas of the Church were then definitively fixed by the decisions of the Œcumenical Councils of Nice, Constantinople, Ephesus, and Chalcedon. Notwithstanding the oppositions which will manifest themselves, the doctrine of these councils is to prevail to the end of the middle ages. In modern times it will be professed by all the trinitarian churches, whether Catholic or Protestant. Despite the dissensions of which we have given a sketch, Christianity had not ceased to extend as well in the interior of the empire as among foreign nations.

We have seen the Goths and other barbarians accept Christianity under the form of Arianism which then dominated in the East, and whose last defenders they were. The evangelical faith had made progress also in Arabia and Persia. In the beginning of the fourth century the Christians were very numerous in the principal cities of the latter country. They had enjoyed toleration while they were open to persecutions from the Romans ; this ceases to be when the emperors have adopted the new worship. The Kings of Persia then became hostile to it. It is offensive to them as early as the days of Constantine. But on a letter from that prince their ill-will dissimulates to reappear under his successors. About the year 343 a violent persecution rages against the Christians of Persia. It is several times renewed, in the midst of the incessant wars which divide the two nations.

In the bosom of the empire, Christianity, protected by the civil authority, makes rapid conquests on all sides. In countries where Greek is spoken, the Christians, as early as the end of the fourth century, equal in number the adherents of the ancient religion. The differences springing from the Christotheism (Christ worship), the Trinity, and the incarnation, far from injuring the trinitarian church bring into repute a crowd of superior men who vivify and illustrate it. It suffices to mention, in the midst of many others, the names of Eusebius of Cesarea, Athanasius, Basil Gregory Nazianzen, Gregory of Nyssa, John Chrysostom the two Cyrils of Jerusalem and of Alexandria. The Latins, who had had so little to do with the formation o dogma, and among whom the Church of Africa had almos alone reckoned some illustrious Fathers, at last see Chris tianity unfold itself in their regions. Africa holds the firs rank, and continues the series of the Fathers by Optatu and by Augustin, the most celebrated of all. Italy glorie in the power of the bishops of Rome and thê splendour c the Church of Milan, the residence of the emperors. I produces Leo of Rome and Rufinus of Aquilea, and appro priates Jerome of Stridon and Ambrose of Gaul. The las country begins to cover itself with churches. Martin d Tours shows himself there the most active agent of cor versions. His miracles surpass in greatness and in numbe those of any monk whatever, if one may believe Sulpitiu Severus, who reports them in a style fit to serve for mos serious narrations. The Gaulish missionaries traverse tl island of Britain. Independently of personages somewha legendary such as German of Auxerre and Loup of Troye Gaul may claim Ambrosius, and with him cite Hilary

Poictiers, Paulin of Bordeaux (Bishop of Nola), Sulpitius Severus of Agen, Eucher of Lyons, Vincent of Lerins, Prosper of Aquitaine, and others. Spain boasts of Osius, Juvencus, and Prudens. However, the success it has obtained under the pressure of the imperial power is not without danger for the Church tself. Its government, its beliefs, its rites, its usages are modified and altered by the forced accession of the Pagan populations. From the day when the emperors are at the head of Christianity they dispose as its masters of everything which concerns it, whether in the interior or the exterior. The exterior care is properly considered as forming part of their functions. Constantine entitles himself bishop of the outside. His successors follow the same road. The emperor convokes the councils, judges ecclesiastical differences or submits them to magistrates of his own choice, receives the appeals brought before him, refers the affairs of the Church either to synods or to governors of the provinces, constrains by force accused or contumacious clerks, deposes and restores bishops, issues decrees on sacred things, on faith, heresy, the churches, gives force of law to the decisions of the councils, takes measures for the destruction of Hellenism, and of the dissident sects. It is by the effect of this omnipotence that we have already seen, as we shall see, this or that point of doctrine admitted or rejected, this or that sect prevail in the Church, or pine in exile, according to the policy or the caprices of the ruling prince. In the internal organisation of the clergy we find the same orders as at the epoch of the Council of Nice—bishops, priests, deacons, sub-deacons, exorcists, readers, singers. In the fifth century mention is made of different ecclesiastical offices, such as *defenders*, either of the Church or of the poor ; *stewards* who administer the ecclesiastical revenues, *Apokrisiaires* who handle external affairs. Divers degrees or dignities are introduced into the principal orders. The first of the deacons receives the title of archdeacon. At a later time, he even aspires, especially in the Latin Chuch, to take rank above the priests ; those who share with the bishop the honour of the priesthood, like him, have in the church a seat more elevated than the others. The most ancient of them bears the title of arch-priest, which the Latin Church in the sequel will make into a name of office or of dignity.

Chorepiscopi (or country bishops supplementary to the bishops of the cities) are mentioned in the Eastern church but not before the fourth century. Certain Episcopal functions are attributed to them for country places. They hold a kind of middle place between the priests and the bishops, while remaining subject to the bishop of the city, as does the district which they administer. One bishop suffices for their ordination. Afterwards they are called vicars, suffragans, vice-bishops. In the Latin Church we do not find Chorepiscopi before the fifth century ; the Church of Africa never had such an officer. In the order of bishops we see changes which correspond to the modifications introduced into the civil Government. The creation of the two empires, one of the East the other of the West, multiplied the provinces and the dignities. There were in the East two Prefectures of the Pretorium ; one called Eastern contained the five dioceses, exarchates or vicariates of the East, of Egypt, of Pontus, of Asia, and of Thrace, the capitals of which were Antioch, Alexandria, Cesarea, Ephesus, and Heraclea, for which Constantinople was afterwards substituted. The other prefecture, that of Oriental Illyria, had been created under Theodosius the elder, and comprised two dioceses, that of Macedonia or of Thessalonica, and that of Dacies. *There were also two Prefectures of the Pretorium in the West ; the Prefecture of Italy, and which were four dioceses and vicariates, that of Rome, of Italy, of Africa, and of Illyria, (total at first, then solely occidental); the other Prefecture, called the Prefecture of Gaul, consisted of three dioceses or vicariates of Gaul, Spain, and Britain. The magistrates placed at the head of the dioceses were called exarchs, vicars, and among the Latins, primates.

The ecclesiastical hierarchy is modified in a similar manner. Over the metropolitans, whose pre-eminence was acknowledged by the Council of Nice, are placed exarchs or primates of the dioceses ; they are the bishops of the principal places of the dioceses or civil exarchates. The name of primate and that of archbishop, who designate the first of the order, were at first given to the metropolitan of each country, and when there existed two or several in the same province, to one of them, as a title of honour. In the fifth century these names are restricted to the Exarchs or chiefs of the nations (Chalc. ix. 17). The bishop of Rome in the west calls himself primate of the primates. After the year 429, the time of the suppression of the patriarchate among the Jews, the name of patriarch begins to make its way into the church. It is first given to all the exarchs or primates of the dioceses. Afterwards it was reserved for the bishops of the five sees of Rome, Constantinople, Alexandria, Antioch, and Jerusalem. The Bishop of Rome is considered by the Greeks as the patriarch of the West. It should be observed that under the emperors the circumscription of the dioceses or exarchates and that of the provinces, are far from remaining uniform, and that the ecclesiastical order is always regulated according to the civil administration; the seventeenth canon of the Council of Chalcedon contains a formal requirement to that effect. From the time of the Council of Nice the power of the bishops increases from day to day. First they exclude the people from all share in the administration of ecclesiastical affairs, and end by stripping the priests themselves of the privileges and the authority which they had always enjoyed. Things go so far in this direction that in the presence of the bishop the priest can do nothing without his order, whether it be prayer, sitting down, or celebrating the sacred mysteries. From that time the bishops have no longer any rein on their ambition and luxury; at their pleasure they dispose of the revenues and benefices of the Church. In the degree in which new dignities impart an hierarchical character to the bishops relatively to one another, the first of the order do their utmost to subject the others to their domination; the latter in their turn oppress the inferior orders, and all taken together oppress the lay members of the Church. No longer do the bishops regard themselves as the delegates of the believers, but as the depositaries and the agents of the public power in religious concerns. They direct against Hellenism and against heresy persecutions not less violent than those of the pagan emperors against the religion of Christ. The clercs are subjected by them to vexations of all kinds, sometimes even to tortures. The episcopate and all the clergy reproduce the intolerance of the Israelite priesthood, whose successors they account themselves, and incarnate for ever the despotic spirit of the imperial government.

The Bishop of Rome holds the first position in his order. He owes it to the importance of his city as capital of the empire, to its opulence, to the external pomp which surrounds it. The rivalry of the Bishop of Constantinople, which begins to show itself, seems as yet only to bring nearer to Rome the chiefs of the churches of Alexandria, Antioch, and Thessalonica, jealous of the new capital of the East. You must, however, take care not to believe that the Bishop of Rome possesses from this time the superiority of power and jurisdiction which he will afterwards obtain in the western provinces. The supreme authority does not cease to reside in the councils, in conformity with the canons of Nice and Constantinople (381). If deference is shown for the advice of the Bishop of Rome in matters of faith and doctrine, if some bishops here and there deposed have recourse to him to get judgments pronounced against them revised in their provinces, it is nevertheless certain that his supreme jurisdiction is far from being recognised at that time even in the Latin regions. The Church of Africa, for instance, among others, stoutly resists his pretensions; they oppose to him the canons of Nice, while complaining that he has forged one, and contest all the rights and privileges of supremacy which he endeavours to appropriate. Notwithstanding opposition, the Roman Pontiff does not discontinue his enterprises. He appoints vicars who act in his name, whether at Thessalonica for oriental Illyria, which he is unwilling to part with, or in different other provinces of the west. A constitution of Valentinian III. finally subjects the bishops of Gaul and all the western churches (445). But this constitution, which went further than the Council of Sardica itself, is published at a time when Africa, Spain, and the greater part of Gaul, are in the power of the barbarians, and remains long a dead letter in those different countries. The corruption of the clergy grows with its power and its wealth. Historians speak of its luxury, its pride, its insatiable avarice. The bishops, especially the powerful ones, have around them a kind of ecclesiastical court. Decrees of councils frequently speak in condemnation of the dissolution of the clergy. Ordinations are habitually made by the bishop and the metropolitan, but with the consent of the clergy and the people. Translations of bishops from one church to another are severely interdicted, although there are some in special cases. Marriage is permitted to the bishops, the priests, and the deacons. The discipline is severe in regard to the simoniacal, and those who live scandalously, frequent taverns, seek illegitimate gains, mix in affairs of the world, keep what are called "introduced females" in their houses. The churches communicate with one another not only by œcumenical, diocesan, or provincial synods, but also by letters called, these canonical, those ecclesiastic. By the side of the clergy, but as yet not in its ranks, we must place monkism, which has made great progress throughout the East. At the end of the fourth century there are in Egypt alone more than 76,000 monks and 20,000 nuns; they people the deserts, and swarm in the cities. At Oxyrinchus their number surpasses that of the inhabitants. There are in the place 20,000 nuns and 10,000 monks. Monks are divided into three kinds; Cenobites, who live in community; Anchorites, who, after forming themselves in society, retire into absolute solitude; Sarabaïtes, who are not so much monks as vagabonds, who observe no rule. Under the name of Anchorites there is a minor class called Hermits, who are free from all obedience. In the second part of the fourth century Basil, Bishop of Cesarea, put forth rules for monkery which from that time have been observed in the oriental Church. Monks have received the name of Christian Philosophers. The monasteries are schools in which science and letters are taught, especially sacred letters. The heads of those establishments are called Archimandrites; in Syria they are named Abbeys, that is fathers. Most of the bishops have also in their own abode a kind of monastery, where instruction is given by reading, teaching, and discussions; thence the colleges of canons proceeded. Among the Latins the monastic life does not take root till the middle of the fourth century. Athanasius is, it is said, the first who made it known in Rome, whither he brought some monks in 341, giving them to read his life of Antony. From that time monks soon propagated in the western lands, especially in Italy and Gaul. Abuses of several kinds soon attach themselves to this mode of religious life. We have just mentioned the Sarabaïtes or vagabond monks who infested Egypt and the East. At the end of the fourth century a crowd of vicious habits appears among the monks. They are accused of insatiable gluttony, immense pride, unbounded superstition; their too intimate connexion with the nuns does not escape criticism; nay, they are charged with sodomy. Egypt is the principal focus of the monastic superstition. Authors that are inclined to the miraculous tell of a multitude of monks and hermits dispersed over the land, where they led a life wholly supernatural. Their sole occupation is to sing hymns in the expectation of the coming of Christ. Do they need things necessary for life, they begin to pray, and their wishes are fulfilled. A good number of them strike wild beasts with death, perform miraculous cures, and many other prodigies, in imitation of the prophets and apostles. The lives of solitaries, written by Athanasius and Jerome, seem to have served as types for all the fables of the same nature; those grave men, in making themselves the echo of puerile tales, opened a road whither they have been followed by crowds.

According to less credulous narrators, the asceticism of the monks consists in avoiding all human society, in leading a life of extreme rigour, and specially in mortifying their body by incredible practices. Simeon Stylites, the pillar saint, embraces the ascetic life at thirteen years of age, and continues it during fifty-six years (403-459). After long exercising himself in the most rigorous austerities, he forms the resolution, in order to withdraw from contact with the crowd, whom his repute attracts, to ascend to the summit of a column, first nine feet high, then eighteen, then thirty-three, and finally fifty-four. There he remained for thirty-seven years, operating, say contemporary authors, a large number of conversions and miracles. At this time monks and nuns were bound by no vow, by no canonical obligation; it is a kind of life that can be entered on and given up at pleasure. The obligation of celibacy is imposed upon them for the first time by the sixteenth canon of the Council of Chalcedon.

The discipline of the Church remains the same until the third century. Nevertheless in a more precise manner distinction is made between four degrees or stations of public penitence. The first degree, that of tears, has its place on the outside of the portico at the entrance of the temple. The second, that of audition, is within the vestibule, among the catechumens, the energoumenes (demoniacs undergoing spiritual therapeutics), the leprous, the Jews, and the Gentiles; in the third, that of humiliation, of genuflexion, of penitence properly so called; the penitents are in the interior of the temple, behind the believers, on their knees during prayer, and when hands are laid on them to dismiss them; they have shared in certain prayers, not in all, nor in the eucharist. In the fourth degree, that of reunion, the penitents are in the rank of ordinary Christians, and are admitted to all the prayers, but not to the Sacrament, although they are present at the great mysteries. The duration of each station varies according to the quality of the persons and the nature of their transgressions; it lasts for a year or two, or several. There are penitents who remain all their lives in the first degrees. Women as well as men are subjected to public penitence. It is forbidden to impose it on transgressions that are not manifest; such transgressions may be confessed in private to the bishops and the priests.

When all the degrees of penitence have been gone through, the penitents are admitted to the eucharistic communion, after the absolution which follows the prayers and the imposition of hands. This reconciliation takes place ordinarily in the anti-paschal week. Independently of the rigorous penalties, incurred by the three chief crimes of idolatry, homicide, and adultery, the canons punish different kinds of sins which seem less grave. Abortion, fornication, concubinage, games of chance, divorce, or repudiation without reason, successive marriage with two sisters, usury, sacrilege, divination, witchcraft, trigamy, or even bigamy— all these misdeeds and others are, but in different degrees, subjected to penitence by the decrees of the Councils. Nevertheless, toward the end of the fourth century the rigour of the canons is relaxed; the bishops have the power to abridge the time of penitence, to diminish the number of the degrees, or even to dispense with all the four, while paying attention to circumstances. At the same time, private confession in the churches of the East is suppressed, as well as the penitentiaries who were appointed for capital crimes, after the persecution of Decius. The abuses brought on by that institution caused it to be abolished under Nectorius, bishop of Constantinople (381-97). Liberty is left to each to approach the table according to the movement of his conscience, as was practised in the time of Origen. The remission of sins is obtained, says Chrysostom, by confession made to God alone, in relation to whom they have been committed. In the West, the discipline of penitence differs in this respect. Previous confession is made to the bishop whose place is filled in case of absence or necessity. As recourse is had to this remedy only in case of capital crimes, the bishop may suffice for the work.

We have in this chapter seen through what vicissitudes and under what influences their adherents established in the trinitarian church the doctrines which prevailed in the middle of the fifth century on the incarnation, the trinity, the two natures in Christ, the Holy Spirit, grace and original sin, as inherent in every human being, *even the Virgin Mary.* Let us go summarily over the other points of doctrine which are admitted in the same period.

The canon of the Old Testament is the same as that of the Jews. The books called ecclesiastic are considered as works of edification, but are not to be employed for the establishment of dogmas.

In matters of belief the Sacred Scripture is the sole authority, the only rule; attention is not paid to unwritten traditions. God alone is the object of religious worship; worship is not paid to his creatures. Mary is simply honoured as a holy woman.

Nevertheless the ever-growing influence of the Platonic philosophy and of the superstitions of paganism, scatters abroad the germs of new beliefs and introduces into the ceremonies of the Church a crowd of practices borrowed from the ancient religion. After the conversion of the Emperors, their example brings to the Church a multitude of people who are far from having thrown off the opinions, the prejudices, and the superstitions of polytheism in which they were nurtured. The confusion is more increased when the latter system is proscribed by the laws of the empire and afterwards by the conquering barbarians. The ministers of the Church are reduced, whether they will or not, to lend themselves to the early habits of the new recruits. Thence arise, with the external pomp of circumstances, a crowd of rites and superstitious usages which are more or less transformed under new names and significations. The splendour of the worship is not less favoured by the luxury which grows with the riches and dignities, as well as the pride and ambition of the priests, whose power that brilliancy throws into relief, and secures their domination over the minds of the multitude.

At the end of the second century the Church, as we have said, believed that human souls even after death were sequestrated in subterraneous places, where they were to remain till the universal judgment. This opinion lasted till the fifth century. The use of prayers for the dead, to which it had given place, continued. Prayers are also put up, as in anterior times, for the patriarchs, the prophets, the Virgin Mary, and other holy personages who were supposed to be in the bosom of Abraham; the same was equally done for sinners in order to bring down upon them the divine mercy. However, in the beginning of the fifth century, that belief in the sequestration of souls in subterraneous places no longer prevails without a rival. Platonic ideas tend to secure prevalence for another system which opens heaven to the just immediately after their death. Origen is the first who completely substituted that new theory for the ancient one. His authority accredits it; it gains ground from day to day. But the transitory abode in the bosom of Abraham is far from being universally abandoned, at the point of time to which we are come.

Those who admit it exempt therefrom as in the second century, the souls of some righteous men, notably those of the martyrs who ascend to heaven straightway from their punishment. This privilege and the annual panegyrics which are pronounced over their tombs raise them greatly in the minds of the crowd. They are naturally supposed to possess great credit in the heavenly places; and the idea soon arises of utilising that credit for the profit of Christians who struggle with the miseries of the world. Thence the invocations addressed to the martyrs in those panegyrics. However, on the part of the orators those requests for intercession are only conditional, and on the hypothesis that the saints take some interest in the affairs of the terrestrial world. Recourse is had to them as to powerful personages without there being any trace of worship. But once on this incline it is easy to descend to the doctrine of the invocation of saints. Toward the opening of the fifth century that practice begins to prevail without being sanctioned by any law. Already anniversary festivals are celebrated in honour of the martyrs; these at first were modest and without pomp, being consecrated to singing hymns and hearing the sacred word. They were observed only in the places where rested the remains of those Christian heroes. Temples or basilicas are raised in their memory. But no festival is yet celebrated, no temple constructed, in honour of the angels, of the Virgin Mary, or of the apostles. At the same time, when a prelude is made in the invocation of saints, there may be seen the exposition of images in the temples, with the mania of relics and pilgrimages. The images show themselves first in Asia Minor and the Hellenic territories of Europe. They are made use of for the purpose either of tracing pictures of the evangelical history or the sufferings of the martyrs, also for ornamenting the temples, and of offering to the Gentiles, habituated to images, examples of Christian virtue, faith, and charity. In principle it is only a local fact in which mingles no thought of religious worship. It even raises active opposition on the part of a great number of believers who blame the usage as contrary to the prescriptions of Scripture, and foresee that it will soon degenerate into veritable idolatry. The mania for relics, imitated from the pagans, takes its source in the extreme veneration felt for the martyrs; and in the credulity of the people who imagine that you are sanctified by the contact of their bones. The discovery of relics is always accompanied by miracles, and preceded by supernatural revelations. The discovery is followed by the transference of the relics, which is not less miraculous, as well as the deposit of them in the churches or other monuments which are dedicated with great solemnity. We may cite as an example in the fourth and fifth century the discovery of the true cross, of that of the relics of Stephen, of Barnabas, of Protais, and of Gervais, of the forty martyrs, to whom we shall return in the chapter on fables and legends. The custom of pilgrimages existed in Hellenism. In their turn the Christians begin to visit the holy places of Palestine, the tombs of the martyrs, the relics of which abound in the temples, and in the cities. The first pilgrimage mentioned in history is that of Helena, Constantine's mother, who goes into the holy land immediately after the Council of Nice. The aged empress finds numerous imitators, notwithstanding opposition from the most sage of the fathers.

Among the new rites that establish themselves after the Council of Nice, some are praiseworthy, others indifferent; most of them are derived from superstitious Pagan practices. The example set by Constantine and his mother cause a great number of temples or basilicas to be arrested in all parts of the empire. They are consecrated to God by hymns, prayers, thanksgiving, and at a later day by the erection of a cross. In order to call the worshippers to prayer a signal was given by loudly beating a piece of board; the use of bells was yet unknown. The worshippers begin to sing in the church the psalms of David, without renouncing the hymns, canticles, and common psalms which are numerous.

Prayer is followed by reading the canonical books, whether of the Old Testament or the New. The bishop or a priest then reads a homily which lasts about an hour. When the discourse pleases the auditors they sometimes applaud, the preaching is forbidden to women and monks. After the sermon prayers are said for the catechumens, the penitents, the energumenes, who are successively dismissed. Then comes the collection of alms, prayers for the believers, thanksgiving, the Lord's Prayer, the Communion, the kiss of peace, the benediction of the people. The solemn festivals are, as in anterior times, Sunday, Passover, and Pentecost. Saturday is also a festival, especially in the East, on that day the holy mysteries are celebrated in all churches, except in those of Rome and of Alexandria. A new festival is introduced, that of the birth of Christ, which is called Epiphany or Theophany. In the beginning it is not kept in the East the same day as in the West. Egypt, Asia Minor, and Syria place it on the 6th of January, while in the Western Church it is fixed on the 25th of December, the day on which the ancient Romans celebrated the new birth of the Sun. This last usage prevails also in the East toward the commencement of the fifth century. From that time the name of Epiphany or Theophany is reserved for the festival of the baptism, which is afterwards confounded with that of the adoration of the magi.

They also celebrate the vigils or previous evenings of the great festivals, specially the Saturday of Passover or of Pentecost. On the vigil of these two last festivals people in the evenings flock to the churches, they light wax candles, which they give to the neophytes to be carried. They administer baptism and the eucharist. The ceremonies are prolonged; they seem to await the resurrection of the Saviour and the coming of the Holy Spirit, while chanting hymns and psalms suitable to the occasion. In the East the vigils begin at midnight and last till day.

Fasts vary much according to the churches. The paschal fast, or Lent, is very solemn, and extends over several weeks—two, three, six, or seven; but they except Saturday and Sunday, when fast is forbidden by the canons. Public shows are forbidden during Lent, also to put criminals to death, to exact a debt, to celebrate marriage, or the festivals of martyrs. Other times of fasting either are not known in the church, such as those of Saturday, Rogations (three days immediately before the festival of Ascension) Four Times, or are accounted for, as the fast or half-fast of Wednesday or Friday.

Baptism is still administered by triple immersion, except for the sick, and ordinarily at the vigils of Passover or Pentecost. New rites are added thereto, such as the injection of salt into the mouth of the baptised person, the kiss that is given him, the foretasting of the wine, milk and honey, the white garments and lighted wax candles carried by neophytes—all things to which a symbolical sense is given, but which are really only imitations of the mysteries of Paganism. The neophyte receives a double unction, one before baptism, the other on quitting the bath; both are administered by the priests. They are accompanied by the imposition of hands and participation in the eucharist, which, they say, seals and confirms the baptism. In the fifth century appears the opinion of the absolute necessity of this sacrament for salvation (the Gentiles said the same thing of initiation into their mysteries); the opinion is in agreement with that of original sin, which dates from the same epoch; one is the consequence of the other. In admitting the necessity of baptism for salvation, the question arose, what became of the souls of children who died without being baptised? It would have been hard to damn them for original sin alone, which did not come from them, and which they were unable to efface. Consequently, imagination created at the entrance into hell the *limbus infantium*, in which their souls were deprived of the divine vision, but without enduring any other penalty. This opinion springs from Hellenism, which also placed the souls of infants on the border of hell.

Infantumque animæ in limine primo.—*Æneid*, vi.

In the celebration of the eucharist we find again the rites mentioned in the preceding book ; the symbols offered by the people ; fermented bread ; its breaking ; its clear and intelligible consecration, the commemoration of the death of Christ ; the reproduction of the words of the institution; the reception of the bread into the hands of the communicants ; the passing round of the cup ; the secret of the mysteries. The Church continues to believe that the bread and the wine do not change their nature by the eucharistic consecration, but that they become the figure of the body and the blood of the Redeemer. According to the expressions in use they are the sign, the symbol, the image, the type, the antitype, the pledge. The eucharist is called the supper, the breaking of bread, the table, the mystic participation, the spiritual nutriment, the symbols, the spiritual sacrifice, reasonable, not bloody, immaterial, without fire and smoke, the sacrifice of thanksgiving. Among the Latins the celebration of the eucharist begins to be designated also under the name of mass (the term is found first in Ambrose). The expression is taken from the Latin word by which the assembly was dismissed. All the laymen present communicate with the priests. The sacred mysteries take place in the East only once or twice a-week, Saturday and Sunday ; but the Latins and the Alexandrines celebrate them on Wednesday, Friday, and Sunday. It is customary to send the symbols consecrated by the bishops to the priests of the other parishes of his bishopric or city ; this is called sending the leaven, not only because the bread is fermented, but also because the present is as a ferment or bond of union.

In the fifth century, the Eucharist, like baptism, is fancied to be absolutely necessary to salvation, and that accordingly infants ought to receive it as soon as they are baptized. The custom arises of putting it into the mouth of the dying, as a sort of viaticum or food for the journey. Sometimes baptism and the eucharist are administered even to the deceased. About the same time, the agapes or love-feasts, were suppressed by the decrees of different councils. The abuses which had made their appearance in the early ages only increase in proportion as the Church extends. Those abuses are the display of wealth, intemperance, dissolution, quarrels. The use of those repasts disappeared by degrees from all the churches; almsgiving is substituted in their place. Celibacy rejected by the Council of Nice, does not the less remain in great favour in the mystic spirit which predominates. The Council of Chalcedon prescribes it for monks and nuns, under pain of excommunication. Different attempts are made to impose it equally on the ministers of the Church. Siricius, bishop of Rome (385-398) desires to render it obligatory for bishops, priests, and deacons, after their ordination. He is followed in this way by Innocent 1st (402-17), by Leo I., and by some western councils; but their decisions are not generally admitted. You may see even in the west married bishops in the fifth century, among others Prosper of Aquitaine, Sidonius Apollinaris, Simplicius of Bourges. In the East, the bishops and the priests are perfectly free to marry or to remain single. Exception should be made to Thessaly, Macedonia, and Achaia, where on occasion of erotical books (Theagenes and Chariclea) composed in his youth by Heliodorus, bishop of Trica in Thessaly, it is enjoined on clercs to cease, after their ordination, from all conjugal relations with their wives. It would occupy too much space to enumerate the usages and the rites that were successively borrowed from the pagan religion, especially after the interdiction of the latter. Let us cite, among a number, wax candles lighted in open day at the meeting of worshippers, even out of the churches, for instance, in funereal ceremonies; the incense which is shed abroad during the prayers and the celebration of the sacraments; lustral water, which passes into holy or blessed water, without losing any of its imaginary virtues for consecrations and purifications; magnificent images, precious vases, altars, and reliquaries of massive silver, which decorate the churches; the sumptuous attire of the ministers, tiaras nitres, crosses, pomp of ceremonies, music in the temples, public processions, rogations, litanies or prayers for the peace of the Church, for the salvation of souls, for the powers of the age. Augustine complains of these new ceremonies. " They rush," he says, " under servile observances the religion which God had made free, in restricting it to a very small number of rites. The condition of the Jews is preferable; if they have not known a time of liberty, at least they are subject only to legal prescriptions and not to human superstitions." While rites and beliefs are thus coming into the Church, it receives also from polytheism a great number of words whose primitive acceptation is more or less altered. Thus it gives to princes, to saints male and female, the name god, and goddess (divi, divae), the bishops are called sovereign pontiffs; we hear speak of altars, priests, litanies, lares, penates, manes; of fortune, destiny, the nuptial genius, &c. Nevertheless, in comparison with coming ages, you yet see in the times where we are, a great purity and a great simplicity in morals and rites. The excesses that ensue are not produced without finding ardent contradictors. The councils of Africa, that of Chalcedon, those of Gaul, publish a great number of canons against the abuses of the monastic life, against the incontinence of clercs, their avarice, their simony, their love of secular things; against the display and the negligence of the bishops. Moreover, the members of the church were more assiduous in their attendance on public worship than in the following ages; they had also more zeal in external matters, more vigour in observing the discipline, more austerity in their manner of life. The Fathers often, and with much force, denounce the growing corruption, the superstition relative to images, to rites, to pilgrimages, to the monkish life, to abstinence from meats; they strongly condemn as well the pompous festivals, ostentation, the luxury of the ceremonies, and other things of the same nature.

But the tide of Paganism rose higher and higher every day.

CHAPTER II.

FROM THE COUNCIL OF CHALCEDON TO THE SCHISM OF PHOTIUS.

(451-891.)

SUMMARY.—Reaction against the Council of Chalcedon—Timothy Elurus—Peter the Fuller—The Henoticon (Unifier) of Zeno—Justinian proscribes Hellenism and Dissent—Neoplatonism at Athens—Closing of the Schools of Philosophy—The Eutychians and James Baradeus—The Barbarians in the West—Attila—Fall of the Western Empire—Odoacer—Theodoric—The Goths—The Franks—The Anglo-Saxons—The Vandals—Belisarius—Narses—The Origenists—The Three Chapters—Vigilius at Constantinople—Œcumenic Council of Constantinople (the Second)—The Incorrupticoles—Disasters in the East—The Lombards in Italy—Precarious Situation of the Popes of Rome—Monothelism—The Ecthesis of Heraclius—The type of Constans—Œcumenical Council of Constantinople (the third)—The Quini-Sextus—The Suevi—The Visigoths and the Burgundians abjure Arianism—The Church of the Franks—Conversion of the Belgians, of the Anglo-Saxons, of the Saxons, and other Germans—Mohamed and Islamism—Abubeker—Omar—Othman—Ali—The Ommiades—The Moslems in Persia, in Syria, in Palestine, in Egypt, in Africa, in Mauritania, in Spain, in Septimania—Invasion of Provence, Burgundy, and Acquitania—Charles Martel—The Abassides—Worship of Images—Leo the Isaurian—Constantine Copronymus—Council of Iconoclasts—Irene—Œcumenical Council of Nice (the second)—Opposition of the Franks—Charlemagne—Michael the Stammerer—Theophilus—Theodora—The new Manicheans or Paulicians—Kalifs of Bagdad—Almamon—Courses of the Saracens in Italy—Martyrs of Cordova—Felix of Urgel—Gothescalk—The real Presence—Commencements of the Græco-Latin Schism—Procession of the Holy Spirit—Conversion of the Bulgarians—Encyclic of Photius—His Deposition—Œcumenic Council of Constantinople, according to the Latins (the fourth)—Photius restored—Œcumenic Council of Constantinople according to the Greeks (the fourth)—End of Photius—His Spirit remains behind—Domination of the Popes in the West—Ignorance, Riches, and Corruption of the Latin Clergy—Monkism—Benedictines—The descent of Jesus into Hell—State of Souls—Superstitions—Mary—Peter—Purgatory—New Festivals—New Rites.

ALL the imperial power had scarcely sufficed to impose the Council of Chalcedon on different countries of the East, and especially in Egypt, where the partizans of Dioscorus prevailed. At the death of Marcian (457) a Eutychian reaction declares itself in Alexandria. The principal people choose for Bishop Elurus, whom his opposition in the last council had caused to be deposed from the priesthood. Proterius is hacked in pieces. The newly-elect bishop establishes bishops of his party in all Egypt, and persecutes the Chalcedonians. These, agreeing with the clergy of Proterius, present a request to the Emperor Leo I. (the elder). The great and the people of Alexandria, as well as the maritime people, speak out in their turn in favour of Timotheus. He himself sends deputies to Constantinople with letters for the Emperor, in which he accuses the Council of Chalcedon and its adherents of Nestorianism. Leo, after punishing the murderers of Proterius, writes to the bishops of the principal sees, and to the most considerable monks, to ask their advice on the difficulties which trouble Egypt. Leo, bishop of Rome, and the other metropolitans, approve the Council of Chalcedon by synodal letters and reject the ordination of Timotheus Elurus. The Emperor banishes him to Gongrae (in Paphlagonia). He is replaced by Timotheus, surnamed Salofaciolis. The Emperor Leo remains still attached to the doctrine of Chalcedon. He confirms the laws passed against the Gentiles, and grants different privileges to the clergy and the monks. Peter, called the Fuller, from having exercised that trade in a monastery, undertakes to usurp the see of Antioch. Confiding in the good graces of Zeno, son-in-law of the Emperor and governor of the East, he accuses Bishop Martyrius of being a Nestorian, and sows division among the people. Martyrius, who finds him supported by the civil power, resolves to give way. He says publicly in the Church—" I renounce an imperfectly submissive clergy, a disobedient people, an impure Church, reserving to myself the dignity of the priesthood." Peter the Fuller takes possession of the see. To the hymn called the *Trisagion* he adds these words —" Thou who wast crucified for us," thus indicating that there is only one nature in the Son. But an order from the Emperor banishes him into the Oasis ; he is compelled to flee for the sake of escape.

Leo, in dying, leaves the throne to his grandson, Leo II. (the younger—474). Zeno, father of that prince, causes himself to be declared emperor with him; and Leo II. dying at the end of some months, he remains alone in possession of the power. His disorderly conduct soon makes him odious. Basilicus, brother of the empress Verina, the mother-in-law of Zeno, revolts next year and obliges him to flee into Isauria with his wife and some faithful friends. He withstands the attacks of the troops of Basilicus, who keep him long under siege.

The new emperor declares against the Council of Chalcedon. He recalls Timotheus Elurus, who had been in exile eighteen years. Peter the Fuller quits the monastery of Acemetes, where he had concealed himself. At the instigation of Timotheus Elurus, Basilicus writes a circular to all the bishops against the Council of Chalcedon and the letter of Pope Leo to Flavian. In this circular he confirms the three first œcumenical councils, and orders all that had been said or done at Chalcedon to be condemned and burnt by the bishops. "These are," he says, " novelties introduced against the faith, pernicious doctrines which have troubled the peace of the Churches; whoever in future shall uphold that council shall be punished as an enemy of God and the prince."

The letter of Basilicus is approved by Timotheus Elurus, by Peter the Fuller, by Anastasius, Bishop of Jerusalem, and by about five hundred bishops. Acacius of Constantinople refuses his assent; to abandon the Council of Chalcedon is in effect to call in question the rights which have been consecrated for his church. Then Timotheus Elurus holds at Athens a council of bishops of the province of Asia; this assembly restores Paul in the See of Ephesus, to which the patriarchial title is restored, which the Fathers of Chalcedon had transferred to Constantinople. Timotheus proceeds to take possession of the Church of Alexandria, while Salofacioles retires into a monastery. Peter the Fuller thus resumes the See of Antioch. Zeno, quitting Isauria, marches on Constantinople, the people and monks of which are aroused by Acacius. Then Basilicus revokes his circular and publishes another totally opposite in sense.

Tardy repentance! Zeno retires into the capital. Basilicus is, with his wife and son, placed in a castle in Cappadocia, where they die of hunger. The acts of the last reign on religious matters are annulled; the patriarch of Constantinople is re-established in all his prerogatives. Peter the Fuller is banished to Pityonte, in the extremity of the Pontus; but he escapes from his guards. Timotheus Elurus is left at Alexandria, on account of his great age; he dies there shortly after. The bishops of Egypt hasten to elect in his place Peter, surnamed Mongus. But the emperor, paying no attention to this election, restores Timotheus Salofaciolis, whose mildness of character makes him a favourite even with dissidents. On his death, those of his communion make choice of John Talaïa (481). Zeno refuses to acknowledge him, and pronounces in favour of Peter Mongus, who offered to subscribe to the Henoticon or Edict of Union. This is a decree which that prince had just published, under the advice of Acacius, and, in view of conciliation it is addressed to the bishops, the clergy, and the people of Egypt, Libya, and the Pentapolis. Zeno therein declares that he receives no other symbol than that of the œcumenical Councils of Nice and Constantinople, followed by the Fathers of the Council of Ephesus. He confesses that the Son of God, who is God, was truly made man, that he is consubstantial with the Father as to the divinity, and consubstantial with us as to the humanity, one and not two. He rejects those who divide, or confound or introduce something fantastic. He anathematises whosoever has sentiments contrary to the symbol of Nice, or had formerly, whether at Chalcedon or in any other council, and principally Nestorius, Eutyches, and their followers. The Henoticon, as you see, without admitting the Council of Chalcedon as equal to the three first, does not reject it altogether; it was necessary to safeguard the prerogatives of the Bishop of Constantinople; they limit themselves to the condemnation of the persons who professed in that council sentiments contrary to the symbol of Nice. But in not specifying what those opinions and persons are, they in fact leave dissidents free to apply the anathema to the whole doctrine of Chalcedon.

Peter Mongus subscribes to the Henoticon, and causes it to be received in Egypt by the two parties, who interpret it each after his own fashion. To reconcile everybody, Peter would have condemned the Council of Chalcedon with these and approved it with those. This equivocal conduct makes him suspected on both sides; but he ends by openly declaring himself anti-Chalcedonian, and removes from the diptychs (registers) the names of Proterius and Salofacioles. John Talaïa, on the other side, was acknowledged as Bishop of Alexandria by Calendion, patriarch of Antioch, and by Simplicius of Rome (467-83). Coming into the last city with synodal letters from Calendion, he had been well received by Simplicius, who had even written in his favour to Acacius of Constantinople; but the latter none the less continued to communicate with Peter Mongus. The successor of Simplicius, Felix II. (483-92) shows more zeal for John Talaïa. He sends to Constantinople three legates with letters for Acacius and for the emperor, in order to secure the rejection of Peter Mongus as a false bishop and a partisan of heresy. On the order of Zeno those delegates are arrested at Abydos; the papers which they have received are taken from them. Two of them, allowing themselves to be seduced, consent to communicate with Acacius, and to recognise Peter Mongus. On their return to Rome, they are brought before a council, deposed, and excommunicated; at the same time the council condemns Peter Mongus. Felix II. writes to Acacius a synodal letter to recall him to repentance. The latter disregarding it, the Roman Pope assembles a council of seventy Italian bishops (484), in which he deposes the patriarch of Constantinople, as much for his conduct in the affair of the Henotic and Peter Mongus, as for having, in contempt of the Councils of Nice, usurped the rights of the other provinces, that is, for having availed himself of the canon of Chalcedon relative to the prerogatives of the See of Constantinople, a canon which they would not recognise in Rome.

Acacius replies to this sentence by removing from the diptychs of his church the name of Felix II. The bishops who do not subscribe to the Henoticon are removed through all the East. Calendion of Antioch is banished to the Oasis, under the charge of having favoured competitors to the empire. Peter the Fuller re-enters that See, after subscribing to the Edict of Union; he remains in it until his death (488). Fravita, successor of Acacius in the See of Constantinople (489), sends synodal letters to the Bishop of Rome and Peter Mongus; but Felix refuses to receive them. Euphemius, who replaces Fravita at the end of some months, separates from the communion of Peter Mongus, and restores the name of Felix to the Diptychs; the Bishop of Rome no longer communicates with him, because he preserves in them the names of Acacius and Fravita. The emperor Zeno dying (491), Ariane, his widow, calls to the imperial throne, Anastasius, whom she marries. The new prince declares in favour of the Henoticon, but without forcing any one to subscribe to it. Specially desirous to maintain peace, he wishes that things should remain in all places in the same state as at his ascension, and shows severity only against the bishops who endeavour to change the usages of their church. Some then declare for the Council of Chalcedon, others against it; others again are attached to the Henoticon.

The Isaurians, in the early days of Anastasius, had made an insurrection in favour of a brother of Zeno. Euphemius, suspected of being in their favour, is deposed and banished into Paphlagonia (495). His successor is Macedonius, who adheres to the Edict of the union. Delivered from the wars which he had had to sustain against the Isaurians and the Persians, Anastasius attacks the Council of Chalcedon and the patriarch Macedonius (506). The inhabitants of Constantinople take part for their bishop. Troubles frequently arise in the city. The emperor removes Macedonius and banishes him to Gangrae (511). The authentic original of the acts of Chalcedon is at the same time stolen and burnt by his orders. Timotheus, the new bishop of Constantinople, communicates with the adversaries of that Council. He causes the Trisagion to be sung with the addition of the clause " Crucified for us." A strong opposition manifests itself at Constantinople. The emperor sees himself on the point of being overturned by a sedition ; but he succeeds in calming it by promises, which he afterwards eludes. Flavian, patriarch of Antioch (512) he drives away and gets ordained in his place Severus, a monk of Palestine, who gives his name to the Severians or Severites, the same as the Acephales (without a head). Vitalian, having put himself at the head of an insurrection against Anastasius, advances to the gates of Contantinople. The emperor obtains peace under the obligation of recalling the exiled bishops, among others Macedonius and Flavian, and of convening a general Council. The Council is convoked for the year 515 at Heraclea in Europe. The Pope of Rome sends legates whom Anastasius dismisses while avoiding to supply their wants. A new legation meets at Constantinople without more result (507). Anastasius sends back about two hundred bishops assembled for the Council which was to be held at Heraclea. About the same time he drives away the patriarch of Jerusalem, who will not communicate with Severus. John, who replaces him, makes a similar refusal ; but Anastasius abstains from employing severity by fear of Vitalian who has recommenced the war. John of Cappadocia succeeds Timothy in the See of Constantinople after having condemned the Chalcedonians (517). Anastasius dies at the age of eighty-eight (518), he had reigned twenty-seven years. His successor is aged Justin, a soldier of fortune, who cannot read, but who is favourable to the Council of Chalcedon.

In the early days of his reign, the patriarch of Constantinople celebrated, with the acclamations of the people, the festival of that Council. An assembly took place of forty bishops who restored to the Diptychs the names of Euphemius and Macedonius, as well as the titles of the four œcumenical councils, together with the name of Leo of Rome ; the assembly anathematises and deposes Severus of Antioch. The emperor puts the Council of Chalcedon into the Diptychs of all the churches. Those whom Anastasius had banished are recalled. Some had died during their exile, among others Macedonius of Constantinople, Flavian of Antioch, and Elijah of Jerusalem. The emperor writes to the Roman pope in order to prepare the way for the re-union of the two churches of Rome and of Constantinople. Hormisdas then occupied the chair (514-523), he sends a third legation to Constantinople, with the consort of Theodoric, king of the Ostrogoths, then masters of Italy. The demands of the church of Rome are acquiesced in, from the Diptychs are effaced the names of Acacius and of his successors, Fravita, Euphemius, Macedonius, and Timothy, as well as those of the emperors Macedonius and Anastasius. The re-union of the two churches is effected after thirty-five years of separation.

Severus of Antioch and the principal bishops of his party are expelled from their sees. Severus seeks safety under Timothy of Alexandria who is not disquieted although he holds the same sentiments. The emperor punishes the Manicheans with death. He forbids all charges of dignities to the dissidents as well as to the idolaters. He even desires to convert the Arians and to seize their churches; but the intervention of Theodoric obliges him to abandon the design.

On the death of Justin (527), the empire devolves on Justinian, his nephew, who under his uncle's reign, had had the principal direction of affairs. That prince, full of religious zeal, pursues the extinction of Hellenism and heresy. The dissidents and the Pagans are excluded from public offices. Their goods are confiscated: they are themselves put on their trial; terror reigns everywhere. Some feign conversion; others flee into foreign lands; others have recourse to sedition; some put themselves to death from despair. In the proceedings against Hellenism the philosophers are not forgotten, especially the Neo-Platonicians, who, under the emperor Julian, had undertaken the restoration of the ancient worship. During the supreme struggle Neo-Platonism, disappearing from the scene of the world, took refuge in the interior of the schools; but in the East its adversaries had not left it in peace. The sanguinary persecutions of Valens were succeeded by the destruction of the Hellenic temples, and the dispersion of their ministers, with whom the philosophers had more than once been confounded by the intolerance of the new priesthood. The neo-Platonicians had fallen back in Greece. Athens had for a century again been the principal seat of science. Their minds were not, as in the East, agitated by the violence of religious quarrels. The school of Athens, estranged from the passions of the world, freely taught all the sciences and all the arts; it was a kind of learned republic, which lived in peace under the imperial protection. The neo-Platonicians pursued there the course of their speculations. They had for their principal men Plutarch of Athens and Syrian. Proclus, their disciple, about the year 450 puts himself at the head of the school, of which he became the most illustrious Coryphæus.

The Alexandrines, we have said, had combined the divine schools of Greek philosophy into a vast whole, of which Platonism was the base. Plotinus, in laying the foundations of the system, had abstained from descending to details. Porphyry, and Jamblicus after him, had comprehended in their explanations only some of the difficulties that needed solution. The same thing remained to be done for other points of doctrine. It was necessary to bring to identity the texts of the ancient philosophers, which often seemed to exclude each other; it was also necessary to identify the different myths of Hellenism, so as to bring them into unison with the Neo-platonic conceptions. Such was the work reserved for the school of Athens, a task resolutely undertaken and completely executed by Proclus. He proves with methodical perspicuity what Plotinus and others had enunciated obscurely, and developes in its principal parts the Neo-platonic doctrine, which at times he enlarges. He takes special pains to establish the ternary theory. With Plotinus all the principles of things are comprised in the trinity of the One, of the Intelligence and the Soul. Porphyry recognises other distinct hypostases; Jamblicus multiplies them indefinitely. Proclus wishes to co-ordinate the yet vague conceptions of his predecessors. He explains the hierarchy of the hypostasis. From the principles of the Ternarium he deduces trinities of trinities, series of trinities. Every essence, being complex, may be conceived of as a trinity. The elements of each trinity decomposing themselves in their turn, new trinities arise, and so on indefinitely. In the explanation of the myths Proclus embraces the entire of the Hellenic beliefs. He accepts all the traditions, and takes pains to find a sense in apparently the absurdest things, even in the superstitions of magic and astrology.

His successors, following the same road, limit themselves to labours of pure erudition. They add few novelties. Neo-platonism seems to have run its career. Marinus, Isiodore of Gaza, Damascius, who successively taught in the school of Athens, are disciples of Proclus, and tend only to complete some points of his explanations. Damascius, however, attempts to probe the nature of The One more than his predecessors. In his theology he does not confine himself to the myths of Hellenism, but he speaks with some precision of the doctrines of the Chaldeans, the Magi, the Sidonians, the Egyptians. New horizons would have opened before him, if, following this road to its termination, he had made himself acquainted with the religious science of the Brahmans and of the Buddhists. But what the school of Alexandria did not do in this respect, the school of Athens was much less in a position to accomplish. Simplicius, disciple of Damascius, pursues to the end the reconcilement of the philosophers of Greece, he harmonises the nominalism of Aristotle with the realism of Plato. In this state of things an edict, issued in 529, requires the closure of the schools of Hellenic philosophy. The school of Athens shuts its lips, like all the others. Its last masters, Damascius, Isiodore, Simplicius, take refuge in the kingdom of Persia. But the caste of the Magi are not less intolerant than the Christian priesthood; at the end of some years they return into their native land to cultivate in secret their philosophical and religious doctrines. With them ended the teaching of Neo-platonism. If it still appears in the schools of the East, it no longer speaks there in its own name, its commentators are Christians. The influence of its doctrines nevertheless continues through the centuries until the revival of letters, when it succeeds in again seizing a veritable dominion.

The violent measures of Justinian do not stop at Hellenism. They extend also to the Samaritans, and occasion grave disorders in Palestine. Some persons in the cities become converts in appearance; but the people in the rural districts fly to arms, pillage and burn the churches, and massacre the Christians without distinction. The insurrectionists having made themselves masters of Samaria, slaughter the bishops and the priests. They choose an emperor out of their own body. They send regular troops, who slay a great number and subdue the country. Justinian puts their leaders to death, he forbids the Samaritans to have synagogues, to exercise public charges, and to receive inheritances and donations.

The emperor at the same time makes an effort to bring the Church of Alexandria back to the official doctrine. Timothy, who had governed it for eighteen years, was not a Chalcedonian. Severus of Antioch and other dissidents had found an asylum under his wing. Among these refugees there arises a schism on the question whether the body of Jesus Christ was corruptible or incorruptible. Severus maintains the first view, the pure Eutychians declare in favour of the second. The patriarch Timothy alternately favours both. At his death two bishops are elected, Theodosius by the Corrupticoles, Gaian by the Incorruptibles. The first has on its side the civil authority, the other the majority of the population. At the end of some months, Gaian is sent into exile by an imperial command; Theodosius remains in possession. The next year, wearied by the seditions which are ceaselessly renewed, he retires to Constantinople; he is all but immediately expelled, on his refusal to receive the Council of Chalcedon.

The Eutycheans, ill-treated by the emperor, find support in the empress Theodora, who shares their opinions. She names to the patriarchate of Constantinople, Anthinius, bishop of Trebizonde, who belongs to the sect of Acephales (headless, 535). Then the chiefs of the party betake themselves to that capital, where they hold assemblies, among others Severus, Peter of Apamea and Zoara, a Syrian monk. Their meetings are soon troubled by Agapetus, bishop of Rome (535-36), who had come to prevent the war which Justinian was preparing against the Goths. That pope deposes Anthimus, consecrates Mennas his successor, and dies shortly after at Constantinople. Anthimus is summoned before a council presided over by Mennas. On his refusing to appear, he is deprived of the Church of Trebizonde; Anathema is pronounced also on Severus of Antioch, Peter of Apamea, and the monk Zoara. The sentence is confirmed by Justinian, who forbids the condemned to dwell in Constantinople or any other important city. In place of Theodosius of Alexandria, the emperor calls to the patriarchate Paul and Zoilus successively, both of them are Chalcedonians. From that time the official doctrine is everywhere preached without any one daring to raise a voice against it. There is no means that was not put in request to reduce the Eutychians or Monophysites. Every day new divisions break out among them; twelve varieties are mentioned— the Theopachites, the Acephales, the Severians, the Corrupticoles, the Incorruptibles, the Agnoetes, the Thritheists, and others. The sect threatens to fall into dissolution, when an obscure monk, James or Jacob, surnamed Baradeus or Zanzalus, undertakes to raise it by uniting the different factions. Some captive bishops confer the episcopate upon him. Seconded by Theodosius, patriarch of Alexandria (535), he traverses all the East, establishes bishops and priests of his communion, reanimates the ardour of the Monophysites, puts an end to controversies which separate them, and, at his death, leaves the sect in the most flourishing state in Syria, in Mesopotamia, in Armenia, in Egypt, in Ethiopia, and in other regions. He had placed all his church under the jurisdiction of the patriarchs of Alexandria and Antioch, by whom it is still governed. The Monophysites, regarding James as a new founder, take thence the name of Jacobites under which they are yet known. In the midst of these sophistical miseries to which the Greeks had been led by false ideas on the deity of Christ and the incarnation of the Word, the Western Empire finally falls under the blows of the barbarians.

The Huns had extended their dominion over all Scythia, and reduced into vassalage the most powerful people of those lands—the Gepidi, the Alani, the Ostrogoths. Theodosius the younger paid them an annual tribute. In the year 451, Attila, their king, turns his regards toward the West. At the head of 500,000 men he enters Gaul, puts everything to fire and sword, captures Treves, Mayence, Metz, and besieges Orleans. He is on the point of getting possession of it when the Romans and the Visigoths force him to leave go his hold. Aetius, the able Roman general, collects all his troops, to which are added, as auxiliaries, the Visigoths, the Burgundians, the Franks, and other barbarians settled in Gaul. With them he marches against the innumerable hordes of Attila. Those masses come into collision on the Catalaunic fields. The Huns, overcome, leave on the field of battle 200,000 slain. Attila, entrenched in his camp, awaits with a firm foot the attack of his enemies. He might have been crushed; but the Visigoths, who had lost their king in battle, hasten to return home, and leave the Huns free to fall back on the Rhine. Attila re-enters Pannonia, where he repairs his forces. In 452 he falls upon Italy, destroys Aquilea, devastates Milan, ravages Pavia, and all the countries around. He returns to the Danube with an immense booty, after imposing an annual tribute on Valentinian III. The next year he summons Marcian to pay to him the tribute promised by Theodosius the younger; then, directing his steps afresh towards Gaul, he penetrates to the borders of the Loire. He there finds the Visigoths ready to give him battle, and returns into his country where he dies in 454. After his death, division breaks out among his children, the barbarous nations whom he had subjected revolt against them and recover their independence. The same year that Attila died, Valentinian III. kills with his own hand Aetius, the conqueror of the Huns. This crime does not remain unpunished long; the people of Aetius massacre Valentinian (455). Maximus, having got himself made emperor, constrains the widow of that prince to marry him. She takes her revenge by calling to Rome Genseric, king of the Vandals. At the approach of the barbarian, a great number of persons take to flight. Maximus is cut to pieces by old servants of Valentinian, who throw his members into the Tiber. Genseric, after pillaging Rome during fourteen days, returns with rich spoils and several thousands of captives. He carries off to Carthage the empress and her two daughters, Eudoxia and Placidia; the first marries his son, Huneric; some time after, Placidia and her mother are sent back to Constantinople. Avitus, prefect of the Pretorium, makes himself proclaimed emperor in Gaul. He is the next year conquered in Italy by the patrician Ricimer, and becomes bishop of Placentia. This Ricimer, a Goth and an Arian, governs as master what remains of the Western empire; he makes and unmakes the emperors, refusing the honour for himself in consequence of his being a foreigner. After a short interregnum, Majorian is called to the empire (457), and put to death four years after by order of Ricimer. Power passes into the hands of Severus, who is poisoned in 465. Anthemius ascends the throne (467), with the consent of the emperor Leo and Ricimer, who marries the daughter of the new prince. The son-in-law kills the father-in-law in 472, and is himself carried off by a disease a short time after. The title of emperor passes successively to Olybrius, son-in-law of Valentinian III., who dies almost immediately after; to Glycerius, who is deposed at the end of fifteen months, and ordained bishop of Salone; to Julius Nepos, who is driven into Dalmatia (475), and finally to Romulus or Momylus, called Augustulus, in whom it becomes extinct. Odoacer, king of the Heruli, invited by the party of Nepos (476), seizes Rome, banishes into Campania the young Augustulus, and proclaims himself King of Italy. In 493 he is dethroned by the Ostrogoths. These last, becoming again independent by the death of Attila, establish themselves first in Pannonia, with the consent of the emperor of the East, from whom he receives an annual gift. In later times they spread into Western Illyria; Theodoric is then at their head. This prince, given as a hostage to the Emperor Leo at the age of seven years (461), passed ten of them at Constantinople, where care had been taken of his instruction. Become King of the Goths, he rendered great services to the Emperor Zeno, who, in his gratitude, had called him near his person, adopted him for son, and in 484 created him ordinary consul. The Ostrogoths could hardly maintain their existence in the Illyrian provinces. Theodoric obtains from the emperor permission to lead them into Italy against the Heruli. He enters the peninsula in 489, beats Odoacer several times, shuts him up in Ravenna, and after a siege of three years, compels him to capitulate. The conqueror makes Ravenna the capital of his states. The monarchy of the Ostrogoths, besides Italy properly so called, comprehends Sicily and Western Illyria; on the side of Gaul it borders toward the Alps, the possessions of the Visigoths. Theodoric becomes the greatest prince of his age. His justice inspires full confidence. The Consubstantialists submit to him, though an Arian, the decision of their disagreements. Nevertheless he does not show himself indifferent in regard to his Church. Towards the end of his reign he takes in hand the defence of the Arians persecuted by Justin, and obliges the Pope of Rome, John I. (523-26), to repair to Constantinople to solicit toleration in their favour. This Pope, who perhaps had not shown much zeal in the accomplishment of his mission, is arrested on his return, with the senators that accompanied him; John dies in prison. At the same time, on accusations doubtless ill-founded, Theodoric, become suspicious, puts to death Boetius and Symmachus, the son-in-law and the father-in-law, both illustrious senators and former consuls. He dies in 526, leaving for successor Athalaric, son of Amalsonte, his daughter, aged only eight years. This young prince having ceased to live (534), his mother alone remains at the head of the Government; she marries her cousin Theodotus, who shortly after has her strangled in a bath. The other nation of the Goths had not succeeded to a less degree of power. Established in 412 in the middle of Gaul and in a part of Spain, the Visigoths succeeded in driving out of the last region the other barbarians, excepting the Suevi, who were in barracks in Gelicia. They profit by the agony of the Western empire so as to aggrandise themselves in Gaul. Under the leadership of Evaric or Euric, they get possession of Clermont in Auvergne, devastate Berry and

Tourraine, and extend their kingdom to the banks of the Loire. They afterwards penetrate into Provence, make themselves masters of Arles and Marseilles; the Burgundians give way before them. Evaric dies at Arles in 485. Alaric II., his son, finds himself possessed of a monarchy which extends from Cadiz to the Loire and the Alps. His father had persecuted consubstantialism in Gaul; the son follows quite an opposite course, and shows himself full of humanity. He publishes in Aquitania and at Toulouse a collection of the Theodosian code and of several other works on ancient right (506), which he authorises for the Romans of his states, with the consent of the bishops and the principal persons of each province. With his permission, there convenes at Agda a council, in which assembles twenty-four bishops of the Gaulish provinces which obey him. This prince died in 507 in a war against the Franks. Those of Germanic origin had passed the Rhine about the year 418, and had by little and little made their way in Gaul. At the time of the fall of the empire of the West, they have not passed the borders of the Aisne and the Somme. Some years later Clovis, a young king, nineteen years of age, marches against Syagrius, a Roman general, beats him, and seizes Soissons, which he makes into his capital (486). He becomes Christian and is baptised in the Consubstantialist Church (494). The populations between the Loire and the Seine place themselves under his laws. Clovis attacks Burgundy and imposes a tribute upon it. He afterwards gains over the Visigoths the battle of Nouillé, in which he kills Alaric with his own hand, and takes possession of nearly all their provinces in Gaul; they retain no more than a part of Languedoc and of Provence. Arles is on the point of falling into the hands of Clovis when Theodoric comes to the aid of the Visigoths. That prince was the maternal grandfather and guardian of Amalaric, son and successor of Alaric. He takes in hand the defence of his states. The Goths, beaten before Arles, are driven from the provinces possessed by the Visigoths between the Rhone and the Pyrenees. At the death of his grandfather, Amalaric, reigning by himself, resides in Narbonnaise Gaul.

At continual war with the Franks, he dies as a consequence of a defeat (531). Theudis, his successor, governs till 548. Although beaten before Arles, Clovis none the less preserved the greater part of his conquests over the Visigoths, that is the Aquitanian provinces. After his death (511) his states are divided among his four sons. Clodomir, one of them, reunites Burgundy to the monarchy of the Franks, of which Clotaire I. becomes sole possessor in 558. At the time of the invasion of Attila into Gaul, the Roman troops had been withdrawn from the island of Britain, which was left to itself. Too weak to withstand the Picts of the North, and the Scots come from Hibernia, the Britons call the Anglo-Saxons to their aid. The enemy being repelled, disagreement arises between the nations and their auxiliaries. The latter subjugate the greater part of the island, and found seven kingdoms of idolaters. The British Christians seek refuge in Gaul, Cornwall, and on the Continent; a part of them settle in the lands of Gaulish Armorica which has since been called Little Brittany. In Africa the Vandals continue to persecute the Consubstantialists, especially those who are of the imperial church. Genseric forbids them to ordain bishops in Africa proper and in Zengitana. He closes the Church of Carthage, and banishes the priests and the ministers. His persecution extends into the surrounding countries—Spain, Italy, Sicily, Sardinia, Greece, and Dalmatia. After the death of Valentinian III., he, every year, sends troops into one or the other of these lands, giving up everything to pillage, and carrying away a multitude of captives Huneric, his son, moderate at first (477), is not slow to follow his father's footsteps. He is severe on the Consubstantialists. The Churches are closed; the bishops, priests, and a crowd of laymen are exiled or subjected to cruel punishments. The Bishop of Carthage and all his clergy, to the number of more than five hundred, are tortured and banished. Baptism is resumed by force. The persecution stops only at the death of Huneric (485). Gontamond, his successor, recalls the Bishop of Carthage, and allows his flock to breathe. Nevertheless the churches open only in

494, after being closed during more than ten years. Trasamond, who reigns after him (496), tries to seduce the partisans of Consubstantialism by promising them charges, dignities, money, or other favours. He forbids the ordination of bishops. Far from obeying, zeal is employed in consecrating them in the vacant Sees. Then it is that Fulgentius is raised to the episcopate of Alfachusæ or Ruspe, a place in Byzacium (Africa proper). He is banished into Sardinia with more than sixty bishops of the same province and others of the rest of Africa, to the number of two hundred and twenty. This exile had lasted ten years, when Trasamond, informed of the merits of Fulgentius, sends for him to Carthage to confer with him on questions of faith. The Bishop of Ruspe resolves to profit by his stay to write and speak in favour of Consubstantialism; but the Arian episcopate soon obtained his being sent back into Sardinia, where he remains till the death of Trasamond (523). That prince has for his successor, Hilderic, son of Huneric and the princess Eudoxia. The new king, full of tolerance for Consubstantialism, re-opens its churches, recalls its bishops, allows bishops to be ordained in all places, in a word restores freedom to that communion, which, in Africa, had been deprived of it from the year 457. But the reign of Hilderic is of short duration; Gilimer dethrones him in 532, and puts him to death. The emperor, Justinian, then sends an army into Africa under the command of Belisarius, already celebrated for his victories over the Persians. That general defeats Gilimer in a great battle, and compels him to surrender (534). Africa is delivered from the yoke of the Vandals after a hundred and seven years of oppression. In the triumph of Belisarius at Constantinople, they display sacred vases of the temple of Jerusalem which Titus had brought to Rome, and which Genseric had taken possession of at the time of the sack of the capital. Africa had been reconquered under the pretext of avenging the death of Hilderic; that of Amalasonte furnishes Justinian with the occasion of driving the Ostrogoths from Italy. Belisarius being sent against them (535), takes possession of Sicily. Theodotus is put to death by the Goths themselves, who substitute Vitiges. Belisarius enters Rome and then Ravenna; Vitiges and his wife fall into his hands. He would have put an end to the war if the emperor had not recalled him (540) to oppose the Persians, who had ruined Antioch and a number of other cities. After his departure, the affairs of the Goths are re-established by Totila, their new king. He beats the imperial army and recovers the country which Belisarius had occupied. The last returns, but with too few troops to keep the field (544). He fortifies himself in Ravenna, while Totila besieges and takes Rome. Belisarius soon returns into it, and attempts to put it into a state of defence. It is attacked by Totila, who finds himself compelled to lay a regular siege to it. Belisarius confides it to his lieutenants, that he may go and fight in Sicily. He finally obtains his recall to Constantinople. Rome falls into Totila's hands (549). The eunuch Narses comes into Italy with a new army and the Lombards for auxiliaries (552). He defeats the Goths in a rencontre in which Totila perishes, arms in hand. After delivering Rome, Narses fights near Mount Vesuvius a sanguinary battle, which lasts two entire days. The Goths being conquered, capitulate and abandon Italy.

While his generals combat the barbarians, Justinian continues the prosecution of heresies. The doctrines of Origen are so described to him. From their condemnation by Theophilus of Alexandria to the commencement of the fifth century, they are generally considered as suspected, as well in the East as in the West. Nevertheless they had adherents more or less decided, such as Theodoret, Socrates, Sozomen, Sidonius Apollinaris, without any trouble arising on their account. But from the time of Justinian their progress became manifest in Palestine, especially among the monks. Complaints, thereupon, are carried to the emperor (538). On the demand of the patriarch Mennas, supported by the legate of Rome, he publishes an edict in which he sets forth the errors ascribed to Origen, classing them under six heads:—1*st*, The Father is greater than the Son, and the Son greater than the Holy Spirit;

the Son cannot see the Father, or the Holy Spirit the Son. 2d, God's power is limited ; he could make only a certain number of spirits and a certain quantity of matter ; genera, and species are co-eternal with God ; there are several worlds, there will be others, so that God has never been without creatures ; 3d, Human souls were pure intelligences, which, having given themselves to evil, were put into bodies as a punishment for their sins. 4th, Heaven, the stars, and the higher waters are animated and reasonable. 5th, Men will rise in bodies round in form. 6th, The punishment of the damned will not last for ever, and the devils will be restored to their first estate. After refuting these propositions, the edict enjoins on the patriarch Mennas to convene the bishops and the abbots who are in Constantinople, to get them to anathematise Origen and his dogmas, and then to give general advice in order that all the heads of the Church may do as much, and that in future no one is to be ordained bishop or abbot unless he has previously condemned Origen with the other heretics. Then come nine anathemas against the pre-cited opinions and against some others which refer to the incarnation, that is to say, that the soul of Christ existed before it was united to the Word ; that his body had been formed in the womb of the Virgin Mary before it was united to the Word and the soul ; that the Messiah was in the future to be crucified for the devils as he had been for men. Finally a tenth anathema applies to the person of Origen and his followers. The patriarch Mennas and the bishops present at Constantinople having subscribed this edict, it is sent to the patriarchs of Rome, Alexandria, Antioch, and Jerusalem, by whom, as well as by the generality of the bishops, it is approved.

Let us again remark that most of these propositions of Origen come from Platonism, as well as the doctrines of the Word and the Trinity. Origen, in recurring to that philosophy, meant to give, not as dogmas, but as simple speculations, the things which the Church had not sanctioned. Of those hazardous opinions some were received among the trinitarians ; others have divided men's minds, the greater number of which finally pronounced against those which are anathematised in Justinian's edict. That edict is not at first accepted in all the monasteries of Palestine. The monks becoming divided, the Origenists have the majority; they are supported by Theodore, bishop of Cesarea in Cappadocia, whom the protection of the empress Theodora, and important services made welcome at court. The emperor at the same time pursues by all sorts of ways the subjection of the Eutychians or Monophysites, but without meeting with the desired success. The measures which he takes in regard to them call forth in certain parts strong and persistent opposition. What offended many people in the Council of Chalcedon, what gave an appearance of reason to the reproach of Nestorianism addressed to him by his adversaries, was the glorification of Theodore of Mopsuesta, the approbation of a letter from Ibas to Maris, and the approbation of a writing of Theodoret against Cyril. Justinian then forms the resolution to employ fire by sacrificing the persons and the writings which seem to incur the reprobation of the greater number. In an edict or letter addressed to all the church, and bearing the title of a Confession of Faith, he expounds his belief in the trinity and the incarnation, declares that he receives the four œcumenical councils, and ends with thirteen anathemas, the three last of which bear on those who defend or do not anathematise either Theodore of Mopsuesta, his works, and his partizans, or the writings composed by Theodoret in favour of Nestorius, and against the twelve articles of Cyril, or finally the letter of Ibas to Maris the Persian. This is what has been called The Three Chapters. Under urgency from Justinian, the four patriarchs of the East consent to subscribe this new edict, and cause it to be accepted by the majority of the bishops of their countries; those who resist are punished by deposition and exile. But the legate of Rome abstains from communicating with Mennas and the other adherents. The edict is ill received in the Western Church, where they know neither Theodore of Mopsuesta nor the writings of Ibas and Theodoret; all revision of what was decided in the Council of Chalcedon is peremptorily refused.

The Roman pope, Vigil (538-555), is sent for to Constantinople, where he arrives in January 547. His position is difficult; Rome and Italy are under the power of Justinian. Could he run counter to his will? All the Westerns declare against the edict; could he approve it? He first refuses to communicate with Mennas; then, at the end of some months, he changes this determination. In April 548 he addresses to him a decision by which he condemns the Three Chapters, without prejudice to the Council of Chalcedon. This unfortunate determination displeases everybody; the adversaries of the Three Chapters are offended with the reservation *saving the authority* of the Council of Chalcedon; the others are indignant that a Pope of Rome should consent to the condemnation of those Chapters. All the bishops of Africa, Illyria, and Dalmatia withdraw from his communion; two of his deacons declare against him. A Council in Illyria decides in favour of the "Three Chapters" (550); a council in Africa excommunicates Pope Vigil, and supports the "Three Chapters" by letters addressed to the emperor (551). The Bishop of Rome demands the convocation of an œcumenical council, and withdraws his judgment. None the less is the edict published, and people are pressed to subscribe to it. Then Vigil repudiates the communion of the orientals, and takes refuge in a church. An effort is made to drag him out by force, but the crowd intervenes in his favour. Promises and oaths induce him to return to his dwelling. He soon perceives that its outlets are guarded, and escaping by night, he retires into a temple in Chalcedon, and this refuge he refuses to quit, until the peace of the Church is restored.

The fifth œcumenical council (the second of Constantinople) meets on the 4th of May 553, at the convocation of Justinian. It is presided over by Eutychius, successor of Mennas. Vigil, who refuses to attend it, promises to give his opinion separately. In effect, he sends to the emperor a decree called *Constitutum;* in this act he condemns the doctrines attributed to Theodore of Mopsuesta, but not his person, not thinking it right to pronounce anathema against dead persons; he maintains the respect due to the memory of Theodoret, while condemning the writings current under his name which agree with the errors of Nestorius; in regard to Ibas and his letter he refers to the decisions of the Council of Chalcedon. Justinian refuses to receive this *Constitutum*, which remains without result. The Council, after declaring that it adheres to the four first œcumenic councils, of which the belief is the same, condemns Theodore of Mopsuesta and his writings, as well as the impieties contained in various writings of Theodoret, and the letter said to have been written by Ibas to Maris the Persian; it anathematises those Three Chapters and their defenders. On a letter from Justinian the assembly also, with one voice, pronounces the condemnation of Origen and his errors, as also that of Didymus and Evager, his partizans. Vigil seeing that no attack is made on the authority of the Council of Chalcedon, and from the letter from Leo to Flavian, that there was no question touching persons, ends by surrendering to the decision of the council, while in the terms of his adhesion, he mitigates it in regard to Ibas and Theodoret (554). He is then left free to set out for Rome, carrying with him some favours from Justinian; he dies on his journey to Syracuse. The fifth œcumenical council is received in all the East by the monks of the new foundation in Palestine; they revolt against the condemnation of Origen. The Patriarch of Jerusalem, who cannot reduce them, drives them from their home, in which he places other monks. In the West, the majority of the churches reject this council as contrary to that of Chalcedon. A schism follows in Aquilea and Upper Italy, which subsists for a century. A number of bishops, especially in Africa, are deposed and banished for their resistance.

The success of these two edicts against the Origenists and against the "Three Chapters," encourages Justinian in his theological enterprises. But in the end fate turns; he clearly yields to a Eutychian opinion. We have said a word of a schism which broke out in Alexandria between Severus of Antioch and other Acephales who had taken refuge in that city, on the question whether the body of Jesus was corruptible or not; a schism which had produced the sects of the corrupticoles and the incorrupticoles or phantasiasts.

Justinian, in search after controversies, is taken with the view of the incorrupticoles, supported by the pure Eutychians; it is inspired, it is said, by Theodore of Cappadocia and the Origenists. He publishes an edict in which he maintains that the body of Christ was incorruptible, that is to say, that from the moment of conception, he was not susceptible of any alteration, not even for natural wants such as hunger and thirst. The emperor demands subscriptions to this edict, as he had done for those which condemned Origenism and the "Three Chapters." But the bishops to whom he applies answer by a positive refusal. The patriarch Eutychius resists him, saying that it would hence follow that the incarnation was but imaginary. Justinian, far from surrendering, arrests the patriarch under frivolous pretences and banishes him to Amasea in the Pontus (565). John the scholastic is ordained in his place. All the oriental patriarchs and bishops equally make opposition. One cannot say what would have taken place had not the emperor died the following year at the age of eighty-four. Justin II., his nephew, lets the matter drop, and recalls all the exiles except Eutychius.

Under the reigns of Justin II., Tiberius, Maurice, Phocas, and even during the first part of that of Heraclius, religious discussions sleep (566-628). The ruinous wars that are carried on in the East leave little leisure for theological cavils. The Persians in the time of Justin invade the empire with impunity. On one side they advance to Antioch, and on another to Cesarea in Cappadocia. Afterwards they are repelled by Tiberius and kept back by Maurice. But under the reign of Phocas, Chosroes II., on the pretext of avenging the murder of Maurice who had re-established him on the throne, commenced an implacable war which continues long after the death of Phocas. The Persians ravage Palestine, Egypt, Libya; they get possession of Jerusalem (614), and carry off, with a multitude of captives, the cross which was said to be that of Christ. Their devastations extend also into Cappadocia, Phrygia, Bithynia, and the other provinces of Asia Minor. They besiege and capture Chalcedon, in face of Constantinople (616). Heraclius succeeds in collecting an army which he transports by sea into Asia and gains over them a series of victories. Chosroes is dethroned by Syroes, his eldest son, who makes peace with the emperor; the war had lasted twenty-four years. The captives are restored, among others Zachary, patriarch of Jerusalem, as well as the pretended cross of Christ. Heraclius has it carried before him in his triumphal entry into Constantinople; he himself goes next year to replace it in Jerusalem. While these calamities afflict the East, the western provinces also have their disasters.

Narses, after expelling the Goths from Italy, governs that country in peace till 567. He is then recalled by Justin II.; the empress writes to him injurious words. In his resentment, he invites, it is said, the Lombards to come into Italy, and dies at Rome shortly after. The Lombards arrive under the lead of Alboin (568). The country is destitute of forces capable of resisting them. In three years they get possession of Upper Italy, Tuscany, Umbria, and proceed as far as the gates of Rome and Ravenna. Pavia becomes the capital of the new kingdom. The Greek emperors retain no more than the Exarchate of Ravenna, Sicily, Sardinia and different countries of Southern Italy. During the three centuries which pass away between the fall of the Western empire and the end of the kingdom of the Lombards (476-774), the bishops of Rome find themselves in a precarious position. They are first subjects of barbarous Arians; the Gothic kings do not always treat them with entire deference; they employ them according to the wants of their policy, make themselves judges of accusations brought against them; decide difficulties relative to their election, and make provision for vacancies in the see. After the expulsion of the Goths, the Roman popes are exposed to competition with the patriarchs of Constantinople. The latter, for whom the Council of Chalcedon has acknowledged privileges equal to those of the bishops of Rome, except priority of rank, raise their heads from day to day. Acacius and his successors are little disquieted at the anathemas of the Latin patriarch. Justinian himself observes in regard to Pope Vigil very disrespectful conduct in the affair of the "Three Chapters." When the Lombards are masters of Upper Italy, and when the Greeks no longer possess the exarchate of Ravenna, things become worse. Rome is nothing more than a dependence of that small province, while the emperors reside at Constantinople. The patriarch of that city claims the title of universal bishop. John, the faster, first takes it in a council held in 589. Pope Pelagius (577-590) cancels the acts of that council, in virtue, he says, of the authority of Saint Peter (whose Roman seat then begins to prevail) and forbids his nuncius to share in John's mass. But in Constantinople little account is made of his decision. The patriarch, supported by the emperor Maurice, does none the less continue to style himself the universal bishop. Gregory I. called the Great (590-604), writes to him to recall him to sentiments of Christian humility (595). "The Council of Chalcedon," he says, "had offered the title of universal bishop to the bishops of Rome, not one of whom was willing to receive it." At the same time Gregory addresses the emperor and the empress, begging them to oblige John to renounce the pretension. He invites the patriarchs of Alexandria and Antioch to unite with him in order to resist the pope. John dies shortly after in the odour of sanctity, but without having heeded Gregory's exhortations. Cyriacus, who occupies his place, takes in his synodal letters the same title of œcumenical bishop. Gregory rejects neither his letter nor his legates; but he writes to him that for the sake of peace, he ought to renounce that presumptuous and profane word. The bishop of Constantinople persisting none the less, Gregory forbids his nuncius to celebrate mass with him. The other eastern patriarchs do not seem to have troubled themselves with supporting that of Rome in this rivalry. A council assembling in Constantinople (599) Gregory writes to the principal bishops who are to attend it, to exhort them not to consent directly or indirectly to the title of œcumenical, "for," he says, "if one bishop is universal, the others are not bishops." He threatens to cut off from the communion of Saint Peter those who shall act in opposition to the recommendations of his letter. All his efforts remain fruitless.

But some years later, Cyriacus, having drawn on himself the animadversion of Phocas, for having protected the family of Maurice, pope Boniface III. (606) obtains from the tyrant the maintenance of the primacy of the bishop of Rome and interdicts the patriarch of Constantinople to take the title of œcumenical. From that time the popes have arrogated to themselves that profane and presumptuous title of universal bishops, which, according to Gregory I., they had refused to receive from the Council of Chalcedon. But the Greeks are not the only ones to trouble the Roman bishop, during the existence of the exarchate. The bishop of Ravenna also attempts to augment the importance of his see. That city had from the time of Honorius, been the abode of the Western emperors, the kings of Italy, and finally of the Exarchs. Its bishops take occasion to put themselves above the others, even the metropolitans. The pope of Rome, obliged to have recourse often to their influence with the exarchs, the bishops of Ravenna abuse the consequent dependence of those of Rome for their own aggrandisement and for combating the Roman see itself. In the East the religious discussions, which were silent during the calamities of war, soon recommence when times become less disastrous. In the time of the first victories of Heraclius over the Persians, a new sect makes its appearance in the Church. While recognising two natures in Jesus, with the Council of Chalcedon, some ask whether those two natures have each an operation and a will of their own, or whether there is only one operation resulting from unity of person. The latter opinion, the originator of which seems to have been Theodore, bishop of Pharan in Arabia, is adopted by Sergius, patriarch of Constantinople, born in Syria, of Jacobite parents. The Emperor Heraclius receives it from him and communicates it to Cyrus, bishop of Phasis (629). The latter, promoted the following year to the patriarchate of Alexandria, unites with Theodore of Pharan to propagate it. Their followers are called *Monothelites*.

Aided by this doctrine, Cyrus succeeds in uniting to his Church the Theodosians or Acephales, very numerous in Alexandria (633). The latter give it out that they did not receive the Council of Chalcedon, but that the council came to them; that to admit a single operation is in the act to acknowledge only one nature in Christ. Sophron, a famous monk, attempts in vain to dissuade the patriarchs of Alexandria and Constantinople against this opinion; both of them maintain that the only Christ, the only Word incarnated produces divine and human things by a sole theandric or deivirile operation, that is divine and human at once. Sophron being elected patriarch of Jerusalem (633), Sergius hastens to prepare Honorius, Pope of Rome (626-638), by setting before him the whole affair in his point of view; he ends by inferring that instead of one sole, or of two operations in Christ, it is better to say, as do the œcumenical councils, that one and the same Christ operate things divine and things human, that all his operations proceed undividedly from the same incarnate Word and refer to him alone; for in speaking with some of a single operation, you make these fear that you are tending to the suppression of the two natures, and in speaking of two operations (not brought forward in any Father) you lead many to think that you recognise two different wills. Honorius replies to the patriarch of Constantinople that he entirely approves his doctrine and his conduct; he commends him for having removed the novelty of words which may scandalise the simple. "We confess," says he, "one sole will in Jesus Christ, because the divinity took, not our sin, but our nature such as it was created, before it was corrupted by sin. The councils and the Scripture speak not of two operations or one, but everywhere in Scripture Jesus is one sole being operating by divinity and by humanity. Whether we should understand one operation or two is of small consequence; it is an affair for grammarians. We must reject new words in order not to appear in the eyes of the simple, Nestorian by recognising two operations, or Eutychean by admitting only one. In his synodal letters Sophron announces his profession of faith by undertaking to prove the unity of person against Nestorius, and the distinction of natures against Eutyches. Each of the two natures, he says, preserving its properties, has its real, natural, and suitable operation. To say that they have one sole operation is to reduce them to one substance and one sole nature, following the error of the Acephales; for we know the natures only by the operations. None the less does Honorius persist in imposing silence on both parties. He writes with this view to the three patriarchs of Constantinople, Alexandria, and Jerusalem. Despite his exhortations, Sophron continues to oppose the Monothelites; he publishes six hundred passages from the Fathers which he has gathered against them. The evil still increasing, he sends to Rome the first of his suffragans to demand the condemnation of the new doctrine. Meanwhile Jerusalem is taken by the Moslems (636). Sophron dies soon after. However, Heraclius, inspired by the patriarch of Constantinople, publishes on the agitated question an edict which is designated *Ecthesis* or Exposition (639). He wishes people to say that it is one sole and the same Jesus Christ who operates things human and divine, and forbids any one to speak of one operation or two. Sergius solemnly approves this Ecthesis in a council held at Constantinople. He excommunicates whoever permits himself to teach either one will or two in Christ. The patriarch of Alexandria also gives in his adhesion. But Pope John IV. (640-642) formally anathematises the Ecthesis. Pyrrhus, successor of Sergius in the See of Constantinople, hastens to command that it shall be subscribed by all the bishops under pain of excommunication. Pope John IV. (639) condemns it afresh in a letter addressed to that patriarch. The emperor, seeing that his edict becomes a cause of trouble, writes to the Pope of Rome that the Ecthesis is not from him, but the patriarch Sergius, at whose request he subscribed and published it. This disavowal does not put an end to the disputes.

The Eutycheans burst out in raillery. They say that the Chalcedonians, after being Nestorians, have recognised in Christ one sole operation, consequently one sole nature, and that now, ashamed of having done well, they confess neither one operation nor two.

After the death of Heraclius (641), John IV. writes to Constantine, his son, a letter in which he endeavours to exculpate Honorius, his predecessor, and asks the prince to suppress the Ecthesis, which scandalises the Westerns and even the people of Constantinople. This letter produces no result. The patriarch Pyrrhus, odious to the people, abdicates and retires to Chalcedon, and thence he goes into Africa. Paul, a Monothelite like him, is ordained in his place (641). He sends to Rome synodal letters in which nothing is said on the Ecthesis. They are received by Pope Theodore (642-649). In his reply the Roman bishop invites Paul to condemn that exposition of belief and to depose his predecessor Pyrrhus.

Africa in its turn declares against the Ecthesis. A conference takes place in that province on the question of Monothelism, between the patriarch Phyrrus and an abbot named Maximus. Pyrrhus, disabused, goes to Rome and presents a retractation to pope Theodore, who receives him then as patriarch of Constantinople. Several councils are held in Africa against the Ecthesis and the Monothelites. The African bishops write about it to the patriarch Paul. Pressed by them and by the legates of Rome, he sends a dogmatic letter to pope Theodore ; he believes, he says, that there is only one will in Christ, for fear of introducing two persons. There are certainly two natures in him ; but his soul, enriched with divine gifts by the close union, has a will that is divine and inseparable from the Word. This letter does not satisfy the Westerns ; the Ecthesis is still written against.

Paul then persuades the emperor Constans to suppress it and to publish an edict to impose silence on both sides. This edict is published under the name of *Type* (648). In it the emperor forbids all future discussion on the question of one will or two, of one operation or two, requiring that people should hold to the Scriptures and to the decisions of the five œcumenical councils. He threatens opponents with deposition, excommunication, destitution, confiscation, corporal punishments and banishment. The pope Theodore, convinced of the inutility of these remonstrances, pronounces in council a sentence of deposition, as against Paul so against Pyrrhus, who had returned to Monothelism. By way of reprisal, Paul overturns the altar of Theodore at Constantinople, and persecutes the Roman legates. Pope Martin I. (649-655) begins by collecting in the Lateran palace a council composed of bishops of imperial Italy, and of some of those of Africa. In this it is declared that the two natures in Christ preserving their properties, he has two wills and two operations, the divine and the human. In consequence, condemnation is passed on those who acknowledge only one sole will and one sole operation, as well as those who will not speak either of one will or two; anathemas are also pronounced against the heretics, namely, Theodore of Pharan, Cyrus of Alexandria, Sergius of Constantinople, as well as his successors, Pyrrhus and Paul, and also whosoever receives the impious Ecthesis and the impious Type.

The acts of this council are sent into the East as well as into the West; a synodal letter is addressed to the emperor. The latter hastens to take his revenge for the contempt which has been thrown on his Type. By his order, the pope of Rome is carried off and embarked for Constantinople (653). There he dwells three months in prison. He is brought before the Senate, charged with having conspired against the prince with the Exarch Olympius. He is laden with ill treatment, kept in prison till 655, and banished to Cherson (on the left bank of the Dnieper), where he dies the same year. An imperial order places Eugenius in the see of Rome (655-58). Constantine Pogonat, become emperor (668), forms the resolution to convene a general council to settle the question of Monothelism.

The sixth œcumenical council (third of Constantinople) meets on the 7th of November 680, under the presidence of the emperor. There are seen the legates of the pope of Rome, and those of his council, George, patriarch of Constantinople, Macarius, patriarch of Antioch (Monothelite). The legates of the sees of Alexandria and Jerusalem had not been able to quit their country, of which the Arabs were the masters; for the same reason there comes to the Assembly no bishop of these two patriarchates, or of the African regions. More than one hundred and sixty bishops assemble at the last session which is held in September 681. Then the definition of faith by the council is read.

After declaring adhesion to the five first œcumenical councils, it decides that there are in Christ two natural wills and two natural operations, and that nothing else is to be taught on pain of deposition for clergymen, and anathema for laics. It condemns as authors of Monothelism, Theodore of Pharan, Sergius, Pyrrhus, Paul, and Peter of Constantinople, Honorius of Rome, Cyrus of Alexandria, Macarius of Antioch, and Stephen his disciple. Those of the condemned that are still alive, are banished to Rome on their request. This œcumenical council, like the preceding one, limits itself to decree on the questions in debate; neither of them passes any canon touching order and discipline. To supplement this, Justinian II. convokes in the dome of the palace a council which hence takes the surname of *In Trullo* (692). It is also called in Greek, Penthecte, and in Latin, Quini-Sextus; others completely confound it with the Sixth Council. The object proposed here is to draw up a body of discipline for all the Church. They determine what canons shall be followed, whether proceeding from œcumenical councils or others, or from canonical epistles of the Fathers; in the number appear the eighty-five canons attributed to the apostles; but they reject the apostolical constitutions as having been altered by heresy. From these different sources are drawn the rules of discipline which are distributed in one hundred and two canons. A certain number of them offer arrangements contrary to several usages of the Roman Church. Each country, it is known, had long had its own particular customs. To draw up a code common to the whole official church, some must be sacrificed. The council, composed of Greek and Oriental bishops, preferred the usages of the East to those of the Western Church. We will indicate the principal divergencies. The Quini-sextus consecrates on the marriage of clerics, the following points, which have since served as the rule for the Greeks and all the Christians of the East:—
Sub-deacons, deacons, and priests are forbidden to contract marriage after their ordination. Those who were married

before their ordination may keep their wives and live with them, except on the days when they have to approach the sacred mysteries or say mass. Whoever has been married twice, or has had a concubine after his baptism, whoever has married a widow, a repudiated woman, a courtesan, a slave, or a comedian cannot be ordained a clerk in any rank. The bishops are bound to complete continence, whether they had been married before or not. In the Roman Church at this time married men were ordained priests or deacons, but they were made to promise to no longer have commerce with their wives—which the Quini-sextus condemns as contrary to the perfection of the apostolic canon. Among the other contradictory articles is canon two which confirms the eighty-five apostolic canons, while the Roman Church receives only the first fifty; canon fifty-five, which condemns the Saturday's fast, even in the time of Lent, except Holy Saturday; canon sixty-seven, which sanctions abstinence from blood and the flesh of strangled animals; canon seventy-three which forbids tracing the figure of the cross on the soil or on the pavement that is trodden under foot; canon seventy-nine, which forbids making at the time of the nativity representations of the virgin; canon eighty-two, which requires that Christ should be represented under the human form, and not under that of a lamb; canon ninety, which forbids bending the knee on Sundays until the evening and every day between Passover and Pentecost; canon one hundred and one, which commands that the Eucharist be received not in a vase, of whatever material, but in hands crossing one another. Of all the decrees of the Quini-sextus those which displease at Rome most and which most contribute to cause it to reject this council, are doubtless canons thirty-six and thirty-eight. Canon thirty-eight reproduces the requirement made by the seventeenth canon of Chalcedon, namely conformity in the ecclesiastical order to the rank and dignity of the cities in the civil order. Canon thirty-six, confirming the twenty-eighth of the same council, decides that the See of Constantinople shall have privileges equal to those of the See of ancient Rome, except the priority of rank. The Church of

Rome, it will be remembered, had refused to recognise this twenty-eighth canon of Chalcedon. Less than ever was it disposed to recognise it in the time of the Quini-sextus; all the West being then in the power of the barbarians, Rome, a simple dependence on the exarchate of Ravenna, was thrown down to the lowest ranks in the political order, while its rival sat on the throne at the head of the empire.

Nevertheless, the quality of œcumenical cannot be seriously denied to the Quini-sextus. It rests on the summons of the emperor; all the patriarchs are present or represented; the legates of the Pope of Rome and the Roman Council approve it and subscribe to it. Nevertheless Pope Sergius (687-701) does not hesitate to charge it with nullity. He even refuses to open the copy sent by the emperor. The latter gives orders for removing the recalcitrant pope; but the people and the troops oppose it. Justinian II. is dethroned the following year, and things remain where they are. The Quini-sextus in the sequel is approved by the second Council of Nice, by Hadrian I., by Nicholas I., and by other Latin authorities. Several of the bishops of Rome receive it, except on the points contrary to their Church. In the Greek and Oriental Church its canons are still in full vigour. The questions of which we have spoken are discussed between the Church of Rome and the oriental Christians; the other countries of the West, subject to the yoke of the Barbarians remain on the outside of the debate. In Spain the conversion of the conquering Suevi and the Visigoths was accomplished in the sixth century. The Suevi, who have occupied Galicia for one hundred and fifty years, accept consubstantionalism about the year 56▶. That region is, shortly after, conquered by the Visigoths, whose king attempts to re-establish Arianism. But his successor, Recarede (587) becomes Consubstantialist, and his example prevails with all the nation. In continual conflict with the Franks, the Visigoths must have felt the need of intimately connecting themselves with the Spanish people by identity of worship. On one side, the so-prompt fall of the Arian Vandals and Ostrogoths, on the other, the power of the Consubstantialist Franks, so solidly founded by the adhesion of Gaul, indicated sufficiently that this was the best means of preserving their monarchy. Gaul, torn by successive divisions, is the incessant victim of the unbridled passions of the descendants of Clovis. The Burgundians abjure Arianism at the beginning of the sixth century; the provinces occupied by the Visigoths persist in it until the reign of Ricarede. But whether they hold consubstantialism or not, these different peoples are no longer penetrated by the spirit of the gospel. In the countries between the Rhine and the Loire, where civilisation, even in the time of the Romans, was less advanced than in the south, frequent invasions, then the definitive establishment of the barbarians, had everywhere deposited a thick layer of superstitious ignorance. Christianity degenerated then into mummeries of all sorts, into veneration for relics, into daily miracles, into monastic institutions, with which the soil is soon covered. Among the most celebrated communities at this time was the monastery of Luxeuil, founded by Columban of Ireland, a missionary of the faith in Gaul and Germany (590) and the monastery of Sainte Croix at Poitiers, the establishment of which is due to Queen Radegonde, who afterwards retires thither, and there keeps up benevolent relations with the most distinguished men of the country, such as Gregory of Tours and Fortunatus of Poitiers. In the midst of disorders, from which it has often to suffer, the clergy increases in power from day to day. In many a council canons are published to protect clergymen from violence, and to augment their credit and fortune. Numerous endowments enrich the church and the monks. The bishops become great Lords; most of them pass for saints in the eyes of the people; many of them bear sway in the courts of kings, among others Gregory of Tours, Arnoul, Faron, Loup de Sens, Eloi, Leger d'Autun.

Northern Belgium, peopled with unbelievers, is converted by Amand and his disciples (626-79); they found there a great number of monasteries. From the middle of the fifth century, when the British Christians had withdrawn into Gaul, the greater part of their island was occupied by the Anglo-Saxons, an idolatrous race. Pope Gregory I. sends thither Augustin and forty other monks, who convert Edelbert, King of Kent, and a part of his subjects (596) Augustin, ordained Bishop of the Angli, establishes his episcopal seat at Canterbury, where he dies in 607. His work is continued by his disciples and their successors in the midst of divers vicissitudes. Christianity triumphs definitively over idolatry in that country only about the end of the seventh century. The success obtained in the island is due to means adapted to the gross ignorance of the population; it is specially by the virtue of relics, and by a multiplicity of miracles, that minds are overcome; the missionaries are also seconded by the influence of some pious natives of Christian lands. The Anglo-Saxons, converted by the monks of Rome, become in their turn the principal agents of the conversion of the German nations, of whom they are the issue. Towards the end of the seventh century they preach the gospel among the Frisons and the other peoples of the maritime coasts between the Rhine and the Elbe. Among the most zealous, Willebrod and his eleven companions may be mentioned. Disembarking in Zealand in 694 they are well received by Pepin d'Heristal and instruct a large number of idolaters. Willebrod, sent to Rome by Pepin, brings back the title of Apostle of the Frisons and Archbishop of Utrecht. But the true apostle of Germany is the Anglo-Saxon Winifried, better known under the name of Boniface. In the year 719 he goes to Rome, where he obtains from Gregory II. (715-31) with a good supply of relics, the mission of preaching among all infidel nations. On his return he seconds, during three years, the efforts of Willebrod in Frisia; then he carries the gospel into Hesse and Thuringia. In a second journey to Rome (723) the Pope ordains him bishop, changing his name of Winifried into Boniface. He returns into Germany with letters from the Pope and Charles Martel, and brings back to Christianity the Hessians and the Thuringians, who had abandoned it during his absence. Gregory III. (731-44) honours him with the title of archbishop, giving him power to place bishops in all the spots where it should appear necessary (732). Boniface builds a number of churches and monasteries. As the Pope's vicar, he presides over several councils, convened by Carloman and Pepin, in Germany and in France, for the restoration of ecclesiastical discipline, and at last dies in Frisia, massacred, with fifty other persons, by Pagans furious to see their religion persecuted and their temples beaten down (754). His disciples pursue his footsteps, especially in Frisia and toward the country of the Saxons. But this last people are soon to encounter a terrible converter in the person of Charlemagne.

Let us return into the East, where the seventh century saw a revolution prolific in political results. By successive councils and by heaping no-sense on no-sense, the imperial church had at last succeeded, under the inspiration of Plato and Hermes, in constituting its three and one God, and its god-man Christ. It had formularies sanctioned by the civil power. To them whose reason rebelled against the result, the Church replied by exile or other penalties. To such as were simple and timid it said: "These are mysteries which human intelligence cannot comprehend; submit and believe." But in the very time when they were putting the last hand to the work a formidable negation arose against it in the depth of the provinces of Arabia. That vast peninsula, protected by deserts on the north, surrounded by the sea on other parts, had always preserved its independence. The Egyptians, the Chaldeo-Assyrians, the Persians, the Greeks, the Romans, those successive despots of Western Asia, had been able only to repress the incursions of the contiguous Arabs; sometimes they had subdued them or driven them back into the deserts, but without being able to settle in the interior of those regions. Religion among the Arabs seems to have begun with idolatry, as among most nations of the world. At a later time Zabaism arose, and progressively gained the greater part of the peninsula. While admitting the existence of one only God, the Zabians at the same time worshipped the stars, or rather the angels who were supposed to reside in them, and hence govern the universe under the direction of the supreme God. They were honoured as inferior divinities, the companions of God, and their intercession with him

was implored by human beings. The Zabians read onl
the Psalms among the books of sacred scripture; but the
possessed other books which they regarded as equally sacrec
Travellers have given them the name of John the Baptis
Christians, and in truth the Zabians called him their apostle
Several Arab tribes had already ceased to be idolaters befor.
Mohamed's coming. The religion of the Magi was observe
in different places; the new prophet was well acquainte
with it. When Palestine is devastated by the Romans i
the first and second century of our era, a multitude of Jew.
flee into Arabia, make proselytes among different tribes, an
seize several cities and fortresses. At an anterior day, th
religion of Moses had penetrated into certain Arab pro
vinces; a hundred years before Christ, a king of Yeme
had caused it to be adopted by the Hamyarites, wh
possessed the greater part of that region of the peninsula
It was also embraced by some of his successors. At th
beginning of the sixth century one of them named Dh
Nowas persecutes those who refuse to be converted t
Judaism. This persecution extending to the Christians c
the land, the king of Ethiopia sends troops to their aid
Dhu Nowas loses his crown and his life. Yemen is the
governed by Ethiopian princes. But in the time of th
emperor Heraclius the Hamyarites drive them away wit
the aid of the king of Persia, who establish the princes o
Yemen until the conquest of the country by Mohamec
Among the Jews who sought an asylum in Arabia, in th
first centuries of our era, there were doubtless Nazarenes o
Judeo-Christians, who had not sundered their fortune fron
that of their nation. A crowd of Pagan Christians mus
also have taken refuge in those parts, at the time when per
secutions and disorders disturbed the Eastern churches
The decrees issued against the partisans of Paul of Samosata
Arius, Nestorius, Eutyches, as well as the proscription o
all the dissident sects by Theodosius, Justinian, and othe
emperors contributed to spread Christianity among th
Arabs; the Eutycheans or Jacobites generally prevailec
there, as in Egypt and Syria. The independence of th
tribes allowed all religious opinions to propagate themselves

One of the most ancient and noble, the tribe of Koreish, had accepted Mazdeism, according to some; Zabaism according to others. It is believed that before Mohamed some members of that tribe professed a kind of theism, abstaining from the idolatry and the other forms of worship observed in the country. The Koreish were Ishmaelites, and as such practised circumcision. Mecca, their metropolis, was regarded as a sacred city; its temple was venerated, and it was visited by considerable numbers every year. With the supreme God, most of the Koreish worshipped Venus and the other planets, of which they had idols in stone under different forms; they also paid homage to the angels whom they considered as the sons and daughters of God and his associates. They gave alms on a large scale, practised frequent washings, and abstained from drinking wine. Mohamed is born at Mecca the year 569 A.D., in the tribe Koreish. The commencements of his life are difficult. The death of his father leaves him an orphan when two years old. Brought up by Abutaleb, one of his uncles, he travels in commercial caravans from Mecca to Damascus, traversing Syria and Palestine. Returning into his native land, he enters as an agent the service of Khadidjah, a noble and rich widow, who at length marries him. This marriage gives him an advantageous position in his tribe. Some years after, the thought comes into his head, to use his own language, he is inspired with the idea of establishing a new religion among the Arabs. Mohamed was illiterate. He makes his ignorance a source of proof that the Koran is a divine revelation. But in his travels and in Mecca he may have become acquainted with Jewish and Christian ideas. What is said of his relations with Jacobite or Nestorian monks seems an hypothesis without foundation: these two sects believed in the incarnation and the Trinity; Mohamed was opposed to both. The Moslem prophet was rather a disciple of the Nazarenes or Judeo-Christians. There is a striking analogy between his doctrine and theirs. Like them, he regards Jesus as a pure man, although born of a virgin by the divine will, and his mother as a righteous person whom no particular advantage distinguishes from other women. As they were, he shows himself much attached to the law of Moses. On that law the Koran is modelled, excepting what concerns the future life, of which the prophet of Israel has not spoken. On this point, Mohamed receives his inspirations from the Judeo-Christians; his sensual paradise comes from the reign of a thousand years, of which they had transmitted the belief to the primitive church. Resembling the Judeo-Christians again, Mohamed owns only the gospel among the books of the New Testament. That of which he makes use, differing from ours in certain points, may have been in use in the Nazarene sects; it is attributed to Barnabas. The Koran contains several of the legends which were current on the infancy of Jesus and his mother. But for the acts of the Apostles, the Epistles of Paul and the other parts of the New Testament, Mohamed does not appear to have known them: the Koran makes no mention of the apostle to the Gentiles; now Paul was unknown to the majority of the Nazarenes, and detested by others as a renegade from the law of Moses. When forty years of age Mohamed undertakes the execution of his designs. He first opens his mind to his wife Khadidjah, who believes in him. He has then for proselyte his slave Zeid, his young cousin Ali, son of Abutaleb, and Abubekr, a man of great credit among the Koreish, who draws to him Othman and four others of the principal men of Mecca. During the three first years Mohamed preaches in secret; a small number of persons unite with his first adherents. This time over, he publicly publishes his mission, to which the Koreish make opposition more or less active. In the sixth year he sees come to him Hamza, his uncle, and Omar, a man highly esteemed, who till then had been one of his most violent antagonists. His doctrine makes great progress in several tribes. The inhabitants of Mecca become converts and offer him assistance. In the thirteenth year he commands his followers to withdraw into that city. A short time after the Koreish conspiring against his life, he flees and seeks a refuge. From that flight dates the Hegira or Moslem era, the first day of which corresponds to our 16th of July 622.

Down to that time the doctrine of Mohamed had been spread only by secret or public preaching. Once at Medina, he has recourse to the force of arms against his enemies, and combats them with advantage during several years. The sixth of the Hegira he concludes a truce of ten years with the Koreish. This truce having been broken by them at the end of two years, he captures Mecca, destroys the idols there, and pardons his adversaries who submit to him. After his victory crowds flock to him from all sides. Islamism propagates rapidly in Yemen. On the death of Mohamed, the Arabs, united in the same belief, are in a condition to carry it to a distance by conquest (632). The idea of his mission became grander with his success. From Medina he sends messengers to the neighbouring princes— to the king of Persia, the emperor Heraclius, the king of Ethiopia, and others, to exhort them to accept Islamism. Let us trace a rapid sketch of the Moslem doctrine.

According to Mohamed there is only one true religion. It consists in the worship of one sole God, in the observance of the laws of justice, and some other precepts and ceremonies which are established of God for the present time, according to different ages. God at certain times sends messengers or prophets to announce his will to men, to draw them away from false worships, and to lead them to the true religion. Thus revelation was given to Noah, and the prophets which followed him, among others, to Abraham, Ishmael, Isaac, Jacob, Moses, David, Solomon, Elijah, Yahia (John), to Jesus, and finally to Mohamed, who is the seal of the prophets. Each nation has had its own; there is a multitude of them, among whom some have received the special mission of apostles. Six of the last established a new law; that is, Adam, Noah, Abraham, Moses, Jesus, and Mohamed. The book of the law was given to Moses; God chose him, in preference to all other men, to convey his word to the world. Jesus is born of the Virgin Mary by an effect of the divine will. God formed him of dust like Adam, then he said, "Be," and he was. Jesus is the divine Word, the Messiah, one of God's trusted servants, his apostle to the sons of Israel; but he is only a man like the apostles who preceded him. He was laden with celestial favours, and set forth as an example to the Israelites. His mother was righteous. They nourished each other with food. One day, so you read in the Koran, God, assembling the prophets, will say to Jesus: "Hast thou ever said to men, Take for gods me and my mother rather than the only God?'" "Far from thy glory be this blasphemy," Jesus will reply, "I said to them, 'Worship God, my Lord and yours.'" God gave his revelation to Jesus. He taught him the book and the wisdom, the Pentateuch and the gospel. His mission was to confirm the law of Moses, to bring wisdom to men, to explain to them the object of their disputes, to allow them the use of certain forbidden things. The gospel contains light and direction; it confirms the Pentateuch, and serves for admonition to them who fear God. Jesus was not crucified and put to death. Another, who resembled him, was substituted for him; God delivered Jesus from the infidels and raised him to himself. Mohamed is God's apostle, his envoy to the Arabs, and the seal of the prophets. He was chosen among the people of his city, an unlettered apostle to unlettered men. He was sent to teach a people who before him had no apostle and no book, and to direct them in the right way. The Koran descended from heaven, in the moon Ramadan and in the night of Alkader; it came down in portions. Gabriel brought it and placed it on Mohamed's heart, that he might be an apostle and teach the mother of cities (Mecca) and its surroundings; the original of this book is in the hands of God, in the hidden volume. It is a revelation of the sovereign of the universe; it is a book blessed, right, glorious, clear, which contains the truth and confirms the scriptures given before it. It is written in Arabic in order to be understood by those for whom it was destined. It ought not to be touched except by the pure. God's religion is Islam. The faithful believe in God and the Koran; they believe also in the scriptures sent to other nations, in the Pentateuch and the gospel. All these religions are but one, their God is the same. The religion revealed to Mohamed is that which was entrusted to Noah, Abraham, Moses, Jesus. The believers—the Jews, the Zabians, the Christians who have faith in God and in the last day, and practise virtue—all these will receive a recompense from their Lord. But the men of the scriptures, says the Koran, do not observe the Pentateuch and the gospel and the books which the Lord has given them. Mohamed indicated to them many passages which they hid, and he passed over many others. They have interpolated and altered their scriptures, and have removed all the passages relative to the coming of the prophet of Islam. We will state the principal dogmas of the Koran. There is only one God. He has neither son, nor daughter, nor associates, nor equal. He is neither two, nor several, nor a member of the Trinity. He is one, immense, knowing everything, present everywhere, the light of the heaven and the earth. He is eternal, the living, the wise, the merciful, the pitiful; he is also the powerful and the avenger. He is God the creator and the former. He brought forth all things from nothing. He created seven heavens and as many earths. He effected the creation in six days, which are six thousand years of our calculation; and he afterwards sat on his throne above the heavens. All that is in the heavens and on the earth publishes his praise. Even the shadows of beings bend before him morning and evening. He is the creator, the God, the king of men. He pardons and chastises at his pleasure; he alone has the right to forgive. He can do without the whole universe. He will make the creation return into himself, and will reproduce beings by a new creation. He is the God of Abraham, Ishmael, and Jacob. The angels are the honoured servants of God, but not his sons nor his daughters. They tremble with fright in his presence, and execute his orders in silence, without having the right of intercession. God employs angels with two, three and four wings. He makes the angels with the spirit (Gabriel) descend on him whom he wishes to be among his servants.

Every man has angels who succeed each other ceaselessly, placed before and behind him. They watch over his person by order of the Lord. When the two angels charged with gathering the words of man apply to their task one sits at his right hand and the other at his left. A certain number of revolted angels became the angels of evil, or the devil and his demons. After the creation of Adam, the angels bowed before him by order of the Lord. Eblis (the same as Satan) refused to do so, saying that he was higher than Adam, since he was made of fire and man of clay. God drives Eblis from his presence, and grants him respite until the day of resurrection. Eblis prepares to watch and tempt the human race. God banishes him, threatening him with hell, him and those who shall follow him.

The stars guard that part of the heaven nearest the earth against the rebellious demons in order that they may not come and listen to what goes on in the sublime assembly. Satan seduced Adam and Eve, and drew on them the divine malediction. He occupies himself incessantly, as well as his angels, in corrupting their posterity. He suggests bad thoughts, inbreathing evil into men's hearts. He threatens them with poverty, and commands them to do infamous deeds. Wine, gambling, idols, and casting lots are abominations invented by him. Below the angels God created Genii (Djin) to worship him like men. He created them of pure fire without smoke. The Genii will answer for their actions in the day of judgment, and go with men into paradise or into hell, according to their deserts. God created men in order to be worshipped by them. Man is superior to woman. God made man first, and of man he formed his companion. She, like him, is invited to the future life. After death the body is examined in the tomb by two angels with a terrible aspect. If the examination is favourable, the body reposes in peace, refreshed by the air of paradise. In the contrary case, the angels smite it in the countenance and on the back ; it is bitten and gnawed by venomous beasts until the day of resurrection. In regard to souls, the Koran says (xxxix. 43) that God receives them at the moment of death. In the opinion of Moslems, they, in the interval between death and the resurrection, are treated diversely according to the lives they led on earth. The souls of prophets go straightway into heaven; those of the martyrs remain in the gizzards of the green birds which are fed on the fruits of paradise and refreshed with the water of their leaves. For the souls of the rest of believers there are different opinions as to the position they receive. Those of the wicked are shut up in the dungeon called *Sadjen*, situated under a green rock, where they will be tormented till the resurrection. The hour of the resurrection is known to God alone. It comes, it is near, nearer, and nearer still; it comes in the twinkling of an eye. The trumpet shall sound (Paul), and all the creatures of heaven and earth shall expire, except those whom God shall dispose of differently; the trumpet shall sound a second time, and lo! all things shall stand up and await the judgment. The heavens shall break up and crumble into pieces. The sun shall be folded up; the stars shall fall; the mountains shall move; the seas shall boil. Souls shall be re-united to the bodies recalled to life (Rabbinism and the Apocalypse). The day of judgment shall last a thousand years, according to one passage of the Koran, fifty thousand according to another. One sole matter shall occupy all thoughts. Man will abandon his brother, his father, his mother, his companion, and his children; the nurse her infant at her breast; women with child will be delivered; the hair of children will whiten with fear; men will be as if intoxicated. All creatures will be gathered together. Every man will repair thither accompanied by a witness and a conductor. Then a soul will not satisfy for another soul; there will be no intercession, no compensation, no succour. Then will be seen countenances radiant, smiling, joyous, and countenances covered with dust, veiled with darkness; countenances white and countenances black. The avaricious will bear the objects of their avarice attached to their neck. An open book will be presented to each man; he who receives his book with his right hand will read it. The angels and the spirit (Gabriel) will ascend the celestial ladder; they will place themselves on each side, and eight of them shall in that day carry the throne of the Lord. God will separate the good from the bad (the sheep and the goats). The good will occupy the right hand, the bad the left. These and those will first pass over the bridge *al Sirat*, which, narrower than a hair, sharper than the edge of a sword, is extended over the middle of hell. The light of the good shall run before them and at their right hand. There will be put into their right hand the book of their good deeds. For them God reserves the future life. The life of this world is a game, a frivolity, an usufruct. That of the other world is better and more durable; this is properly life. The righteous will obtain an eternal reward with God. They will be his guests in paradise, which is vast as the heavens and the earth. There they will find their parents, their wives, and their children which shall have practised virtue. They will have charming habitations in the Garden of Eden, with infinite grace from God. In the midst of these gardens flow rivers of water which ever remain sweet; rivers of milk always delicious; rivers of mild wine; rivers of pure honey. The righteous will have there abundance of fruit, and the rarest food, and everything to suit their taste. They will repose under delicious shades, among fountains of running water. They will sit on seats decorated with gold and precious stones, supported at their ease, seeing each other face to face, and addressing each other questions. They will be clad in silk and satin, with bracelets of gold and pearls; they will lie on carpets made of silk and fringed with gold. They will be served all round by children possessed of eternal youth, resembling strung pearls. There will be offered to them plenty of delicious fruit, the flesh of the rarest birds, all things they can desire. They will be served with exquisite wine, flavoured with musk and tempered with water from the fountain of Tasnim. Not far from them, under pavilions, are the houris with their fine black eyes, like pearls, virgins of paradise, created by a special act of creation, with modest aspect, charming bashfulness, cherished by their husbands, and of an age equal to theirs. The eyes of the righteous will plunge to the bottom of hell, and they will congratulate themselves on their happiness. As to the wicked, God, after separating them from the good, will heap them the one upon the other, will bind them in bundles, and hurl them into hell or Gehenna.

Gehenna has seven gates. At each of these will remain a troop of the wicked. Nineteen angels are charged with watching at the mouth of hell, which will be filled at once with genii and men.

On the day of judgment, the wicked will be assembled before the fire, and advance in bands. There their ears and their eyes and their skin will testify against them. When the fire shall see them at a distance, they will hear it bellow with rage. They shall be thrown into a narrow prison, bound one with another. Then they will call for death, and it will be said to them—"Do not call for one death, call for deaths of several kinds." They will be in the midst of pestilential winds and boiling waters, under the shadow of smoke with three columns, which will not protect them from the fire, and will cast sparks like towers. The fire will seize their hearts and surround them like a vault. Their garments will be cut by fire; their coats will be of pitch. The flame will cover their persons, and the boiling water will be poured upon their heads; their entrails and their skin will be consumed. They will be struck with blasts of fire. Every time that in their agony they shall try to escape, they will be thrown back with the words—"Endure the punishment of fire." They shall be fed on the fruits of Zacoum, a tree which grows at the bottom of hell, and of which the branches resemble the heads of demons. This fruit shall boil in their bowels as melted metal. They shall have for drink filthy and boiling water. Their faces shall be black like dark night. Death shall rush upon them from all sides, and they shall not die; they shall neither die nor live. They shall be plunged into despair. In the fire they shall utter sighs and sobs. They shall remain there eternally; without intercession or succour, except God change his mind; there shall be succour for those only whom God shall pity. They shall cry to the inhabitants of paradise—"Send down on us a little water and some of those delights which God has granted you." "God," they will reply, "has interdicted both to the infidels."

They will cry to the angel who presides over their torments—" O Malek! would that thy lord would put an end to our punishments." " No," Malek will reply, " you will remain in it."

The principal points of religious practice taught by the Koran are prayer, alms, fasting, and pilgrimage to Mecca. Prayer is preceded by ablutions and purifications. They are made at the two extremities of the day, afternoon and at the entrance of night; you ought to consecrate to it also the time of your nocturnal vigils. To pray, you turn your face toward the temple of Mecca, wherever you are. Women pray in the house, or, if they wish to go to the mosque, they wait till the men are no longer there. Friday is the day of the week specially consecrated to the Lord. Fasting is prescribed on believers. It begins at the moment when you can distinguish a black thread from a white thread, and is observed strictly until night. The fast properly lasts during all the month of Ramadan, in which the Koran came down from on high.

Whoever does a good work shall receive a reward tenfold. You ought to succour your parents, your relatives, orphans, the poor, travellers. You should give alms of what you value most. To do alms openly is laudable; to do alms secretly is more meritorious. Pilgrimage is not a new institution of the Koran. It was in use among the Arabs before the coming of Mohamed. The prophet preserved it, while regulating the rites and ceremonies to be observed. Circumcision existed among the Ishmaelites; it has been retained among the believers, although Mohamed says nothing about it. The Koran forbids wine, gambling, usury, lots, rash oaths, defamation, prodigality, avarice. It prohibits the eating of animals that die of themselves, blood, pig's flesh, as well as that of victims offered to idols. You may eat any unprohibited animal.

But good works and pious practices are powerless to procure salvation, if the divine mercy does not give you aid. You may even contest their utility in presence of the dogma of absolute predestination, which the Koran admits. All that takes place in the world, it is said, whether of good or ill, proceeds entirely from the divine will, and is written from all eternity in the reserved tablet. Independently of religious observances, the Koran also contains civil laws, after the manner of the Pentateuch and divers other books of the East. These laws are the more stable because it is believed that they emanate from God. The major part of the political or civil requirements of Mohamed are borrowed from those of Moses. They are full of the same spirit, and very often they are identical. The Koran authorises polygamy, like the law of Israel; but it is restricted to four legitimate wives, without limitation as to the number of concubine slaves. Marriage is prohibited between relations within certain degrees. It is forbidden to believers to marry a woman already married to another, unless she has fallen into their hands as a slave, or, married to an infidel, she has left him to take refuge among them; it is equally forbidden to marry an idolater. They are to marry virtuous girls of believing parents or of those who received the scriptures before them. They are bound to assign dowers to the women whom they marry. The husband has the right to correct his wife; he may reprimand her, he may send her into another bed, he may beat her. The husband has also the right of repudiation. He who has repudiated a wife may take her again; but after a third repudiation, he is not permitted to take her again, except she has been married and repudiated by another man. The Koran regulates the conditions of repudiation. It equally fixes the rights of widows, and the time after which they may re-marry. The prophet, like the Jewish kings, had the privilege to take as many legitimate wives and concubines as he wished. None of his wives, repudiated, or widows could be married to another. Women ought to cast down their eyes, be chaste, cover their bosom with a veil, not display their ornaments except to their husbands or their nearest relations.

Adulterous men and women receive a hundred blows each, and cannot marry except to adulterers or idolaters. In the order of successions fixed by the Koran men are always better treated than women; a son receives the portion of two daughters.

The penal laws are equally based on those of the Pentateuch. The penalty of talion is appointed for murder; life for life. Nevertheless, the criminal may obtain his pardon from the family of the defunct, by paying a certain sum as the price of blood and emancipating a slave. The vengeance of an injury ought to be equal to the injury received; but reconciliation with your enemy is rewarded of God.

During the first years of his mission, Mohamed, as we have seen, restricted himself to preaching his doctrine. He said at first (ii. 257), "No violence in matters of religion; truth distinguishes itself from error. God understands and knows everything." But after his flight to Medina, he repelled force by force. His victories contributing more than anything else to the extension of Islamism, he then made a formal order for religious war. "Combat," he said, "in the way of God, those who make war on believers; fight until every form of worship is that of the only God. Make war on those who believe neither in God nor in the last day, and on those among the men of the scriptures who do not profess the true religion, until they pay the tribute and are submissive." He nevertheless forbids the violation of engagements taken with unbelievers, as long as their term is not run out. In imitation of the ancient Arabs, the Koran establishes four sacred months, during which war is not permitted among Moslems. Mohamed left, to dispute his succession, his son-in-law Ali, husband of Fatima, his only child, and three fathers-in-law, Abubekr, Omar, and Othman. Abubekr, father of Aïsha, the most beloved of his wives, is recognised as his successor (632), and takes the title of Kalif (vicar or lieutenant), calling himself the prophet's vicar. His first care is to put down the revolts raised by pretended prophets who had been rivals of Mohamed. The principal are Museilama and Aswad. The latter was killed by conspirators during the life of Mohamed. Abubekr sends against the other an army led by Khaled, a skilful general. Museilama is defeated and falls in battle.

The frontiers of Persia and those of the empire of the

East are then invaded by the Arabs, who are called also Saracens, from the name of one of the tribes bordering on the empire. Abubekr dies after reigning two years. Under the Kalif Omar, who takes his place, the Moslems ruin the monarchy of the Persians, and take from the Romans Syria, Palestine, and Egypt. Heraclius, not in a condition to defend those countries, retired into his capital with the pretended wood of the true cross, which he had carried off from Jerusalem. This last city is taken by Omar in 636. The Kalif enters the holy city clad in a hair shirt. He clears the ground on which the temple of Solomon stands, on which he builds a mosque some years later. Omar gives a guard to Jerusalem and goes to Bethlehem to make his prayers in the grotto where Jesus was born, according to the legend.

Damascus becomes the capital of Moslem Syria. The Arabs take possession of all Egypt. Alexandria surrenders after a siege of fourteen months (640), and its library is burnt by Omar's orders. The patriarch of the Jacobites, who had hidden himself for ten years, returns into that city, where resides also a Melchite patriarch, that is, a patriarch of the imperial Church. Omar is assassinated during public prayer (644). Othman, his successor, gives the government of Egypt to Abdala, with a large amount of troops. That general advances by land beyond Tripolis and penetrates into Africa proper or proconsular. He defeats the patricius Gregory, imposes a considerable tribute, and after an expedition of fifteen months, returns laden with a rich booty. Moaviah, who commands in Syria, takes there several cities from the Greeks; he also attacks the isle of Cyprus (648). The conquests of the Moslems restore liberty to the dissident churches. The Nestorians rise again in Syria, the Eutychians in Egypt. The Melchites are treated worse than they. It is not that the Mohamedans care about the divisions existing among those churches, who all three hold the trinity; but the Melchites are suspected of being in favour of the Emperor of Constantinople. The Arabs continue to increase. The last King of Persia is killed (651) and his kingdom entirely conquered. The

Moslem power then extends over Arabia, Persia, Mesopotamia, Chaldæa, Armenia, Syria, Palestine, Egypt, and a great part of Africa. Othman is massacred at Medina in his own house (655). His adversaries proclaim Ali, son of Abutaleb, cousin-german and son-in-law of Mohamed. But, a considerable party declare against the new Kalif, at the instigation of Aisha, the prophet's widow, who is called the mother of the Moslems. The head of this party is Moaviah, who commands in Syria from the year 634. After several combats, peace is concluded on the condition that Persia and the East belong to Ali, Syria and the West to Moaviah (660). Ali is assassinated the same year. His son Hassan succeeds him, and, six months after, yields the empire to Moaviah, who is recognised as the sole Kalif. This is the head of the family of Ommiah.

From these divisions between Ali and Moaviah proceeded the schism which still separates the Sonnites from the Shiites or partisans of Ali. The Sonnites, or traditionalists, acknowledge as having canonical authority the *Sonna*, a collection of traditions and of unwritten sentences of Mohamed and his first successors. The Shiites reject this book as apocryphal and unworthy of credence. The two parties accuse each other of having corrupted the Koran and of neglecting its requirements. The Shiites regard as usurpers the three first Kalifs, Abubekr, Omar, and Othman, while the Sonnites account them legitimate Imauns. In the eyes of the Shiites, Ali is greater than Mohamed himself, or at least his equal; the Sonnites allow neither Ali nor any other prophet to be equal to Mohamed. The Persians and the Fatimites of Egypt are the principal followers of Ali; the other Moslems declare in general for the Sonna; each of the two parties maintains itself to be alone the orthodox. Civil war had suspended the conquests of Islamism. They resume their course as soon as Moaviah governs alone. He advances on the provinces of the Roman Empire, devastates them, and carries off numerous captives (662). A part of Sicily falls into the power of the Mohamedans. They carry off from proconsular Africa eighty thousand prisoners (668), ravage Greece, Thrace, and go to attack Constantinople. Then it is that to destroy their vessels the Greek fire, which burns in the water, is invented.

Yesid succeeds Moaviah, his father (680).

Carthage and the province of Africa are definitively conquered (696). In the ensuing years the Moslems occupy Mauritania, and spread as far as the Atlantic Ocean. They pass into Spain (712), the monarchy of the Goths ceases to exist; Cordova becomes the capital of the conquerors. They pass over the Pyrenees and seize the Spanish possessions in Gaul; Narbonne succumbs in 719. During several years the Arabs struggle against the Aquitanians with diverse success. In 732 they make a last effort under the leadership of Abd-el-Rahman. One of their armies, going up the Rhone and the Saone, occupies Avignon, Valentia, Lyons, Maçon, Chalons, Besançon, Dijon, and Auxerre; it is repelled under the walls of Sens. Other bodies of troops, led by Abd-el-Rahman in person, defeat Eudes, duke of Aquitania, and take Bordeaux, Agen, Perigueux, Saintes, Poitiers. Near the last city Charles Martel gives them battle, in which Abd-el-Rahman perishes (732). The Arabs are driven from Aquitania and other provinces of France which they had invaded; none the less the war continues in the following years.

In Spain the Saracens bear sway in all the countries except Asturias. A certain number of Christians, retired into the mountains of that province, succeed in maintaining themselves there in independence under the lead of Pelagius, whom they elect for king. In 737 the power passes to his son, and two years later, to his son-in-law, Alphonse the Catholic. The latter finding the Saracens enfeebled by the defeats they have suffered in France, beats them in several conflicts and takes from them a certain number of cities. Nevertheless the new state remains in a precarious situation till toward the middle of the ninth century. In the East a new war rises between the Arabs, under the reign of Meruan (744). Ibrahim is acknowledged for Imaun in Mecca. He descended from Abbas, Mohamed's uncle, while Ommia, head of the reigning dynasty, was only distantly related to the prophet. Meruan seized his competitor and had him put to death (748). Abdalla Saffah succeeds his brother Ibrahim. Meruan is driven from Syria and Palestine ; he is pursued into Egypt, where he is at last taken and slain (750). In his person the dynasty of the Ommiades comes to an end in the East. But it succeeds in maintaining itself in Spain, where Abd-el-Rahman, grandson of the Kalif Hescham, is proclaimed Emir-al-Mumenin, that is, prince of the faithful (756). He reigns thirty-three years in Cordova. Under the Abassides, Damascus ceases to be the capital of the oriental Moslems. Almansor (735-75) builds Bagdad, which becomes the residence of the Kalifs, toward the end of his reign. While the Moslem power extends over the moiety of the Roman empire and the greater part of the other provinces undergoes the domination of the barbarians, the Greek emperor, embarrassed in the religious quarrels, is reduced to fight against the pagan and monkish superstitions which make eruption into the official Christianity. The questions relative to the incarnation were resolved for the imperial Church. The sixth œcumenical council had definitively come to a conclusion on the last, that of monothelism. Hardly is it necessary to mention an attempt made by Philippic (711) against the decisions of that council, an attempt which fails, owing to the Emperor's deposition (714).

A new schism breaks out on occasion of the images that were displayed in the churches. The Christians of the first centuries followed the requirements of sacred scripture against statues and images. (Exod. xx. 4, 5 ; Deut. iv. 15-19 ; Is. xi. 18-20 ; Acts xvii. 29). But after the conversion of the emperors, the customs of Paganism gradually introducing themselves into the Church, images begin as early as the fourth and fifth century, to show themselves in some parts of Greece and the East. The usage spreads in the sixth and seventh century, when Hellenism is proscribed. To satisfy and attract the multitude, still Pagan in heart, their eyes are fed by the representation of external objects. Nevertheless not as yet is worship paid to the images. No genuflexions are made, no incense offered, no wax candles lighted, no prayers addressed. Historic paintings of the saints and martyrs are placed in the temples, oratories, sacred porticoes, by the side of the portraits of emperors, bishops, fathers of the œcumenical councils, without any idea of adoration being connected therewith. In the West the custom of images has more difficulty to obtain prevalence. In the commencement of the seventh century, Serenus, Bishop of Marseilles, seeing some person worshipping before those of his own church, breaks them and throws the fragments on the outside. Pope Gregory I. writes to him that he is to avoid scandal by excess of zeal, and to tolerate the exposition of images, while proving from scripture that they are not to be worshipped. In the degree in which the Pagan beliefs and ceremonies strike root in the official church, the veneration for paintings degenerates more and more into superstitious worship. The doctrine of the intercession of the virgin and of the saints making them into veritable divinities, their images are worshipped like those of the gods of heathenism; incense is offered to them; wax candles are burnt before them; they are invoked in prayer. This idolatry established itself about the time of the birth of Islamism. The rapid conquests of the Moslems throw it into relief. The disciples of Mohamed, like the Jews and the Persians, proscribe paintings and statues. The superstitious usage of the Greek Church calls forth at once their mockery and indignation. The Kalif Yesid suppresses the paintings and sculptures exposed in the churches of his States, whether on wood or mosaic on the walls, or on sacred vases and ornaments of the altar, as well as all those that decorate the public places of the cities (723). His successors seem to have shown more condescendence. The emperors of Constantinople undertake themselves to efface the images in the churches. Leo III. (the Isaurian) first decides against them. He declares publicly, in an assembly of the people, that their use is idolatry (727). The patriarch Germain resists him with force, and writes to several bishops, among others to the Pope of Rome, Gregory II. (715-31), who gives him his approbation. Greece and the Cyclades rise against Leo. Conqueror of the rebels, he assembles a council where a decree is passed against images (730). Germain, who refuses to subscribe to it, is driven away and replaced by Anastasius. Moreover, Leo not only speaks against images; he also rejects as Pagan superstitions the invocation of the saints and the worship of relics; but he honours the cross, provided it is not in the shape of a crucifix.

His enterprise excites also troubles in Italy, Gregory III. (731-41) calls on him to repent. The emperor paying no attention to the call, the Pope assembles at Rome a council of ninety-six bishops, and excommunicates whoever shall attack the images (732). Leo, irritated, sends troops into Italy, augments by one-third the capitation tax of Calabria and Sicily, and confiscates the patrimony of St Peter of Rome.

Constantine Copronymus persists in the same views (741). Artabasus, his father-in-law, proclaimed emperor at Constantinople (742), re-establishes the worship of images in all the cities under his sceptre. The following year, Constantine, re-entering into his capital, tears out the eyes of Artabasus and his two sons. The suppression of images is maintained. It is pursued with still more vigour after some success obtained over the Moslems (751). In 754 the emperor brings together a council of three hundred and sixty-eight bishops, which entitles itself œcumenical. A decree is passed against the partisans of images, who desire, they say, to restore idolatry, which Jesus condemned when he ordered men to worship in spirit and in truth. To paint Christ is, according to the council, to yield to Nestorianism; the true image of his natural flesh is the bread in the Eucharist. They reject also the images of the virgin and the saints, who recall the Pagan worship of idols. The saints live with God; they ought not to be represented in dead matter. The decree terminates by anathemas against images and their worshippers, notably against Germain of Constantinople, George of Cyprus, and John of Damascus. The decree is published in Constantinople and in the provinces. The Iconoclasts change the sacred vases, burn the images, deface or cover the painted walls. This zeal is stimulated by the emperor. He persecutes specially the monks, those great defenders of every superstitious practice; soldiers are placed in different monasteries; other monasteries are pulled down. The monks of Constantinople retire to the Euxine, Cyprus, Rome, and Italy, the sole countries where the image worshippers prevail.

The governor of Natolia assembles at Ephesus all the monks and nuns of Thrace, to compel them to marry (770). Those who refuse have their eyes plucked out or are sent into exile. The following year he sells all the monasteries and nunneries, with their movable and immovable property, and puts the result into the imperial treasury. He burns the relics, and punishes their possessors as guilty of impiety. In all his territory there does not remain a person that wears the monastic garb. The emperor approving his zeal, he is soon imitated by other governors. Leo IV. (Chazare) shows himself at first better disposed toward the virgin and the monks (775), but none the less the interdiction remains on the worship of images. After a reign of five years this prince is poisoned by his wife Irene. She governs in the name of her young son Constantine, and shows herself a jealous protectress of monks and images. Tarasius, created by her care patriarch of Constantinople, demands the convocation of an œcumenical council (784). Irene writes on the subject to the Pope of Rome. Hadrian I. (773-95), in his reply, claims the restitution of the patrimonies of St Peter; he at the same time protests against the title of universal patriarch which the letters of Irene gave to Tarasius. The empress attempts to bring her council together at Constantinople in the Church of the apostles (786), but the old soldiers of Copronymus, impelled by the iconoclastic bishops, enter the Church sword in hand and drive out the image worshippers. Irene calls other troops into the capital, whence she sends the discontented soldiers, who are then broken up. The council convoked afresh assembles at Nice in Bithynia (787). After the legate of Rome and the patriarch of Constantinople there figure three monks who call themselves legates and vicars of the patriarchs of Alexandria, Antioch, and Jerusalem. Three hundred and seventy-seven bishops are present, all come from countries that obey the emperor. When the letter of the Pope of Rome is read, the part referring to the restitution of the patrimonies is left out as well as his other pretensions and claims. This seventh œcumenical council, the second of Nice, decides that the images of Christ, of his mother, of the angels and the saints shall be placed, like the figure of the cross, in the churches, on the sacred vases and vestments, on the walls as well as in houses and on the highways. Salutation and worship of honour is due to them, but not veritable latreia (adoration) which befits only the divine nature. But incense and light may be used in veneration of them, as they are used for the cross, the gospels, and other sacred things. In regard to those who remove from the churches the images or the relics of the saints, who profane the sacred vases or the monasteries, the penalty of deposition is pronounced if they are bishops or clerics, and that of excommunication if they are laics. The council moreover draws up twenty-two disciplinary canons, in one of which it is ordered that the episcopal houses and monasteries which the Iconoclasts had converted to profane purposes should be restored.

In the execution of these decrees Constantine and his mother re-establish the images in the Churches and in their palaces.

Three monks, we have said, represented in this assembly the sees of Alexandria, Antioch, and Jerusalem. These pretended legates had, to say the truth, received authority only from their monasteries. The Christians of the East, and especially the Melchites, were then under oppression which did not permit them to communicate openly with Constantinople. They were persecuted in order to compel them to abjure, and rarely were they allowed to elect patriarchs. The see of Antioch had remained vacant during the first forty years of the eighth century. At the same time the Melchite patriarch of Alexandria was a poor man, not knowing how to read or write, a needlemaker by trade.

The Jacobites of the last city were much more numerous and in a better position. The success obtained by Constantine Copronyonus during the civil wars of the Moslems (750) had brought new rigours on the Christians of their territory. The Melchite patriarch of Alexandria was sent into exile. The governor of Syria forbade new churches to be built, crosses to be set up in public, and the Christian faith to be discussed with the Arabs (756). Tribute was imposed even on the monks, the hermits, and the stylites; the treasures of the church were sealed and sold. In other places the Christians were forbidden to teach letters and to assemble by night in their temples. At the end of his reign Almansor, visiting Jerusalem, branded the Jews and the Christians in their hands. His successor, Mohamed Almahadi, commanded in the same city that all the Christian slaves should apostatise, and the churches be deserted (780). At Emesa he cruelly tormented the Christians and the Jews who would not abjure. Different churches in Damascus were closed, in contempt of treaties made by the Arabs with the Christians. As there were in the last Council of Nice only Eastern bishops, the pope of Rome had to cause it to be received in the countries of the Latin Church. The Christians of Africa and Spain, subject to the Moslems, were not in a condition to raise objections. Those of England, newly converted barbarians, would accept anything at the hands of the pope. It was not the same with the Francs, governed by an illustrious chief, who had just added to his kingdom Germany and the Lombard States. Numerous motives obliged the bishop of Rome to humour those peoples; they had already rendered him eminent services, and he hoped for yet greater advantages in future. Rome had had more than once to suffer from the wars of the Lombards with the exarchs of Ravenna, who received from Constantinople only insufficient succours. In the year 741 Gregory III., besieged by King Luitprand, asks protection of Charles Martel, while offering to withdraw his obedience to the emperor, and to confer on the Frank prince the title of Consul of Rome. But the offer is declined by Charles, who then had need of the support of the Lombards to repel the Saracens. Some years later, when Pepin aspires to the royalty, pope Zachary (741-52), to conciliate his favour, zealously approves and supports the enterprise, the new king is consecrated by Boniface, archbishop of Mayence, and legate of the pope in Germany (752). Meanwhile Astolfe, king of the Lombards, after making himself master of the exarchate of Ravenna, attacks the duchy of Rome. Pope Stephen II. (752-57) asks aid of the emperor, who satisfies himself with sending an embassy. The pontiff then addresses himself to Pepin, whom he finds well disposed. From Pavia, whither he accompanies the Greek ambassador (753), Stephen goes into France, and is there received with the greatest honours. He consecrates afresh Pepin, with his two sons, and confers upon them the title of Patricians of the Romans. Pepin passes over the Alps twice and constrains Astolfe to surrender Ravenna and several other cities. At this moment is placed a pretended gift of several parts of Emilia and the Pentapolis which the Frank king made to Saint Peter and the Roman Church, a gift which was the source of the temporal power of the popes. This act is for the first time mentioned by the librarian Anastasius, who wrote more than a hundred years afterwards. On the death of Astolfe (756) Stephen II. forthwith seized the duchy of Ferrara and two other places. Paul, his successor (757-67), continues to lean on the Franks against the Lombards as well as against the Greeks. His letters, nevertheless, as those of his predecessors, are always dated with the reign of the emperor as sovereign of Rome. The Senate and the people give to their bishop only the title of pastor and father. Didier, king of the Lombards, seizes several cities of the exarchate, and marches on Rome. Hadrian I. (773-95) implores succour from the Franks. Charlemagne defeats the Lombards, makes himself master of Pavia, and banishes Didier into a monastery in France (774). The monarchy of the Lombards ceases to exist after lasting two hundred years. Charlemagne entitles himself king of the Franks and the Lombards. The Roman Church, on the authority of the same Anastasius, supposes that he then confirmed the donation of his father, adding thereto the exarchate of

Ravenna, Venetia, Istria, the duchies of Ferrara and Beneventum, Liguria, Corsica, Sardinia. The king of the Franks makes again other journeys into Italy; in one of them (780) his two sons are consecrated by the pope, Pepin as king of Italy, and Louis as King of Aquitania; in another (787) he brings back with him two singers to teach the French the Roman notes, as well as masters of grammar and arithmetic to found schools in all places. Charlemagne, though he knew not how to read, felt the value of letters and science. He made laudable efforts to spread some instruction among the barbarians of Germany, and to dissipate the profound ignorance which their invasions had spread in the regions of Gaul. His zeal for religious matters was not less ardent, especially in regard to discipline and good morals. He frequently assembled councils, and the bishops took part in the national consultations. Such were the relations of Rome with the Franks at the time of the second council of Nice; such was the prince who there reigned over those peoples. Hadrian I. sends him the acts of the Council to have them examined and approved by the bishops of his states. They find that the decision is contrary to their usage. There were indeed among them images in the churches, but no worship was paid to them. Charlemagne declares himself of the same point of view. He gets written against the worship of images four books, which are known under the name of the Caroline Books. In them the Council of Copronymus, as well as the second council of Nice, are rejected; the title of œcumenical is denied to the latter because the bishops of all countries were not invited to it, and because its resolution is contrary to the doctrine of the universal Church; in conclusion it is said that in France it is permitted, according to the letter of Gregory I. to Serenus, to put images into the church and on the outside, but without obliging any one to worship them, as also without authorising their demolition. In the body of the work several reproaches are incidentally made against the Fathers of the Second Council of Nice, among others the patriarch Tarasius, for having said that the Holy Spirit proceeds from the Father through the Son. Charlemagne assembles at Frankfort-on-Maine a council of all the provinces under his control, at which two legates of the pope are present (794). Determinations are there come to on different points of faith and discipline. In regard to the worship of images, the Fathers of Frankfort, under the influence of the Caroline books, declare that they despise and reject that worship and that servitude, which they condemn unanimously. The Caroline books had been sent to the pope. Hadrian replies in a long letter addressed to Charlemagne. He begins by maintaining what Tarasius had said, that the Holy Spirit proceeds from the Father through the son, in resting on the authority of several Fathers; the Church of Rome was then on that point of the same opinion as the Greek Church. Coming to the question of images the pope, under the most obsequious forms of language, defends what he calls the ancient tradition of the Church. He mentions two councils held at Rome against the Iconoclasts, one in 732, the other in 769, and reports the examples of several popes who had placed images in the Churches. He, however, approves that no one should be constrained to worship them. He ends by in some sort excusing himself for having received that council of Nice; his refusal might throw back the Greeks into their error. He adds, however, that he has not yet given any reply to the emperor on the subject of the council. He has asked, he says, that the jurisdiction of the Roman Church should be restored over certain bishoprics and patrimonies of which it was despoiled at the time of the abolition of images; he insists afresh on his request, and in case of refusal, he will declare the emperor heretical. Hadrian, it is obvious, contrives a pretext to give or refuse his definitive approbation, according to circumstances; he subordinates the question of faith to that of the restitution of his jurisdiction and the patrimonies of his Church. Shortly after death comes to relieve him of the embarrassment (795).

Leo III. (795-816) lets the question of images sleep. His first act is to send to Charlemagne the keys of the Confession of St Peter and the standard of the city of Rome, begging him to send some one of the lords of his court to receive the oath of fidelity of the Romans. Some years after (800) Charlemagne proceeds into their city himself, and on Christmas day, he is crowned emperor by Leo, amid the acclamations of all the people. Rome separates from the eastern empire to become the capital of the west. One may then perceive that the two churches, the Greek and the Latin, will also separate, each under the direction of its patriarch. However, the work of the Second Council of Nice is questioned in Constantinople. Power escapes from the hands of Irene (802). Nicephorus, without interdicting the worship of images, hinders the Iconoclasts from molesting their adversaries. After him, Michael Rangabé (811) leaves all power to the priests and the monks. Leo V., the Armenian (813) after dissimulating some time, declares himself against the images in the second year of his reign. Michael the stammerer recalls the exiles; he believes in the intercession of the virgin and the saints; he reveres relics, but he does not honour the images, without, however, interfering with liberty of opinion on the point. To put an end to the superstitions of the Iconoclasts, the images are removed from the low places and set up on high, where they serve for the instruction of the people without their being able to worship them. Michael, however, ends by persecuting the monks whom he despises and detests. His opinion on the images resembles that of the Franks sufficiently for him to seek to come to an understanding with them. He in effect sends an embassy to Louis the good natured (824); it also carries letters and presents for the Roman bishop. Louis causes it to be accompanied to Rome by two deputies who obtain for himself permission to have the matter examined by bishops. Their assembly, which is held in Paris, rejects as insufficient the reply of Hadrian I. to the Caroline books, and decides with them that it is necessary neither to worship the images nor to destroy them; he asks of Louis to recommend to the pope and to the emperor Michael the adoption of the usage of the Franks in this respect (825). It is not known what ensued from this request. In France the same doctrine on images is maintained still some time, but without interrupting communion with the See of Rome, which follows that of the Second Council of Nice. Then the authority of the Pope increasing day by day people submit insensibly to his opinion. Toward the end of the ninth century, the Gallican clergy prostrate themselves before the images, and their example is followed by the other peoples of the west. To say the truth, the medium line of the Caroline books could not be of any long duration. To set up images in the churches is to invite idolatry. Some minds may make a distinction between to pay homage and to give worship. But such nice distinctions escape from the multitude; it naturally yields to a superstitious worship, and its ascendancy soon draws all the world to their practices. The law of Moses, more wisely conceived, not only forbids worshipping images, it forbids their appearance on sacred places. The emperor of the east, Theophilus (829) goes farther than Michael the stammerer, his father. Openly hostile to images, he forbids their preservation. The paintings are effaced from the churches or publicly burned, the prisons fill with image worshippers, the monks are exposed to persecutions. But at his death (842) the power passes into the hands of Theodora, his widow, who governs in the name of her young son, Michael III. (the drunkard). This empress, overruled by the monks, definitively restores the worship of images, so dear to the Greek populations.

The same spirit of superstition led Theodora into excesses far more deplorable; into bloody executions, the recollection of which will always lie upon that woman whom the official church honours as a saint. We refer to the massacre of the Paulicians or new Manicheans, on which it is proper to enter into some particulars.

A certain time after the death of Manes, his doctrine was carried as far as Samosata in Armenia. Two brothers of that city, Paul and' John, receive from heads of the sect a mission to preach it in the Armenian lands. They obtain full success, especially among the inhabitants of Phanarea, and establish themselves in a neighbouring village called Episparis. From one of these brothers comes the term Paulicians given to their adherents. Down to the time of

Constantine Pogonatus (668-85), the sect continues to extend without at all changing its doctrine; neither exhortations nor severities can stop its progress. Some time after, the assembly sends into those regions a new teacher, by name Constantine, a native of Mananale, a neighbouring village to Samosata. He fixes himself at Cibossa. As he sees his religion a butt to the public hate, and condemned by the laws of the empire, which proscribe the books and punish with death those who read them, he forms the design of getting away from those perils. He suppresses all the books of the Manicheans, contenting himself with keeping the dogmas in his memory, and, by frequent lessons, engraving them on the mind of his disciples. He puts into their hands the veritable text of the Gospel and the Epistles of Paul; but the sense is perverted to adapt it to the beliefs of the sect. A certain number of dogmas and fables are at the same time eliminated from those beliefs. Constantine, acting as a legislator, creates new doctrines, and takes up the position of supreme director of his religion. Accordingly, the new Manicheans voluntarily anathematise Scythian, Buddha, and Manes; but they venerate Constantine and his successors as apostles of Christ, not to say more. In order to avoid suspicions, Constantine gives himself the name of Sylvanus, of whom mention is made in Paul's Epistles; he declares himself sent to them by the apostle. His successors after his example take the name of the different co-workers with Paul, and give to their churches that of the regions whither the gospel was carried by him. The Paulicians, who are regarded as followers of Manes, notwithstanding sensible differences, seem to be equally connected with the ancient Gnostics. They acknowledge two principles, one good, the other bad. According to them, Jesus was not conceived in the virgin's womb; but his body descended from heaven, passed through that of Mary as by a canal. After the birth of Jesus, she had children by Joseph. By the body and the blood of the Lord in the supper, they understand his word and teaching, of which the bread and the wine are only symbols. They deny the virtue and the efficacy of the wood of the cross. They reject the books of the Old

Testament; but they admit all the New, except the Epistles of Peter, to which they have a strong dislike. They also read the Epistles of Sergius, one of their principal leaders. In order to protect themselves from persecution, they in word confess the official dogmas, but give them a hidden sense. Thus under the name of orthodox faith they understand their own doctrine. The cross is for them Christ himself who forms it by stretching out his arms. The mother of God is the heavenly Jerusalem into which Christ has entered. The body and the blood of Christ is his doctrine. Baptism is Jesus Christ, that living water. Constantine, the author of the renewed sect, after having taught twenty-seven years at Cibossa, died of stoning by the emperor's order. He who had presided at his death, Symeon, is seduced by his disciples and succeeds him under the name of Titus. At the end of three years, Justinian II. causes him to be seized and burnt with his companions. One of them, however, a native of Armenia, and by name Paul, succeeds in escaping from death, and flees to Episparis with his two sons Gegnaesius and Theodore. The first is put at the head of the sect, under the name of Timothy. Leo the Isaurian orders him to Constantinople and has him examined by the patriarch. He allows himself to be misled by the answers, two-fold in meaning, of Gegnaesius, who is sent back to Episparis. He flees with his disciples to Mananale, the country of Constantine, where he dies after having governed the sect during thirty years. Division arises amongst the Paulicians. Some take sides with Zachary, son of Gegnaesius; others attach themselves to Joseph, his servant, who bears the name of Epaphroditus. They all form a resolution to emigrate into another country. During the journey the Saracens massacre the companions of Zachary, who alone makes his escape. Joseph eludes the Moslems and reaches Episparis with his friends. They are soon discovered by the public force. Joseph flees to Antioch in Pisidia; he there converts many people and dies after having taught his beliefs for forty years. Bahane, his successor, mingles obscenities with the dogmas of the sects. Sergius rises against him and a schism takes place. The

Paulicians divide into two parties, the Bahanites and the Sergiotes. Sergius, who calls himself Tychicus, surpasses all his predecessors. He traverses a great number of cities and countries in which he makes a multitude of proselytes. He calls himself the Paraclete, the bright star, the good shepherd, the head of the body of Christ, the light of the house of God. He directs the sect during thirty-four years, from Irene to the emperor Theophilus; most of the Manicheans attach themselves to his doctrines. They are exposed to violent persecutions under Michael Rhangabé and Leo the Armenian. The sword strikes all those who do not retract. In Armenia the Manicheans massacre Thomas, bishop of Cæsarea and the exarch Paracondace, charged to inflict suffering on them; they flee to Melitine, occupied by the Saracens. They are settled in a place called Argaous. Their co-religionaries gathering from all parts, they are soon in a condition to ravage the frontiers of the empire. After sojourning at Argaous for some years, Sergius dies by the hand of an assassin (835). His principal disciples, without electing a chief, direct the sect in common with equal power; they have under them servants whom they call notaries. Such is the situation of the Paulicians when the empress Theodora forms the resolution to extirpate them. The officers whom she sends for the purpose hang, decapitate, or drown one hundred thousand persons. Their goods are confiscated.

A warrior, named Corbeas, whose father was in the number of the victims, flees to Melitine with some others. They combine with the Moslems in order to combat their oppressors. Soon the city of Argaous is not sufficient; they found a new one which they name Tephrica. Situated between Armenia and the Roman frontier, it is well fitted for making incursions and collecting the fugitives. Corbeas does not limit himself to pillaging; he makes regular war either alone or with the aid of the Moslems. He has for successor Chrysocheris, his son-in-law, who continues to fight and perishes in a rencontre with the imperial troops (872). His death does not interrupt the envenomed struggle of the Paulicians against the empire. Several

Greek provinces are the theatre of frightful desolations. The doctrine of the Paulicians penetrates near the end of the ninth century, to the newly converted Bulgarians and strikes deep roots into the soil. Thence we shall see it extend into the rest of Europe. The cruel executions of Theodora had then ended only in occasioning an implacable war against the empire. In the year 854 the emperor Michael, her son, wishes to compel her to become a nun with her daughters. On the opposition of the patriarch Ignatius, he shuts them up in the palace of Carian. The Cæsar Bardas, brother of Theodora, governs under the name of his nephew. He applies himself to the task of raising again the studies which have long been fallen and almost annihilated by the gross ignorance of the preceding emperors (859). Schools are founded in Constantinople under the direction of the philosopher Leo. Bardas is put to death in 866. Michael associates in the empire Basil the Macedonian, who, the following year, has him killed and remains himself the sole emperor. About the same time a change takes place in the education and the tastes of the Moslems. Under the Ommiades they study only their law, their language, and a little medicine. Under the Abassides they initiate themselves in letters and the sciences. Almansor had already favoured them ; the same tendency increases under his successors. The premature death of Monça, eldest son of Almahadi, leaves the supreme power in the hands of his brother, the celebrated Aaron-al-Rashid (786). This prince, a zealous Moslem, maltreats the Christians, especially the Melchites, always objects of suspicion ; the Jacobites are less odious to him. At his death (809), his two sons Alamin and Almamon dispute the throne. During the civil war, the Christians have much to suffer. A certain number of them take refuge in Cyprus and Constantinople. Almamon, peaceful possessor of the empire, through the death of his brother (813), extends his protection to the sciences. A taste for study spreads more and more every day. The learned are laden with favours, whatever their religion. This prince searches after and has translated into Arabic, Greek and Syriac books. He applies himself specially to astronomy. But the astronomers of his court giving countenance to judicial astrology, that superstition made new progress. The taste for knowledge survives Almamon. The Moslems give themselves to philosophy, the mathematics, and medicine. These studies are propagated in all the lands under their sway and pass even into Spain, despite the difference of the dynasties.

Oriental Islamism sees a series of princes feeble, cruel, given to pleasure, and governed by their dependents, succeed to Almanon. These, for the most part, perish miserably after a reign of short duration (842-92). Under that of Moutamid, Ahmed, son of Touloun, governor of Egypt, makes himself independent of the Kalif; he captures Antioch in spite of the excommunication pronounced against him in the mosques of Bagdad. This son of Touloun lays taxes so heavy on the Christians of Alexandria that they are constrained to impose on themselves a capitation tax and to sell the property of the monks with the fourth of their churches; even then they succeed in paying only a moiety of their contribution. The Saracens of Africa are in perpetual war with the Christians. They seize Palermo (820), and some years after all Sicily, which depended on the Eastern empire, as well as Calabria. From Sicily they make frequent incursions into different parts of Italy. Several times they approach the very gates of Rome, devastating everything on their march. The churches of Saint Peter and Saint Paul, situated on the outside of the city, are pillaged by them. Leo IV. (847-55) surrounds with walls the church of Saint Peter, builds by its side a new city (the Leonine city), and repairs the walls of Rome, which are tumbling in ruins. This capital in vain seeks aid of the feeble successors of Charlemagne. The pope submits to pay an annual tribute to the Saracens (877). He then applies to the emperor Basil, who sends galleys to defend it (880). None the less do the ravages of the Moslems continue; they attack specially the churches and the monasteries and establish themselves on certain points of southern Italy. In Spain their power still rules over the greater part of the territory. There they find themselves in presence of three Christians states. The Franks maintain themselves in Catalonia, which they conquered under Charlemagne. A new prince rises on the Pyrenees (830); his successors take Pampeluna, which becomes the capital of the kingdom of Navarre. In that of Oviedo, peace is maintained by Ramir, successor of Alphonse the chaste (842). Ordogno, his son, undertakes (849) to re-people the cities conquered by Alphonse. Alphonse, called the great, gains numerous victories over the Saracens, whom he drives back towards the south (866-912).

Under Abderame III., who studies to live in peace with his neighbours, the Moslems of Spain make courses by sea (821-52). They land on many islands left without defence by the Greeks, seize Crete, devastate the coasts of Italy in concert with the Saracens of Africa. Abderame has been reproached with having persecuted the Christians of his states, but the pretended martyrs of Cordova are in truth madmen who were punished for insults to Mohamed and Islamism. In order to moderate this indiscreet zeal, Abderame collects in council the metropolitans of different provinces, who dissuade the believers from voluntarily running to punishment. Mohamed, his son, shows himself more ill-disposed in regard to them (852-87). In the beginning of his reign he strips of their charges and drives away those who are employed in his palace. He demolishes the recently constructed churches, overloads the Christians with imposts, and resolves to banish them from his kingdom together with the Jews. Some martyrs are spoken of; but they are people who take pleasure in outraging Islamism in face of the officers of justice. Such is the state of things in 859. After that time there remain few monuments of the Church of Spain in the provinces subject to the Moslems. France, since the time of Charlemagne, remains at peace with the Saracens. But it is a prey to the depredations of the Normans. The public power weakens every day in the hands of the Carlovingian race; the lords and the bishops divide the wreck. In the midst of the troubles with which their reigns are agitated, Louis the debonnaire and Charles the bald continue to the learned the protection which

Charlemagne had accorded to them. Like him they frequently convene councils. Whether from fervour of zeal or knowledge ill-directed, opinions which have divided the Church are reproduced and new questions arise whence schisms and heresies will soon arise.

In the time of Charlemagne, Felix of Urgel, and Elipand, archbishop of Toledo, preach a doctrine touching Jesus which savours of Nestorianism. It is, they said, according to his divine nature that he is truly son of God, begotten of the Father; while, according to his humanity, he is son of God only by adoption. Felix spreads this opinion in Septimania, whence it passes into the Gaulish and Germanic provinces. Elipand propagates it in the countries of Toledo, Asturia, and Galicia. The pope writes to the bishops of Spain in order to put them on their guard. Charlemagne convokes a council at Ratisbone (792), by which Felix is heard and condemned. He is sent to Rome, where he abjures his sentiments in the church of Saint Peter. Returning to Urgel, he begins to maintain them again. The pope will excommunicate him if he does not renounce his error (799). Ordered to Aix la Chapelle, Felix there retracts; he is deposed and banished to Lyons, where he passes the rest of his days. It was not so easy to repress the acts of Elipand, who lived under the Moslem power. The council of Frankfort refutes his opinions by a synodal letter (794). Charlemagne writes to invite him and the other bishops of Spain, to yield to the opinion of the pope and the whole Western Church. Elipand nevertheless does not cease to preach his doctrine; but his death follows soon after the exile of Felix of Urgel. Their enterprise does not seem to have had other results. Toward the middle of the ninth century Gothescalk, a monk of the diocese of Soissons, revives the questions relative to free-will and predestination. Imbued with the writings of Augustin, which he comprehends well or ill, he affirms that there is a double predestination, one for the elect, the other for the reprobate. On returning from a journey into Italy, he spreads that doctrine at Mayence. The archbishop Raban Maur assembles a council before which Gothescalk is allowed to explain himself (848). He is condemned and sent to Hincmar, archbishop of Rheims, that he may keep him confined within his diocese. By the order of Charles the bald, thirteen bishops, among whom figures the bishop of Soissons, assemble at Quiercy-sur-Oise to judge the affair. Gothescalk is declared an incorrigible heretic, deposed by the sacerdotal order, condemned to be beaten and imprisoned. He is beaten publicly in presence of the king, then he is shut up in an abbey of the diocese of Rheims. From his cell he writes to support his doctrine. It finds defenders and adversaries among the most illustrious men of his time. Combatted by Raban Maur, Hincmar of Rheims, and John Scot, it is supported more or less by Ratramne, Loup of Ferrieres, Prudence, bishop of Troyes, and Remy, archbishop of Lyons. The last complains specially of the bad treatment which this poor monk undergoes, and of his long and inhuman captivity. Even councils declare in favour of Gothescalk. None the less does he remain in prison, where he dies in 868, refusing to retract and deprived, by Hincmar's order, of the Sacraments and ecclesiastical sepulture. At the same time the question of the real presence in the Eucharist is agitated among the doctors of the Church. The Fathers of the five first centuries did not make a mistake in this matter. They were too enlightened, too versed in the Greek and Oriental philosophy to give to figurative expressions a gross material sense. But when the imperial edicts, proscribing Hellenism, had forced the Gentiles to enter the Church imbued with pagan superstitions, when the invasions of the barbarians, the suppression of the schools of philosophy, the predominance of ignorant monks, had lowered the intellectual level of the nations, then the literal sense of the words of Jesus in the Eucharistic institution could prevail in the bosom of the masses, and thence glide by degrees into the doctrine of the official church.

The first author who put forth such an opinion was the monk Anastasius the Sinaite in the seventh century. It is reproduced in the eighth by John of Damascus, the great defender of the superstition of images. The two opposed sentiments are put forward in the Council of the Iconoclasts in 754, and in the Second Council of Nice (787), but the question is put only incidentally and without leading to any decision.

It is reproduced in the West, as a sequel to a treatise on the body and blood of our Lord, published by Paschasius Rathbert, monk of the Abbey of Corbey (831). He teaches the following points :—The bread and the wine, after consecration, became the true body and the true blood of Christ ; it is the same body that was born of the Virgin, suffered, and rose ; Christ is immolated every day, because every day we sin ; he ought to be in us not only by faith, but also by the natural union of his flesh and blood with ours ; the Eucharist, a truth and a figure at the same time, is not subject to the consequences of digestion.

Rathbert's writing made little noise at the first. But the author, having become the abbot of his monastery, offers his work to king Charles the bald, and then public attention is awakened (847). Its several propositions are combatted by the most distinguished men of the age, among others by Raban Maur, John Scot, and Ratramne. The composition ascribed to Raban Maur, denies these two assertions of Paschasius :—the body of Christ in the Eucharist is the same as was born of the Virgin ; Jesus suffers afresh every time mass is celebrated. The work of John Scot, now lost, was condemned two hundred years after in the Council of Verceil (1050); if we may judge from a passage in Hincmar, he maintained that the sacrament of the Eucharist is not the true body and the true blood of the Lord, but solely the memorial of the true body and the true blood. The book of Ratramne on the body and the blood of the Lord exists still. He explicitly shows that the bread and the wine figure the Lord's body ; that Christ is in the Eucharist spiritually, mystically, by figure and image, but not in a material substance, in a body endowed with a veritable existence.

The question at that time does not seem to have quitted the domain of controversy and the bosom of the Gallican Church ; but the opinion of Paschasius Rathbert, appropriate to the ignorance of the age, will strike root day by day, until it ends by passing into a dogma in the eleventh century. This ardent zeal, which raises in the Gallican

Church discussions, the sense and tendency of which it comprehends more or less, expresses itself at the same time by laudable efforts to spread the faith among the nations of the north of Europe. Ebbon, archbishop of Rheims, goes to preach in Denmark with a mission from the Pope (824), and baptises a great number of unbelievers. But Anscarius, or Ansgard, is the principal apostle of the Scandinavian regions. After a first journey into Sweden (829), he obtains from the emperor the creation of an archiepiscopal see at Hamburg, to which are subject the peoples that dwell on the north of the Elbe, and the rest of the northern countries. Promoted to the See, and having become legate of the Pope in those regions, he labours efficaciously till 865 by himself and by his vicars, to plant the faith in Sweden, Denmark, and all the countries of the north.

In the course of this same century commence the debates between the Greek and the Latin Churches which determined the schism of their churches. The real cause of their separation is, as has been said, the rivalry of the Sees of Rome and Constantinople. The pretext on the occasion was the disagreement of the two churches on certain religious practices, and principally on the dogma of the procession of the Holy Spirit.

The Fathers of the Council of Nice (325) contented themselves with saying in their symbol : "We believe also in the Holy Spirit," without speaking on his origin, nature, and functions, on which, as yet, minds were not well made up. The first Œcumenical Council of Constantinople, more explicit, expressed itself in these terms (381) : "We believe in the Holy Spirit, lord and life-giver, *proceeding from the Father*, and who ought to be worshipped with the Father and the Son ; who spake by the prophets." This belief that the spirit proceeds from the Father, agreeable to a passage of the Gospel according to John (xv. 26), was then professed by all Trinitarian Christians. The Oriental Church which has never varied in this point, said, and says still, that the Holy Spirit proceeds from the Father through the Son. The same doctrine was held by the Church of Rome, and also, without doubt, by all those of Italy and Africa. It is found consigned in the reply of Hadrian I. to the Caroline books (794). The author of those books reproached the patriarch Tarasius with having said in the Second Council of Nice, that the Holy Spirit proceeds from the Father through the Son. Hadrian formally approves the words of Tarasius; the Roman Church was, at that time, in agreement with the Greek Church on the procession of the Holy Spirit. The opinion of the Caroline books, that the Holy Spirit proceeds from the Father and the Son (*Filioque*) was, on the contrary, admitted by Spain, Gaul, England, and Germany. It is found mentioned for the first time in a council held at Toledo in 419. There it is said: " The Father is not begotten, the son is begotten, the Paraclete is not begotten, he proceeds from the Father and from the Son." Spain was then under the dominion of the Arian Visigoths. At the time of the conversion of the latter (589), Recarede, their king, convokes at Toledo a national council of all the provinces on this side and on the other side of the Pyrenees. This council rejecting Arianism, declares that it receives the four Œcumenical Councils; it pronounces anathema against whosoever does not believe in the Holy Spirit, or does not believe that he proceeds from the Father and the Son, and that he is co-eternal and co-equal with them. In order to corroborate the faith of the people, it is ordered that in the mass the symbol of Constantinople should be sung in imitation of the oriental churches. But in their version of that symbol, the Spaniards say that the Holy Spirit proceeds from the Father and the Son, while the Greek text has only that he proceeds from the Father. Whence the difference? Spain does not seem to have the thought of putting itself in disagreement with the Imperial Church. Did it regard its version as the true one? Was there an error of translation? or rather in order to affirm against the Arians the consubstantial equality of the Father and the Son, did it think it its duty to say that the Holy Spirit proceeds from both, without any feeling that thus it would put itself in opposition with the Œcumenical Council of Constantinople? However it may be, the same phraseology is found in the other Councils of Toledo. It passes the Pyrenees with the bishops of Septimania and spreads over Gaul. The *Filioque* is already seen in the confession of Gregory of Tours (Hist. I.). From Gaul it passes into England and Germany. It is to be added that it is after the invasion of the barbarians that it establishes itself in Spain and in Gaul, at a time when those countries had little communication with the Church of Rome, which depended then on either the Ostrogoths or on the Empire of the East. The two opinions come into collision in a council held at Gentilly, near Paris, in presence of the legates of the Pope, and of ambassadors sent from Constantinople to the king of the Franks (767). There the Greeks reproach the Latins with having added to the symbol *Filioque*. It is not known whether the council came to any decision on the point ; but each church persists in its own usage. The question is reproduced at the period of the Caroline Books (794). They censure, as we have just said, the procession of the Father through the Son, and Pope Hadrian defends it.

The monks of Jerusalem, taking part in the controversy, send to Charlemagne one of their order to complain of the interpolation of *Filioque*, which they regard as a very criminal fraud. That prince convokes at Aix-la-Chapelle a council in which the question is debated (801). He sends to Rome a bishop and an abbot to submit to the pope the passages of scripture and of the Fathers by which they try to prove that the Holy Spirit proceeds from the Father and the Son. Leo III. finds himself in a delicate position. He confesses that he shares their opinion on the substance of the question, but he refuses to add *Filioque* to the creed, the œcumenical councils having forbidden any addition to them ; as the symbol was chanted in Spain and in France, while at Rome they confined themselves to reading it, the Pope advises that they should gradually cease to chant it in the churches of France, in order not to perpetuate the abusive custom of adding *Filioque*. The conference remains without result ; but Leo, to protect the faith, suspends in the Church of St Peter two silver shields, on which the symbol is engraven, in Greek on one, on the other in Latin, such as it was promulgated by the œcumenical council in

381. The discussion reposes until the time when Ignatius is expelled from the See of Constantinople (858). That patriarch, son of the emperor Michael Rhangabé, had drawn on himself for different reasons the animadversion of Michael III. and of Cæsar Bardas. He receives as successor Photius, grand-nephew of Tarasius. He had a superior and well-cultivated mind; he passed for the most learned man of his age. The Church chose him while yet a layman, a custom then frequent in the oriental church. The clergy are divided between the two patriarchs; the bishops of the province depose Photius, and anathematise him with his adherents. He replies by assembling a council which deposes Ignatius and the bishops of his party. Imperial ambassadors go to Rome with rich presents for the Church of St Peter. Photius asks Pope Nicholas I. (858-67) to send legates to Constantinople to put an end to the heresy of the Iconoclasts and to conciliate all things. Legates in effect arrive with the Pope's letters to the emperor, and to Photius. Nicholas complains in his reply to the emperor that they have deposed Ignatius without consulting the See of Rome, and that they have appointed a layman for his successor; he will give his decision after the report of the legates. At the same time he requires the re-establishment of his jurisdiction over Eperus, Illyria, Macedonia, Thessaly, Achaia, Dacia, Maesia, Dardania, and Prevale, with the Bishop of Thessalonica for vicar, and finally the restitution of the patrimonies of the Church of Rome in Calabria and Sicily. A council meets at Constantinople (861). Three hundred and eighteen bishops and the legates of the Pope of Rome are present. There Ignatius is put upon his trial. He is deposed with the assent of the legates, and Photius is confirmed in his patriarchal functions. A letter is read from Nicholas I., but without his demands being attended to, for the re-establishment of his jurisdiction and the restitution of the patrimony. This council is accounted œcumenical by the Greeks. The emperor writes to the Pope of Rome confirming the deposition of Ignatius and the ordination of Photius. The latter sends letters of the same import; to the reproach of having been elected

although a layman, he replies that the Church of Constantinople has never received the canons which are said to have been violated (those of the Council of Sardica); he cites old and new examples of similar elections among the Greeks and even among the Latins. In regard to jurisdiction over the churches of Illyria, he affirms that he could have asked nothing better than the lightening of his burden; but that, as it was a question of country and frontiers, it is an affair the decision of which belongs only to the emperor. Nicholas, who sees himself overcome, if not deluded on the question of jurisdiction, forthwith disavows his legates. In presence of the whole Church of Rome and of the Greek ambassador, he declares that he has not authorised the acknowledgment of the deposition of Ignatius and the promotion of Photius, and that he will never consent to the one or the other. He writes in the same sense to the emperor, and to Photius, whom he treats as a mere layman (862). In another letter addressed to all the faithful of the East, he explains the prevarication of which he accuses the legates, adjuring the bishops to join him and to publish his protests in their dioceses. To secure justice for the complaints of Ignatius, the Pope assembles at Rome a council which declares Photius deprived of all sacerdotal character, forbidding him to intrude again into the concerns in which that quality is required, under pain of excommunication and anathema; Ignatius, on the contrary, is re-established by that council in his dignity and his functions, as well as the bishops and clerics exiled or deposed on his account.

The emperor Michael writes to Nicholas a letter full of insults and threats to make him revoke the condemnation of Photius (865). In his reply the Pope accuses of nullity the last judgment rendered against Ignatius; extolling the pretended privileges of the Church of Rome, he demands that the two competitors should betake themselves to that city, or, if they cannot go thither, that they state the reasons by letters and send deputies. A new subject of division arises at the same time between the See of Rome and that of Constantinople. The Bulgarians converted in 865 had been instructed and baptised by bishops and priests of the Greek Church. The year following, their king deputes to Rome his son and several lords, with offerings for St Peter; he charges them to consult the Pope on several religious questions, and to ask of him bishops and priests. Nicholas in his reply contradicts certain usages of the oriental church. He sends into Bulgaria bishops who preach and baptise all over the country; the king dismisses the missionaries of other nations. At the same time three legates of the Pope are directed by that country to Constantinople with letters in favour of Ignatius; but they are stopped at the frontiers of the Eastern empire, and constrained to return to Rome without having accomplished their mission. Photius, informed of these doings, learns that the legates have rejected his operations in Bulgaria and introduced different usages in opposition with those of the Greek Church. A council then meets at Constantinople in which Nicholas is condemned and deposed. Photius addresses to the patriarchs of the oriental churches an encyclic letter against the Pope of Rome and the Latin Church. "The Bulgarians," he says, "had been in the Church of Christ scarcely two years, when execrable men, proceeding out of the darkness of the West came and corrupted the sound doctrines which they had received." The errors which he reproaches the Latins with having taught the Bulgarians are, 1*st*, to fast on Saturday contrary to the canons of the Church; 2*d*, to cancel the first week of Lent in allowing milk and cheese to be eaten; 3*d*, to detest, like the Manicheans, the legitimate marriage of priests; 4*th*, to reserve for the bishop the right of giving the unction of the Chrism, and to forbid it to the priests; 5*th*, to alter the creed by the addition of strange words, saying that the Holy Spirit proceeds not from the Father only but also from the Son. He speaks with special force of the *Filioque*, which he calls a blasphemy against the Holy Spirit, or rather against the entire Trinity. He asks whence the Latins have derived that doctrine: from what gospel? from what councils? from what Fathers?

The emperors Michael and Basil write to the same effect to the Pope of Rome. Nicholas finds himself in an embarrassing situation in regard to the *Filioque*, which the Church of Rome rejects equally. He takes the step of submitting the griefs of Photius to the bishops of France, asking them to unite with him in repelling them (867). We learn from the letter that to the facts mentioned in the Encyclic the Eastern churches added the following inculpations ; that the Latins made the Chrism with river water; that they did not observe eight weeks before Passover without eating flesh, and seven without eating eggs and cheese ; that they imitated the Jews in offering at the Passover a lamb on the altar of the Lord ; that their clergy shaved their beards ; that they ordained bishop a deacon without having ordained him a priest. Nicholas maintains that a part of the reproaches of the Greeks are false and that the rest have always been observed at Rome and in the West. But, continues he, it is not astonishing that the Greeks oppose these traditions, they who dare to assert that when the emperors passed from Rome to Constantinople, the primacy of the Roman Church and its privileges devolved on the Church of that last city. The Pope's letter called forth in France several writings against the Greeks. But the dispute is suddenly quieted by the news of the fall of Photius. After the murder of the emperor, Michael, the first care of Basil, remaining alone in power, was to expel the patriarch who, according to some, had risen against the crime, and according to others, had wished to raise a competitor to that prince (867). Ignatius replaced in possession of the See of Constantinople, demands the convocation of an œcumenical council. The emperor writes about it to the Pope and the other patriarchs. His envoys bring to Rome the acts of the council which deposed Pope Nicholas and declare false the signature of Basil which they bear. Hadrian II. (867-72) assembles a council of thirty bishops ; this council condemns that held by Photius and the emperor Michael against the respect due to the holy See ; it renews the sentence previously pronounced against Photius, yet leaving him lay communion if he repents. The acts of the council which condemned Nicholas are burnt publicly.

The legates of Hadrian II., on arriving at Constantinople,

require that the oriental bishops, to be admitted to the œcumenical council, shall give them a document in which, acknowledging the supremacy of the See of Rome, they approve the councils held against Photius by the popes Nicholas and Hadrian, and reject those which he assembled under the Emperor Michael. The council opens on the fifth of October 869. In the first session there appear, with the legates of the pope, only the patriarch Ignatius, the legates of the Sees of Antioch and Jerusalem (who were easily procured), and finally twelve bishops of the party of Ignatius. In the following session ten others make their submission. But the generality of the Greek clergy remain with Photius. He is brought before the assembly; following the examples of Jesus before Pilate, he refuses to reply to the questions put to him. The bishops of his party undertake his defence spiritedly. The council pronounces anathema against Photius and his adherents. The sittings are then interrupted during three entire months. In the interval some bishops and a legate of the See of Alexandria are recruited. The last session receives the subscriptions of one hundred and two bishops; but in that number stands not one of those whom Photius had ordained, and they were more than three hundred. Such is the council which the Latins hold for the eighth œcumenical, and which the Greeks do not acknowledge. The Roman legates conducted everything as they pleased while they seconded the animosity of the Emperor; it is not the same, some days after, in the question of the Bulgarians. These people had sent ambassadors to obtain a decision to which Church they should be subject. The affair is discussed after the close of the council. Notwithstanding the protests of Hadrian's legates, who wish to leave the decision to the See of Rome, the Eastern legates, constituting themselves judges, decide that Bulgaria shall remain under the jurisdiction of Constantinople. On their return the legates of Rome fall into the hands of the Sclaves, who take from them the original of the acts of the council; there remains only a copy translated into Latin by Anastasius.

Peace was not established in the Church of Constantinople, where the party of Photius still remained powerful. On the request of Basil, Pope John VIII. (872-82) sends two legates to apply a remedy (878). On this occasion he summons Ignatius, by a menacing letter, to restore his jurisdiction over Bulgaria and to recall the Greek priests.

Nevertheless, after eight years of exile, Photius succeeds in regaining the favour of the Emperor. He is recalled to Constantinople. On the death of Ignatius he recovers his see (878). The two Roman legates affirm that they are commissioned to declare him patriarch. Ambassadors go to Rome to carry the letters of the Emperor and of Photius. The circumstances were propitious. John VIII., constantly exposed to the attacks of the Saracens, had pressing need of the aid of the Greek empire. He acknowledges Photius as legitimate patriarch. In his reply to Basil he says that he is favourable to his prayer and to the consent given to the return of Photius by all the Greek clergy, even by the bishops and the priests ordained by Methodius and Ignatius. He absolves Photius and his followers from all ecclesiastical censure, in virtue, he says, of the power given to Peter by Jesus Christ, a power which authorises the See of Rome to absolve even condemnations pronounced by councils. John, however, adds as conditions that after the death of Photius a layman shall not be elected in his place and that the patriarch of Constantinople shall not put forward any claim to Bulgaria. The same clauses are enunciated in the instructions given to the legates; under these reserves, the pope consents that, in the council which is to meet, they shall declare null those which have been held against Photius, in the time of Hadrian II., both at Rome and Constantinople. An œcumenical council opens, in the last city, in the month of November 879. There are present three hundred and eighty-three bishops. The sessions at which the Emperor does not appear are presided over by Photius. The Roman legates enquiring how he has been restored, the legate of Jerusalem replies that Photius has never ceased to be acknowledged by the three patriarchs of the East and by nearly all the bishops. In their letters, the oriental patriarchs disavow as falsifiers those who declared themselves representatives to the council of 869. The assembly, examining the articles of reunion proposed by the Pope of Rome, decides, on the question of Bulgaria, that the decision should be left to the wisdom of the prince, and that, on the ordination of laymen, they should uphold the old customs of the Greek and Oriental Church which has always admitted laymen to the episcopate. They then with one voice pass to the condemnation of the council held against Photius under Hadrian II., and they excommunicate as schismatics those who do not recognise him in the quality of patriarch.

The second Council of Nice touching images is declared the seventh œcumenical council. A special canon determines that persons deposed, excommunicated, or anathematised by Pope John shall be treated as such by Photius, and that those which the latter shall have deposed, excommunicated, or anathematised, shall be considered by Pope John as subject to the same censure. This canon, in consecrating the equality of the two episcopates, denies by implication the right of appeal to his See, which the Bishop of Rome pretended to possess.

In the last session, presided over by the emperor, they publish anew the Symbol of Nice, such as it was reformed at Constantinople (381), and it is forbidden to alter it by additions or retrenchments, under pain of deposition against clerics and anathema against laics. This was to condemn the addition of the *Filioque* made by the majority of the western churches. In a letter reported at the end of the acts of the council, John VIII. declares that Rome has never received that addition, and that it disapproves it, but that it was necessary to employ mildness and consideration to induce the return of the other Latin bishops from a usage confirmed for so many years.

This council of the year 879 has always been considered as the eighth œcumenical by the Orientals who annex to it that of 861; it cannot be denied that it has all the nalities.

Some months after its close, John VIII. writes to the Emperor Basil, praising him for his zeal for the re-union of the Church, and exhorting him to maintain it ; he thanks him for having sent succours against the Saracens, and restored to the See of Rome its jurisdiction over the Bulgarians. For this last point the question without doubt was one of only promises, more or less explicit. John wrote at the same time to Photius, and complains that his orders have not been followed. Nevertheless he declares, in two letters, that he receives the Council of Constantinople, except in what had been done by the legates against his will. These reserves cannot refer to anything but the jurisdiction over Bulgaria, and to the equality of power attributed to the two Bishops of Rome and Constantinople. John lives still two years without ceasing to communicate with Photius and the Greek Church. Marin II. (882-84) had been legate of the Pope Hadrian II. in the council of 869. He condemns Photius, and rejects the œcumenical council held under John VIII. Hadrian III. (884-85) commits the same errors. Photius writes in the time of one of them, a vehement letter against those of the westerns who maintain that the Holy Spirit does not proceed solely from the Father, but also from the Son. He in it reproduces the reasons set forth in his first Encyclic, and invokes the authority of the Popes Leo I. and Leo. III., as well as that of the legates of Pope John VIII. to the œcumenical council of 879. His conclusion is that the Roman Church agreeing on that doctrine with the other patriarchal churches, all those who reject it ought to be condemned. The Emperor Basil irritated that Hadrian III. declares against Photius, writes to him injurious letters, which are handed to Stephen V (885-91). This Pope is of the same sentiments as his predecessor ; in his reply to Basil he makes a distinction between the ecclesiastical and the secular power, but employing caution toward that prince whom he begs to send a well-armed fleet and a garrison for the defence of Rome against the Saracens. This letter does not arrive in Constantinople till after the death of Basil. Leo the philosopher, his son, gives a successor to Photius, in the first year of his reign (886), and confines Photius himself in the monastery of the Armenians. He suspected him, it is said of being the author or the accomplice of a disgrace which Leo had experienced under his father, and of having conspired to put one of his own relatives on the throne. From that time Photius appears on the scene no more; he dies in 891 in the place of his exile. His spirit survived in the Greek clergy, most of whose bishops he had ordained. The new patriarch Stephen, brother of the emperor, had received from him the diaconate. Leo the philosopher and the bishops of the party of Ignatius write to the Pope of Rome to inform him of the displacement of Photius, who had renounced the patriarchal See, according to the prince, and who had been driven from it, according to the Ignatians. All concur in asking the Pope to acknowledge the ordinations made by Photius. Stephen V. requires that bishops should be sent to Rome to explain to him the real state of things. That deputation does not arrive till 891. Formosus then occupied the chair (891-96). He refuses the ways of conciliation. The legates which he despatches to Constantinople are ordered to assemble with the Greek bishops, in order that before all things the condemnation of Photius may be irrevocable. As to those who have received ordination from him, all that can be obtained from the condescension of Formosus, is that after having acknowledged their fault, they shall be admitted to the communion of believers, but solely as laymen. This excessive rigour makes the Greeks resolve to do without the adherence of the Pope. From that time relations between the two churches languish; there remain seeds of discord which will produce the definitive schism of the eleventh century.

Let us now cast a glance on the state of the clergy during the period covered by this chapter, and on the numerous superstitions which are mingled with Christianity. There is but little change in the inferior orders of the Church. The archdeacon has, among the Latins, taken rank above the priests and the arch-priests. In the east their functions have not varied; but there exist, at Constantinople specially, divers other dignitaries below the bishop, such as the syncell or protosyncell (chancellor), the great sacellair

(purser), who takes care of the finances of the Church, th
great economist (steward), who administers the possession
and the revenues, the first defender, who is charged with it
protection and the protection of its ministers, and th
cartophylax or guard of the archives.

The Chorebishops subsist still in the sixth century
The Episcopal authority increases daily; that of priest
decreases.

The patriarchal rights increase in the sixth century i
the four Eastern Sees, and principally at Constantinople
Justinian establishes in European Dardania a new patri
archate, whose duration is ephemeral. After the Mosler
conquest, Alexandria, Antioch, and Jerusalem groan unde
such servitude, that we do not know even who were thei
patriarchs in the eighth century; a similar oppressio
weighs upon Africa, and on other subjugated provinces.

We have spoken of the struggle that took place betwee
the Patriarch of Rome and that of Constantinople, and (
its different phases till the end of the ninth century; but
the pretensions of the Bishop of Rome to dominion over tl
universal Church encounter insurmountable obstacles in tl
East, it is not the same in the Western countries. Acknov
ledged for a long time as patriarch of those regions, he su
ceeds, without much difficulty, in getting himself accepte
there as head of all the Church. Thence to absolu
monarchy there is but one step. That step is soon take
by Rome, with the aid of the new order of things create
by the establishment of the barbarians. Beginning wit
Boniface III. (606), its bishops take the title of œcumenice
in the sense of the universal head of the Church. In tl
eighth and the ninth century they take pains to multip
episcopates, concessions of the pallium, creations of primat
and archbishops. The bishops are required to swear fideli
to the See of Rome. The title of patriarch is given to tl
primates of dioceses and kingdoms; the pope glories
commanding patriarchs. He soars above them. The po
tifical dominion extends from day to day. The pop
assume it no longer as bishops of the capital of the empii
or in virtue of the constitution of Valentinian III., but

of divine origin, by the concession of Christ and the authority
of Peter;—they assume the right to command all the ecclesiastical orders, and even emperors and kings—to bind and
to loose them, to set them up and put them down, to act as
supreme judge in all things without any one knowing their
sentence. They ascribe to themselves a power equal to that
of Christ, and by their acts take on themselves the spiritual
and temporal sovereignty. They cause themselves to be
carried in pomp on human shoulders, and give their feet to
be kissed by everybody, even the Roman Senate. John
VIII., in concert with the people of Rome, disposes of the
imperial crown to the profit of Charles the Bald (875).
This prince, in some way, recognises the sovereignty of the
Holy See, and obliges himself by oath to defend it against
all its enemies. John compares himself with Moses; and
the cardinal priests, or titulars of parishes, are in his eyes
the seventy ancients who judged the people of Israel. Yet
the papal usurpations are not consummated without opposition. Independently of the Greek Church and the emperors
of the East, who have always withstood it, the tyranny of
Rome is more or less strongly combatted in the West by
councils, princes, bishops, and pious and learned men. In
throwing off the yoke of the Greeks, the Holy See passes
under the domination of the Frank princes, who make
ecclesiastical laws, convoke councils, establish bishops. Despite the weakness of Louis le Debonnaire and the abasement of Charles the Bald, the popes are still far from having
attained their object. Two centuries of subjugation and
struggle will pass away for them before their ambitious
thought is realised in facts. Among the causes of the
power of the Western clergy, and of the absolute authority
which the Church of Rome is on the point of seizing, we
must place the ancient religious belief of the peoples of
Gaul and Germany. The barbarians, in their simplicity,
assimilate the ministers of the Church to the priests of
Druidism, and the pope to the head of the Druids, whose
authority had no limits. There still existed vestiges of
that religion about the ninth century. Add to that the
breaking up of the states by the successive divisions among

the sons of the conquerors; the tendency of the oppressed populations to rally round the heads of the Church, the only one of the old powers that remained erect; the incredible ignorance into which society had fallen as a consequence of the invasions; the audacious fraud of the apocryphal decretals which were published in the ninth century under the pseudonym of Isidore Mercator, as well as other pieces of the same nature, whose authenticity no one suspected in those days. The clergy itself did not escape from the common ignorance. With few exceptions, the ministers of worship are scarcely more enlightened than the multitude. He who knows grammar among them, is accounted learned. All their study consists in learning the rules of penitence. To be admitted into their order, it is enough to be able to read and chant; to know the Calendar, the psalter, the creed, and the Lord's Prayer. But however ignorant the clergy, they knew the art and had the skill of amassing wealth. They work on the credulity of the people. The great give them property to buy off their sins. In the eighth and the ninth century they obtain even regal rights. Resembling the popes, the bishops and the abbots possess provinces, cities, castles, fortresses; they are dukes, counts, marquises, judges, legislators, and sovereigns; they bear arms; they give themselves up to hunting, festivities, nocturnal orgies. Their corruption increases step by step with their opulence; they are familiar with usury, simony, sacrilege; they are a prey to pride, ambition, avarice, luxury. Monkism assumes considerable developments in all Christian lands. Before the Moslem invasion, armies might have been raised among the monks of the East without their number being sensibly reduced. Down to the sixth century the institution is everywhere the same. The monks live dispersed in deserts, or inhabit separate cells in small colonies and monasteries. Benedict of Nurscia changes that order of things in the West. He assembles in a community on Mount Cassino monks who take perpetual vows, and submit to certain rules as to dwelling, food, attire, order, and blind obedience (529). The Benedictines spread over different countries of Europe, where they find large numbers of monasteries. In imitation of them are born all the religious orders, which are distinguished by different usages and names. Monasteries and nunneries abound in the Western regions. Admiration for the monastic life, and the liberalities of the powerful, bring them together from all parts. Kings exchange the diadem for the cowl; queens, princesses, noble virgins take the veil.

From the sixth century monks have their heads tonsured like the priests. There are two kinds of tonsure. One is made, it is said, after the example of Paul; the other in imitation of Peter. It is supposed that the latter, to represent the crown of thorns, had the top of his head bared of hair, leaving the lower part with hair round it. Paul, on the contrary, had the whole of his head tonsured. This last method is followed by the Greeks; Peter's tonsure is adopted in the West. In the sequel the Latins shaved the top of the head, instead of cutting it bare. The cloisters and the monasteries serve also for prisons, where penalties or penance were endured. These prisons contain kings, princes, illustrious men and women, who lay aside the secular dress, and whose hair is cut off. In the East, deposed emperors, patriarchs, metropolitans, are confined in them.

The morals of the recluses remain pure in the primitive ages. A number of monasteries are schools of letters and sacred discipline. The abbots intrust the care of them to the most able monks, who are called scholastics. But disorders come with riches, and with the exemption of Episcopal jurisdiction, which the popes grant to the monks, in order to secure their influence. In vain did Charlemagne try to apply some remedy to the corruption. Louis the Good-natured, with the same object, charges Benedict of Aniana to effect a reformation. The latter, at Aix la Chapelle, presides over a council which adopts wise measures. All monks, without exception, are subjected to the rule of the Benedictines; out of the different orders they form a single body, united by a common bond. But this discipline grows weak, and disappears in a little time.

The dogmas of the Official Church on the trinity, the

incarnation, grace, original sin, did not vary from the Council of Chalcedon to the end of the ninth century. The same may be said of the procession of the Holy Spirit; although earnestly supported by the Churches of Spain, Gaul, Britain, and Germany, the procession of the Father and Son is only in a state of private opinion; Rome agrees with the Oriental Church in not admitting the last clause, namely *Filioque*.

The beliefs in the state of souls and in the descent of Christ into hell have on the contrary undergone some modifications. Descent into hell was taught in the primitive church; according to the doctrine of the Jews it was believed that while the body of Jesus reposed in the sepulchre, his soul had descended to hell, that is into the bosom of Abraham, whence it came when he rose again; but they spoke then of no mission to be fulfilled in the infernal regions, no deliverance of the just of the Old Testament. Those, according to the opinion of the time, were to remain in the bosom of Abraham until the universal resurrection, and during the two first centuries it was held that it would be the same with the righteous who died in the Christian faith. The aspect of things is no longer the same, when this last opinion came to be abandoned, and it was definitely admitted that the righteous of the new law rise into the heavens the day of their death; it is no longer possible to leave in the infernal abode the patriarchs, the prophets and the righteous of the Old Testament. Imagination then said that the descent of Jesus into hell had for its object, to subdue the powers of the abyss, and at the same time to take out of the lower places the souls of the ancient righteous persons in order to lead them into the celestial paradise, which from that time is itself designated by the name of "The bosom of Abraham." The compartment of hell which alone was so called in the beginning, takes the denomination of *Limbo of the Fathers* in opposition to the *Limbo of Infants* which was placed below.

These new opinions on the descent of Jesus into hell, and on the transmigration of the ancient righteous persons, are consecrated by the apocryphal Gospel of Nicodemus, which was drawn up in the fifth century, and which obtained full credit in the church of the west in and from the seventh century. The employment of prayers for the dead sprang from the belief that was held in the earliest centuries, that souls inhabited subterraneous places until the day of the resurrection. When this belief disappeared, none the less do the prayers continue; but then their aim was to draw the souls out of purgatory. As early as the fifth century there began to appear in the Latin Church the idea of a fire which purified souls of slight faults before they were admitted to eternal happiness, (Augustin speaks of it in a doubtful manner). This opinion had its source, as so many others, in the philosophy of Plato, agreeing in this particular with the Hellenic and Egyptian beliefs. The existence of purgatory, placed in a particular part of hell, gains belief among the Latins during the sixth and the seventh century; in the eighth it has become a dogma of the church. The monks take pains to spread it. In the absence of the authority of Scripture and the Fathers, they cite visions, dreams, extasies, narratives of the risen dead—objects which easily impose on gross populations. The belief in purgatory gives place to a multitude of masses and oblations intended to deliver souls from their sufferings. This doctrine was then unknown to the Greeks, who afterwards vigorously combatted it. During the eighth century and the ninth, the sacred scriptures gradually cease to be the sole rule of faith. In the west preference is given to the Roman traditions, the authority of Peter, whom the popes make speak, the orders and the decrees of the Sovereign Pontiffs, the decisions of the councils held at Rome. The divers superstitions, which began to germinate in the first half of the fifth century, grow and flourish in all places in posterior ages. Their progress is more manifest from the reign of Justinian. After the closing of the schools of philosophy, intelligence grows weak and dim, and ignorance increases every day. The last followers of Hellenism, thrown violently into the official church, give to superstition a force which nothing can resist. The degeneration of Christianity into a veritable idolatry is perhaps one of the principal causes of the success of Islamism in oriental countries. The emperors of Constantinople, who see the danger, attempt to apply a remedy. During more than a century they struggle with rare energy against the worship of the saints, images, and relics, and against the monkish spirit which propagates all these novelties. Useless resistance! Superstition triumphs in the east owing to two women, Irene and Theodora; it triumphs in the west by the influence of the popes of Rome and monks their emissaries. Toward the middle of the ninth century, it reigns with opposition in the two churches; but its force and intensity are greatest in the western regions, where a profound ignorance prevails. The doctrine of the intercession of saints no longer encounters contradiction. Among the persons to whom prayers are addressed, Mary holds the first rank. She has become the object of special worship. The New Testament, we have said, is silent in regard to her from the time when she prayed with the apostles, before the descent of the Holy Spirit, (Acts i.) In the four first centuries she is spoken of as a wise and pious person, distinguished in nothing from other women. The Miriamnites and the Collyridians, who worship her in the fourth century are considered as heretics. Their opinion seems nevertheless to have continued here and there in the lower strata of Christian society. It overflows in the church after the condemnation of Nestorius by the Council of Ephesus. Mary is then more and more glorified as the mother of God. In the pagan beliefs, which mingle with Christianity, the mother of a god could not be a simple woman, a saint as so many others. The mothers of the Hellenic gods—Latona, Maïa, Semelé, Alcmené, were honoured as goddesses. Apocryphal books soon supplement the silence of Scripture on the last period of Mary's existence. They make her, on her death, ascend to heaven in the arms of angels. Ridiculous as they are, these narratives obtain full belief among the crowd. After the defeat of the Iconoclasts, the fable of the assumption is accepted as an incontestable verity by populations still semi-pagan. It is not enough to reign in the heaven of the one God of the Bible, nor even of the three in one of the trinitarian church. Had not all the ancient worships celestial queens? Mary becomes the queen of queens, the queen of the pagano-Christian heaven. The transformation takes place mostly in the seventh and eighth centuries. Her panegyrics abound in the Fathers of that period. The orators lavish on Mary the names, the titles, and the attributes given in the ancient religions to Isis, Venus-Urania, Cybele, and the other queens of the Empyræum. A more and more ardent worship is addressed equally to the saints and the angels. They take the place of the gods of Hellenism in their different attributes and functions. After the manner of those gods they have foresight of future things, penetrate into the secret designs of men, intercede on their behalf with the Supreme God, protect them against evil spirits, turn aside threatening evils. Peter becomes specially great among all in the Roman Church. He is, as the prince of apostles, the special representative, the immediate agent of Christ and God. He enjoys an unlimited influence in the higher regions. The popes perpetually introduce him in their relations with kings and peoples; they speak in his name, and make him speak in the interests of the pontifical see. Each community of believers has moreover its particular saint. As the gods of old, the angels and the saints are the special patrons of cities, villages, homes, and even of a crowd of uninhabited places. As of old the god, so there is the angel, or the saint of a nation, a family, an individual, and also the angel or the saint which guarantees from this plague or that, heals this or that malady of soul and body, or presides over this or that department of human affairs—over war, hunting, flocks, the vine, &c. Their occupations ceaselessly varying and increasing it becomes necessary to multiply the number of the saints. The priests and the monks do not fail in the task; they people heaven with a crowd of individuals known or unknown, often imaginary.

The worship given to the saints is appropriated to their images and their relics. One cannot enumerate the apparitions, revelations, and miracles which precede, accompany, or follow the discovery and the transferences of relics true or

false; the imagination of the monks is a perennial stream
Everywhere they build churches to the Virgin, the angels,
the apostles, the martyrs, and other saints. The same application is made of the ancient temples of the gods and the
goddesses of Hellenism. Boniface IV. obtains from the
Emperor Phocas the Pantheon of Rome, formerly consecrated to Cybele, mother of the gods, and to all the pagan
divinities. The pope transmutes it into a Panagion (*All
Holy*), which he dedicates to Mary, mother of God and all
the male and female saints. New festivals are instituted in
their honour. Care is taken to fix them at the same time
as the ancient festivals of Polytheism. In the sixth century
they celebrate the purification of Mary, the circumcision of
Jesus, the birth of John the Baptist, Saint Martin, the
Chair of Saint Peter. The festivals of the Ascension, the
Annunciation, the True Cross, belong to the following century. The Assumption and the festival of the Archangel
Michael are referred to the commencement of the ninth
century; about the same time Gregory IV. institutes the
festival of All Saints. It is customary to celebrate the
anniversary of the ordination of popes and bishops. They
continue to celebrate the day of the death of Christian
martyrs. Solemnities without number are born on occasion
of the miracles attributed to the martyrs, confessors, recluses,
bishops, or abbots whom the different churches adopt for
their patrons. The same is done on the discoveries and
transferences of relics. Each saint has his own form of
worship. The festivals connected with this or that church
are afterwards changed into general festivals.

Pope Gregory I. established new rules for the office and
the canon of the mass. But this Gregorian canon is not
admitted in all places. Milan observes the Ambrosian
canon; in Spain there are the Gothic and the Mosarabic
canon; in France the Gallican. It is in the eleventh or
twelfth century that the Roman office prevails in all the
Latin Churches. Superstitious practices increase beyond
measure. As early as the fifth century a crowd of Pagan
ceremonies are imitated, such as processions, stations,
litanies, or prayers to God and to the saints for rain and

fine weather, for the cessation of the plague and other calamities. New rites for consecrations, derived from the same source, are introduced equally with solemn masses, wax candles, perfumes, holy water, &c. The use of bells begins in the seventh century, as well as that of organs in churches. At the end of the ninth century the entire face of Christianity is entirely changed in the official church. Infinite novelties are displayed in the temples, superb altars, magnificent pictures, wax candles always burning, long and brilliant processions, sumptuous attire for the priests, masses with great pomp, masses for the dead, sacerdotal penitences, unction of the chrism, exorcisms, and other things of the same kind. The whole of religion consists in the observance of festivals, fasts, abstinences; in the solemnities of the mass, in the melody of chants, in the intervention of the saints, in prayers addressed to the cross, to statues, images, tombs; in offerings for souls in purgatory; in pilgrimages to different spots; the ideal of Christian perfection is to take the monkish vow and cowl.

All these things, however, are not introduced without opposition. Princes, bishops, learned men, raise their voices against them at different times in the Latin Church. But during the ninth century the opposition grows weaker and weaker. Toward the end of that age all the west seems to bend before the omnipotence of Rome, and before the superstitions of its Church.

CHAPTER IV.

APOCRYPHAL BOOKS, FABLES, AND LEGENDS.

SUMMARY.—Apocryphal Writings—Lives of Saints—Creed of Athanasius—False Decretals—Dionysius the Areopagite—Saint Mary's Assumption; Legend of the Assumption—John—Peter and Paul—Fables—Discoveries and Transferences of Relics—The True Cross—The Body of Stephen—The Head of John the Baptist—Mark at Venice—James at Compostella—Ceaseless Miracles.

ONE cannot tell the number of Apocryphal books, fables, and legends which became current from the Council of Nice (325) to the end of the ninth century, principally from the beginning of the sixth. The ignorance and superstition, which gain greater prevalence every day, especially in the west, leave an open field for the stories of Visionaries, the fictions of monks, the deceits of the sacerdotal class. We shall restrict ourselves to the indication of some of the most known, or the most important, results being considered, Apocryphal books.

There has been attributed

To the Apostle Paul a *Correspondence with Seneca*, first spoken of by Jerome, which betrays itself by its style, the subject, and the date ascribed to it:

To Nicodemus *A Gospel* of the fifth century, the principal object of which is to confirm and glorify the descent of Jesus into hell:

To Dionysius the Areopagite *Works* unknown in the first five centuries:

To Justin Martyr the book of *Questions and Answers to the Orthodox;* an *Exposition of the Faith* on the holy and consubstantial Trinity, and divers other writings which are of the fourth or the fifth century:

To Hegesippus *Five Books of History* written in Latin on the War of the Jews and the ruin of Jerusalem, books supposed to be by Ambrose of Milan or some other Latin author of his age:

To Melito of Sardis, among other works, the book of *The Journey of Mary* or of her *Assumption* in body, and soul, the date of which cannot be anterior to the sixth century:

To Origen a crowd of *Commentaries, Homilies, Dialogues*, as well as interversions and interpolations made in his works by Rufinus and others:

To Gregory the Wonder-worker an *Exposition of Faith* against the Arians, a kind of *creed* revealed to him by John and the Virgin Mary, and *Sermons* on the Annunciation of the Mother of God:

To Cyprian a great number of writings and interpolations which have slipped into his works, in favour of the primacy of the Church of Rome:

To Dorotheus (which is not known) a book on the *Life* and the *Death* of the *Prophets*, the *Apostles*, and *Disciples* of Jesus Christ, in which the episcopates of different countries, whether in the east or the west, are distributed among the seventy disciples:

To Methodius a *History*, in which you read the fable of Veronica's handkerchief:

To Eusebius of Cæsarea *Homilies* and different other writings, which are by an author of the same name:

To Athanasius a number of works, among others, an *Exhortation to the Monks*, written in Latin; the book of the *Passion of the Image of Christ*, crucified at Berytus, a sermon on the *Assumption of the Very Holy Virgin Mother of God*, and different things of the same nature:

To Ambrose of Milan Sermons on divers subjects, for instance, on the *Passion of Agnes*, the *Baptism of Augustin*, prayers for the *Preparation of the Priest, for the Sacrifice of the Mass*, the book of the *Mysteries* or *Sacraments*, which belongs to the seventh or the eighth century:

To Jerome, as well as to Augustin, a multitude of writings, the nomenclature of which would be uninteresting.

We also meet with a number of Apocryphas under the names of Basil of Neo-Cæsarea, Gregory Nazianzen, Epiphanes, Hilary of Poitiers, and other Greek and Latin

Fathers of the fourth and the fifth centuries. In the later ages there were fabricated a countless number of Acts of the Martyrs alleged to have suffered from the reign of Septimus Severus to that of Diocletian. Gelasius refers to the class of Apocryphas those which existed in his own time (494). Eusebius of Cæsarea (fourth century) was the first to make a collection of the ancient martyrs; and his work is the only one which deserves any confidence. In imitation of him, but after the fourth century, there appeared in the east a Monologue and in the west Martyrologies, which were gradually augmented by the lucubrations of Bede, Florus, Usuard, Adon of Vienna, and others. These collections were made with the aid of a multitude of false acts, lives of fictitious saints, legends preserved in monasteries and in churches, fables of all sorts which were found in anonymous authors, or here and there in Gregory of Tours, the Pseudo-Dorotheus, Metaphrastes, &c.

In the time of Charlemagne there was spread in the western countries a profession of trinitarian faith which was called the *Creed of Athanasius;* drawn up first in Latin, this apocryphal production is also known under the name of the creed or symbol *Quicunque*, the word with which it begins. In it are enunciated with an intrepidity of belief which nothing astonishes, all the contradictions and impossibilities of the consubstantial trinity, and of the God-man person of Christ. This symbol, whose origin is unknown, may have been written in Spain, in order to affirm with emphasis the consubstantialist orthodoxy in face of the Moslem Monotheism or the persistent remains of the Visigoth Arianism. As it corresponded to the spirit of the age, it was welcomed with fervour everywhere and bore uncontradicted sway during all the middle ages. Under the names of the popes of Rome of the first four centuries there exist decretal letters which were fabricated between the seventh and the ninth centuries, and published in a collection at the beginning of the last with the pseudonym of Isidore Mercator. The most ancient decretals held to be true do not go back beyond the end of the fourth century. Dionysius the little, who died in the middle of the sixth century, made a collection of decretals which begin with those of Sirisius, elected bishop of Rome in the year 385. Those of Isadore Mercator convict themselves of fraud; their style denotes the eighth century; you find in them a crowd of passages of the popes Leo I. and Gregory the Great (fifth and sixth century), and of other posterior writers; there is error in nearly all the dates; the writers speak of archbishops, primates, patriarchs; of the fast of seven weeks before Passover, of the celebration of the mass on Christmas eve, and at other times, of the hymn of the angels, the privilege of ministers of worship to touch the sacred vases, the prohibition to consecrate virgins before the age of twenty-four; the faith in the holy trinity (at the beginning of the second century) finally, (and here appears to have been the principal object of the forgery) an express recognition of the absolute power of the pope of Rome; it is interdicted to hold any council without his permission; mention is made in every page of appeals to his seat as a thing of common right; and at the same time pains are taken to elevate the episcopal authority and preserve the bishops from the accusations brought against them.

Those decretals and other similar pieces of the same period were absolutely needful to consecrate the supreme prerogatives which the popes wished to arrogate to themselves. No longer is sufficient support supplied by the council of Sardica, rejected by the Latins, or by the other synodal decisions, or even by the imperial decrees by which they had profited till then. Since they had assumed the position of successors to the prince of the apostles, vicars of Jesus Christ, their authority, coming from a divine source, could no longer depend on councils or emperors which they represented as inferior to themselves. But pretensions so lofty run the risk of being combatted as novelties if ancient titles and acts were not produced in their favour, if they were not found in documents emanating from the popes of the first ages. Now as nothing of the kind existed, fraud and falsehood were the sole resource.

When the false decretals appear their authenticity is not questioned by any one in the Latin Church. Everybody is captivated thereby. The pope and the high clergy eagerly draw advantage from documents which favour them. Nevertheless, Nicholas I., relying on them for deciding in the last resort the affair of a bishop condemned by a provincial council (864), the bishops who had pronounced the sentence object, without contesting the genuineness of the decretals, that they are not in the code of the canons. The pope replies that this is not a reason for rejecting them, and that those who would do so, to diminish the power of the holy See, do not fail to make use of them when they are useful to themselves. Criticism was then too ignorant to recognise their fraudulent character. The pope and the bishops, who derived advantage from them, were not disposed to call them in question. They were held to be true during the middle ages. They passed into canonical law and became the principal basis of the papal autocracy. Only at the time of the Reformation was their fraudulence demonstrated. It is now contested by no one; but the institutions and the prerogatives established by the authority of those false acts continue nevertheless to subsist in the Roman Church, with which they are, so to say, identified.

Among the different apocryphal works which we have just enumerated, there are two others which deserve special attention, in consequence of the influence which they have exercised in the official church; we refer to the pretended works of Dionysius the Areopagite, and the assumption of Saint Mary attributed to Melitos of Sardis.

The author, whoever he may be, of the writings published under the name of Dionysius the Areopagite, shows himsel[f] imbued with the neo-Platonic ideas, and endeavours to introduce them into Christianity with the oriental doctrine o[f] emanation. These books seem to belong to the end of the fift[h] century. Their authority was invoked for the first time in th[e] conference held at Constantinople with the Severians in th[e] year 532. They were then regarded as authentic. Yet i[t] appears that they were questioned by some persons, they re[-] marked that no one of the fathers of the foregoing ages ha[d] mentioned them; that Eusebius of Cæsarea does not includ[e] them in his enumeration of ecclesiastical works; that the[y] introduce doctrines, traditions, rites, and ceremonies, whic[h] were not current till posterior ages. Notwithstanding these oppositions, the work is received with transport by the generality of the Greek Church, which revels in mystic thought, and it consecrates the hierarchy of the celestial spirits which it was not then acquainted with. John Philopon declares himself the admirer of Dionysius; Maximus the martyr makes comments on it; John of Damascus profits by it more than once.

These books having been brought into the West by the ambassadors of Michael the stammerer (824) Hilduin, abbot of Saint Denis, takes occasion, in a life of the patron of his abbey, to confound the Areopagite with the bishop of Paris who carried his head after it had been cut off, and this blunder prevailed down to the sixteenth century. By compensation, the works of the false Areopagite find in John Scot an able interpreter and an adept of superior intelligence. In the middle ages they will become a fertile source for the mystics of which Dionysius the Areopagite will be the head and the guide.

The book of the journey of *the Holy Virgin Mary*, which bears also the name of *The Assumption of Mary* or the *Death of Mary*, is acknowledged to be apocryphal by everybody. It is marked as such in the decree of Gelasius (494) though it seems posterior to that date.

The author says that he had learnt the history from the mouth of the apostle John. Let us enumerate the principal features. After the master's death John took peculiar care of Mary. After the dispersion of the apostles she remained in the house of the parents of that disciple near the Mount of Olives. Twenty-two years after the ascension, she one day was weeping alone in her dwelling at the remembrance of Jesus. An angel appeared before her. He announces to her that she will be separated from the body in three days, and puts into her hand an olive branch, gathered in paradise, to be carried before her coffin; "Thy son," said he to her, "awaits thee with the thrones and the angels and all the virtues of heaven." Mary begs that the apostles may be brought together near her at that supreme moment. The angel promises it. She takes the palm branch, goes to pray on the Mount of Olives in order that Gehenna may have no power over her, and then returns into her home. John was preaching one Sunday at Ephesus when of a sudden, about the third hour, a great earthquake takes place. A cloud carries him off, and goes and puts him down at the door of the house inhabited by Jesus's mother. He enters: Mary, glad to see him, discloses to him the bad designs of the Jews, who propose to burn his body, and shows him the luminous palm branch which she will have carried before her the day of her funeral.

John desires to have with him all the disciples and the apostles of the Lord. Then, by the divine will, the apostles are transported in the clouds from the countries where they preached the gospel, and meet each other before the door of the house. They salute each other, asking for what reason the Lord assembles them in this place. Peter invites Paul to pray first, in order that it may be revealed to them; the apostle of the Gentiles replies that it is for Peter to begin, since he precedes the other apostles in the apostolate, while he, Paul, is only the least of them. When they have prayed in common, John comes to acquaint them with the facts. They enter, salute Mary, and pass three days with her in consoling her and praising God. The third day, at the third hour, a deep sleep seizes all the persons who are in the house, excepting the apostles and three virgins, Mary's companions. Jesus comes, surrounded with a company of angels; a brilliant light shines forth; the angels sing a hymn in praise of the Saviour, and the Saviour says to his mother: "Come, my elect one, my precious pearl enter into the abode of the everlasting life."

Mary, prostrating herself, asks Christ to preserve her from the insults of Satan and the evil spirits. Jesus replies that, according to the common law of human nature she will see Satan at the hour of her death, as he himself saw him, but that Satan will not be able to injure her, because he has no right over her, and her son is at her side Mary lays herself on her bed, and dies. A brilliant light shines in her eyes. The Lord orders the apostles to carry the body to the east of the city, where they will lay it in a new sepulchre. He confides his mother's soul to the archangel Michael; the archangel Gabriel follows her. Christ enters into Paradise with the angels. The three virgins wash Mary's body. When stript of its clothes, it throws out a dazzling light, which disappears afterwards in the degree in which she is covered with grave-clothes. The visage of the Virgin is white as lilies. It exhales so sweet an odour, that nothing can be like it. The apostles place the body in the coffin. Peter and Paul carry it off. John, in his quality of verger, walks before with the luminous palm branch. The other apostles sing melodiously. A crown of clouds hovers over the coffin; a choir of angels sing a sweet canticle in the clouds, and on the earth delightful notes reverberate. The people, astonished, leave the city to the number of fifteen thousand persons. When they are told that it is the funeral procession of Mary, mother of Jesus, a prince of the Jewish priests, raging with anger, attempts to overturn the coffin and the body. But his arms are withered, and remain attached to the couch. The apostles, raising the coffin, it remains suspended during the journey, a prey to violent pains. The angels strike all the people with blindness. The prince of the priests implores Peter for his deliverance. The apostle imposes on him the condition of embracing Christianity. The suppliant is eager to comply. The cortege stops; his hands become free, and, after kissing the couch, he obtains a complete cure. Peter causes him to take the palm carried by John, commanding him to enter the city, of which all the inhabitants have become blind. He is to place the palm on the eyes of those who shall believe, and they will be healed. Those who will not believe will remain blind. The things take place as he has said. The prince of the priests then carries back the palm to the apostles. Mary's body is carried to the prescribed spot in the valley of Jehosaphat. The apostles place it in a new sepulchre; they seat themselves at the door, according to the order of the Lord. Jesus comes with an innumerable army of angels. He reminds the apostles that he has promised them that after he had taken his place on the seat of his majesty they should be seated on twelve thrones, and judge the tribes of Israel. He then asks them what he ought to do in regard to that woman chosen among the twelve tribes to bear him in her womb. Peter and the rest reply that as a member of the Trinity he knew all things before the ages; that for them his servants, it seems proper that he should raise his mother's body, and conduct her full of joy into the celestial abode. Jesus says: "Your word shall be done." He commands the archangel Michael to bring Mary's soul. Gabriel removes the stone which seals the monument. At the voice of the Lord Mary rises from the tomb, and, prostrating herself, blesses the name of the Redeemer of the World, the God of Israel. The Lord gives her a kiss, and charges the angels to conduct her into paradise. He embraces the apostles, wishing them peace. Then rising on a cloud, he enters heaven with the angels, who escort the blessed Mother of God. The apostles, in their turn, are carried up in clouds, and taken back to the places of their preaching.

We shall not criticise an elucubration that is purely fantastic. Let us remark solely that this apocryphal piece is the sole basis for the history of the assumption. The author makes Mary die at Jerusalem, in the paternal house of John, which she has not quitted since the ascension of her son. Her death took place the twenty-second year after that event, or in the year 55 of the Christian era. The Virgin was then seventy years of age. Three days after she is raised by Christ, and carried into heaven by angels.

This legend has received a number of additions and variations. Some make the mother of Jesus die at the age of seventy-two; others, on the contrary, represent her as only sixty, and place her decease twelve years after the ascension; according to others, she died, not at Jerusalem, but at Ephesus, whither she accompanied the apostle John; others declare that she did not die in this place or in that, but that she was carried into heaven without ceasing to live. A narrative relates that the apostle Thomas was absent at the moment of the assumption. When he arrives, he refuses to believe what he is told about it. Then there falls into his hands, as coming from on high, the girdle which was round the Virgin's body.

According to another relation, Mary was not raised in view of the apostles. After they had placed her body in the sepulchre, they remain at the door during three days, while the angels sing hymns around to the praise of the mother of God. The third day Thomas joins them. He had not been on the spot at the time of the decease. He requests that the tomb may be opened in order that he may render a last homage to the mother of the Word. An opening having been made, they find in the sepulchre not the slightest trace of the sacred body, but solely the funereal linen. The articles are intact and in order as if the body had just left them. An unutterable odour proceeds from them. The apostles hence conclude that Mary's body has received immortality before the general resurrection, and that Christ has had her carried by the angels into the purest places of the celestial regions, not wishing that she should rise at the same time as other human beings, even the most illustrious and the most worthy of praise. Despite these divergencies, inevitable in a fabulous recital which each modified at pleasure, the supernatural facts of the legend did not lead to its being questioned until the sixteenth century. The middle ages embellished it still more, and made it an object of admiration, as all the other popular and monkish fictions on Christ, the Virgin, and the Saints.

In these superstitious times it was not more difficult to fabricate relics of Mary than to get the legend of the assumption received. They are soon produced in all parts. The Empress Pulcheria (450-57) deposits some in two churches built in Constantinople in honour of the Virgin—namely, in one, her tomb, her grave-clothes, her girdle; in the other, her portrait, which Luke had taken in her lifetime, her distaff, and the linen of the Saviour. Under the reign of Leo the Ancient (457-74) the discovery of Mary's garments took place. It is related that at the assumption she had left them with a Jewess who was either a virgin or a widow. In the fifth century this treasure was in the hands of another woman of Israel, from whom it was stolen. These garments were put into the emperor's hands, who does not fail to construct a temple to receive them.

Different churches fancy they possess portions of the palm branch which was borne by the apostle John at Mary's interment. Some affirm that they possess the Virgin's comb, a small portion of her hair, the belt she put on the infant Jesus. The history of John the apostle naturally connected itself with that of the mother of Christ. The glorification of the one in the fifth and the sixth centuries indicated the other to the imagination of the legendists. As long as Mary was only a simple woman, whose existence was not known in the times after the ascension, they did not trouble themselves with her relations to the disciple to whom, according to the common opinion, her son had entrusted her in his dying moments. But at the time of the apotheosis of the Virgin, ignorance of the least detail of their life is not allowed. The legends undertake to supplement the silence of the Scripture and history in regard to him and her. In the twofold belief held then by the Græco-Latin Church of the dispersion of the apostles over the world, and the identity of the two Johns, the apostle and the presbyter, they represented the former as preaching at Ephesus, ascribing to him all which relates to the second, who had resided in that city during the latter quarter of the first century. Thus they ascribed to Zebedee's son the struggles of the presbyter with Cerinthus, his banishment to Patmos, his return into the province of Asia, events which belong to the reigns of Domitian, Nerva, Trajan, the period in which the presbyter flourished. But the history of this last furnishing nothing for the anterior times, the same void was reproduced in the history or the legend of the apostle who bore his name. During the first four centuries the writers restricted themselves to saying of him that he had preached the gospel at Ephesus after the dispersion of the apostles, without stating at what time, and without citing any fact which went beyond the period of the presbyter. It was thus allowable to believe that the apostle had not appeared in that city till after the departure of Paul, which prevented contradiction with the *Acts of the Apostles*, and the epistles of the preacher to the Gentiles. No longer could this be the case when legend undertook to recount of Mary facts which passed from the day of the ascension to that of her death. We have just seen that the worshippers of Mary do not agree as to the time and place of the last event. Did Mary die at the age of sixty (the year 45), of seventy-two (57), or at some intermediate date? Did she die at Jerusalem or Ephesus? If she died at Jerusalem at the age of sixty, we may imagine that John did not leave her. Do you prolong her existence a certain number of years beyond the legend, the dispersion of the apostles does not permit those who receive it to suppose that Zebedee's son remained in the holy city till Mary's decease; and the confusion of the two Johns then leads to his being made to reside at Ephesus. Thus the legendists, who do not suspect what they do, are eager to install him there with the Virgin or without her. But this fiction is belied by the *Acts of the Apostles*, and by the epistles of Paul, which demonstrate that neither John nor any of the twelve went either to Ephesus or to any other part of Asia Minor, or of Greece, before or during the preaching of Paul in those countries, a work which lasted to the year 59 A.D. The legends which make Mary sojourn in Jerusalem had not much trouble to find her a dwelling there. They simply placed her in the house where Jesus celebrated the last Supper. If we believe them it is in that house that the apostles afterwards remained, and that took place divers facts related in the Acts, such as the appearance of Jesus in the midst of his disciples, the confirmation of the faith of Thomas, the descent of the Holy Spirit, the election of Matthias (Acts i. 23), the choice of the seven deacons, &c. That house, according to the legend of *the Assumption of Mary*, was the property of the parents of John the apostle. Other narratives, however, have it that it was purchased by him after the death of his father. They make Zebedee a rich and illustrious fisherman, and it is with the price of his part in the succession that John acquired the house inhabited by the Virgin. It is added that he sold that hereditary portion to the high priest Caiaphas, which has the advantage of explaining how the apostle was known to that functionary, and was able to introduce Peter into the court of Caiaphas at the time of the passion of Jesus. Various other stories were put forth touching the apostle John. Some see in him the bridegroom of the marriage feast at Cana; while others, that Mary had been confided to his care because he had always remained a bachelor. Others send John to spread the gospel among the Parthians, and even in Hindostan. A passage in the fourth gospel (xxi. 22, 23) gave occasion to several opinions as to the end of that apostle. Jesus in speaking of the beloved apostle, had said, "If I will that he tarry till I come, what is that to thee?" Some have concluded that John, without dying, ascended into heaven with his flesh and bones. Others believe that he died to revive and rise again immediately, in the same manner as Mary. A legend relates that John having come to the age of ninety-nine, Christ came to him to announce that he would die the following Sunday, five days after his appearance. The Sunday being come, a crowd assembles in a church built in John's name. The apostle says mass at cockcrow, and preaches to the people till the third hour; then by his order a square grave is dug near the altar, the earth being thrown out of the church. He goes down into the grave, returns thanks to the Lord, commends the faithful to His care, and entreats him to open to him the door of life without his being troubled with the presence of the prince of darkness. His prayer being at an end, a light whose splendour was intolerable shines upon him during more than an hour. The grave is then found full of incense, and does not cease to produce it. A great number of miracles are performed.

We have seen in the fourth chapter of the first book, what the legendists, at the time of the Council of Nice, said of the sojourn of Peter and Paul at Rome, and of their simultaneous punishment. In posterior ages, there was added a crowd of narratives, more or less stupid, but which we must not pass in silence. The two apostles had then died at Rome, according to the legend of the fourth century, and were interred, one in the Vatican, the other in the Via Ostia. According to Caius, you saw in those places their trophies which Eusebius made into their tombs. Everything goes well in the matter as long as there was no thought of displacing the remains of Peter and Paul. But the superstitious spirit of Paganism, which seized the Church after the conversion of the emperors, brings with it, among other things, the love and the worship of relics. Has a discovery of relics been made, the bones are transferred in great pomp into the churches, and offered to the veneration of believers. It is easy to understand that great value would be attached to the relics of the two chief apostles; accordingly, in the sixth century, if not sooner, the design of transferring the relics of the apostles came to maturity. Then the truth becomes manifest, despite the legend, that the bodies of Peter and Paul are not in the monuments of which Eusebius and Caius speak. What is to be done? The embarrassment is the greater because, at this time Rome has ceased to be the capital of the empire and the patriarch of Constantinople, its successful rival, takes the title of universal bishop. It is then asserted that the bodies were originally deposited in those monuments, but that the bodies had been removed. A legend recounts that about the middle of the third century, Greeks having stolen them in order to carry them into the East, a great earthquake, according to some, the voice of idols, according to others, aroused the people who rushed after the robbers. They, stricken with fear, threw the bones into a well, or into a catacomb, whence they were afterwards taken. This supposition of a robbery made by the Greeks which would have no sense in the third century when Constantinople did not yet exist, is entertainable in the sixth when the Church of that city disputed the supremacy with Rome. These bones found in a well or a catacomb, indicate that the pretended remains of Peter and Paul were, like those of so many other saints, taken at hazard from a common burial ground, or from the vast ossuary of the Roman catacombs. Under the recital of this legend, one discovers the truth, that is, that Peter and Paul were never interred in Rome, from the simple fact, that neither the one nor the other died there. When once it was admitted in the legends that Peter had been for twenty-five years bishop of the capital of the empire, legendists began to invent histories narrating what he did during that long period, the circumstances of the struggle of the two apostles with Simon, and the death of all three. Let us give a brief analysis of these imaginations which are as gross as the ages which produced them. Simon, conquered by Peter in Syria, throws his magical books into the sea and betakes himself to Rome, where he wishes to pass himself off as a god. Peter, following his traces, arrives there in the fourteenth year of Claudius (44), and remains there for twenty-five years. Peter institutes bishops to assist himself, namely, Linus and Cletus, one for the interior of the city, the other for the outside (*extra muros*). He converts a large number of persons, and cures many that are sick; among the baptized persons, mention is made of Livia, Nero's wife, and Agrippina, wife of the governor Agrippa, as well as four concubines of the last. Paul in his turn arrives in Rome, and puts himself in conference with the Jews, who go to inform Peter of his arrival. The two apostles preach the gospel in common. The emperor takes very much to Simon, whom he regards as his support. One day the magician suddenly changed aspect in his presence; he took now the air of an old man, now that of a young one; and Nero believed that he was a son of God. Simon requests that his head may be cut off, announcing that he should rise on the third day. The order having been given, the magician substitutes in his place a ram whose head the executioner cuts off and regards it as that of Simon. The third day, the latter presents himself before the emperor, stating that he has risen; Nero believes him to be veritably God's son. A demon, taking the figure of the magician, harangues the people in his favour. The Romans have such a veneration for this cheat, that they raise to him a statue with this inscription: "To Simon the holy god." The magician kept chained at his door an enormous dog who barred the way to those who did not suit him. Peter, having presented himself, detaches the dog and gives him a human voice, in order that he might announce to his master the presence of the servant of Christ. The animal goes to fulfil his message and returns to call the apostle; he enters and remains for a long time in conference with Simon. Peter and Paul denounce to Nero the enchantments of the impostor, in whom, says Peter, there are two natures, that of man and that of the devil. Simon threatening him with his angels, Peter replies, that far from fearing them, he is dreaded by them. Nero is astounded that a person is braved who proves his divinity by miracles. "If," says Peter, "the deity is in him, let him tell me what I think." Then, speaking in the emperor's ear, he begs him to let him have secretly a barley loaf. When he has received the loaf, the apostle blesses it, and places it under his cloak; then he asks Simon to tell him what he, Peter, has thought, said, and done. Simon, on the contrary, desires that his own thought be disclosed by his antagonist. Peter replies that he will do what the other has thought. Simon, furious, cries out: "Let the dogs come and devour him." Suddenly there appear enormous dogs who are about to rush upon Peter; he presents to them the blessed bread, and forthwith the dogs take to flight.

Simon offers to raise the dead. The two adversaries are conducted to a young man who has just expired. The penalty of death is decreed against that one of the two who does not succeed. Simon, by his enchantments, makes the dead man move his head. The bystanders, astounded, prepare to stone Peter. The apostle demands, that if the deceased is restored to life, he should rise up, speak, and walk. Simon is removed from the corps. The deceased remains motionless. Peter, standing up, makes a prayer, and in the name of Christ, orders the young man to rise and walk; he is immediately obeyed. Then the people are ready to stone Simon. But Peter intercedes, saying, that Simon is punished sufficiently by his defeat. Marcellus, one of his disciples, receives frequent visits from Peter. Displeased at these relations, Simon binds to the door of Marcellus a very great dog to intercept the passage. The apostle being come, detaches the dog, which pursues Simon, throws him down, and is on the point of strangling him. Peter hastens to his aid. The animal, without wounding Simon, tears his clothes to pieces, and leaves him naked on the soil. The magician, ashamed of the affront, remains a year without reappearing. Marcellus, witnessing these things, becomes a follower of Peter. Having regained the good graces of the emperor, Simon informs the people that he is about to rise to heaven, the earth not being worthy to serve for his abode. He ascends to the top of a tower, others say to the summit of the Capitol; whence, crowned with laurels, he throws himself off and begins to fly. (According to another version, he rushes not on wings, but in a chariot of fire, like Elijah). At the sight, Nero accuses Peter and Paul of imposture. Paul then bids the demons who bear the magician through the air not to sustain him any longer, he falls and perishes, his head being smashed (otherwheres, it is said, that he did not die forthwith, but had his thighs broken; going afterwards to Brindisium he was led by shame and grief to hurl himself from an elevated summit.)

Nero, exasperated at the death of his favourite, throws Peter and Paul into the Mamertine prison, under the guard of two soldiers named Processus and Martinianus. They were both converted by Peter. They open the prison and let him out. After having long refused to quit Rome, he finally makes up his mind to it at the urgency of the brethren. At the gate of the city he meets with Jesus, who tells him that he is going to Rome to be crucified a second time. Peter says, " Lord, I will return to be crucified with thee." Jesus re-ascends to heaven, leaving the mark of his foot imprinted on the earth. The apostle, understanding that martyrdom is required of him, returns into the city. Seized by Nero's satellites, he is led before the Governor Agrippa; his person shines like the sun. Peter and Paul are led to death together. One, as a stranger, was to be put on a cross, the other to be beheaded as a Roman citizen. The Jews and the Pagans spit in their faces. They are separated. Peter, being come near the cross, asks to be affixed to it with his head downwards—it not being proper for the servant to suffer crucifixion as his master. The executioners consent. The people are disposed to kill Nero and the Governor in order to deliver the apostle, but the latter entreats them not to hinder his martyrdom. The by-standers shed tears. The Lord opens their eyes. They see angels with crowns of roses and lillies around the cross to which Peter is fastened. The apostle glorifies the Lord, commends the faithful to him, and renders his last sigh. Marcellus and Apuleius, his disciples, take the body down from the cross, cover it with aromatics, and bury it in a place called the Vatican, near the triumphal road. On his side Paul converts three soldiers charged to conduct him to punishment. They desire to set him at liberty, but Paul refuses. Other soldiers, sent by Nero, conduct him beyond the walls of the city. A woman named Platilla, who was of the number of the apostles, lends a veil to bandage his eyes at the moment of the execution. The head of Paul, in falling, pronounces the name of Jesus. Milk flows from his wounds instead of blood; an odour of the sweetest kind exhales from his body; the executioner wraps the apostle's head in Platilla's veil. A female servant of the Lord, called Lucina, embalms Paul's body, and buries it on the Via Ostia, two miles from Rome.

The same day Dionysius the Areopagite (Acts xvii. 34), sees Peter and Paul, who hold each other's hands, and enter the city clad in splendid garments. They show themselves to Platilla in the same vestments, and their heads surrounded by an incomparable light, they bring her her veil all full of blood. Paul had announced to Nero that he would appear to him alive three days after his execution. He keeps his word, and the emperor, affrighted, ceases to persecute the Christians. The soldiers who had led the apostle to punishment are baptised near his tomb by Titus and Luke. Paul's head, mixed with a crowd of others in the midst of a valley, could not be recognised in the number. It is thrown into a common ditch. It was at a later time taken out and abandoned in fields, where a pastor picks it up and carries it into his own house. The bishop recognises it by an ineffable light which radiates around it. The faithful transport it on a tablet of gold. It is placed near the body of Paul; the head adjusts itself. We have said in speaking of the pretended theft of the bodies of the apostles that the plunderers threw them into a well to escape pursuit. It became a question to draw them out. At the moment of their extraction great peals of thunder resound, accompanied with fearful lightning. As they cannot distinguish which are the bones of each of them, a voice from heaven cries that the smaller are those of Peter, and the larger those of Paul—(a tradition of the earliest ages has it on the contrary that the smaller size belonged to Paul). The bones were got together separately, and deposited in two churches erected to receive them. (According to Pope Gregory the body of Peter was preserved in the church of his name). Others relate that Pope Sylvester (314-35) put the bones, small and great, into scales, and divided them in two halves between the two churches.

Such are the old wives' fables which were put forth respecting the apostles Peter and Paul; such are the follies propagated by the Apocryphal books and welcomed by the credulity of the populations. To complete the picture we must mention the fictitious travels of Peter, not only in Asia Minor, Greece, and the islands, but also in Egypt, the Thebaid, Africa, Spain, and even the island of Britain. The aim of these travels had for object, among other things, to ascribe to that apostle the foundation of the principal churches as well as the government of the whole Christian world, and as a consequence to legitimate the universal power of the Bishops of Rome, his pretended successors. The other apostles of Jesus did not escape from the zeal of the legendists of our present period. Without entering into details, we mention the crucifixion of Andrew in Achaia preceded by his different combats; the translation of Bartholomew from the Indies into Armenia, where he suffers death, in what place is not clearly known; the apostleship of Philip in Gaul, the journeys of James the elder in Spain and in other countries of the west. Let us again observe that in regard to Mary and the twelve apostles the student must restrict himself to the information supplied by the Scriptures; all the rest are fictions and fables. We

shall aid the reader's memory by referring here, relatively to
the first century, the tales put forth respecting the Magi,
respecting the infants slain by Herod, the number of which
is fixed at fourteen thousand; respecting one of the two
thieves converted and baptised in anticipation; respecting
the soldier who pierced the side of Christ, and who is perpetuated under the name of Longinus; respecting the
banishment of Pilate to Vienne in Gaul, and respecting that
lake of Helvetia, where every year he appears in the attire
of a judge; respecting the Emperor Augustus, who constructed in the Capitol an altar to the first-born god, who
refused to be called lord because the Son of God was about
to be born, and to whom the Virgin Mary appeared in the
higher air, holding her son in her arms, &c. Among the
fables spread abroad respecting the personages of the second
century, we recall the martyrdom of Clement of Rome with
all its miraculous circumstances—a martyrdom unknown
before Gregory of Tours and the Epitome of the Recogni-
tions; the martyrdom of Romulus, and of ten or eleven
thousand Christian soldiers who, under the reign of Trojan
or Hadrian, were crucified on Mount Ararat. In the
number of fictions which refer to persons of the third
century we mention: The History of the Seven Sleepers of
Ephesus. Seven Christians having hid themselves in a
cavern near that city, at the time of the persecution of
Decius, were discovered and enclosed by a wall built at the
mouth; there they either slept or died of hunger, to revive
near two hundred years afterwards, under the reign of
Theodosius the Younger. They were presented to the
bishop and the emperor, and at last died a natural death.
The extermination of the Theban Legion. That legion was
first decimated not far from the Lake Leman, then entirely
massacred by the order of Maximian for having rejected an
idolatrous form of oath, and refused to persecute the faithful. In this martyrdom Maurice, the head of the legion,
and his companions Candidus, Victor, and Exuperus were
distinguished. Their relics were deposited at Aguane,
where was founded the monastery of Saint Maurice, celebrated by heaps of miracles. The Dukes of Savoy pride

themselves on possessing a sword and a ring which are supposed to have belonged to this Maurice.

The discovery and transference of relics, true or false, of male saints and female saints, of ancient or modern date, have been an abundant source of fables and legends from the time of the Council of Nice. In speaking, according to Eusebius of Cæsarea, of the journey of the empress Helena into Palestine, and of the discovery of the sepulchre of Christ, we have not seen that the author makes any mention of disinterred crosses. Now, Eusebius, Bishop of the metropolis of Palestine, was doubtless on the spot when the diggings took place in the presence of the aged empress. Had he been absent, the discovery of a cross regarded as that of the Saviour would have made too much noise not to reach his ears. His absolute silence in this respect does not allow us to doubt that the whole is a pure fable. Besides, we do not see in Scripture anything which justifies the belief that anything but the body was buried. The wood on which criminals were hung was accursed among the Jews. Each sufferer carried his own cross, and that cross was taken away when it had answered its purpose. Besides, Jesus was put to death on the ordinary place of executions, and they were then frequent. Some years later they crucified around the city as many as five hundred Jews a day; had it been the custom to inter the crosses, not one, or two, or three, but a multitude would have been found there. Nevertheless, the history of the discovery of the true cross soon spreads abroad. Cyril, Bishop of Jerusalem, says, in a letter written to the Emperor Constance about five-and-twenty years after Helena's visit, that, in the time of Constantine, the salutary wood of the cross had been found in Jerusalem, but without entering into detail. Was not this a rumour? Legend soon lays hold of it; the story circulates first in the west. After Cyril, Latin writers speak of it first. Not only the cross of the Saviour is in question, but that of each of the thieves. Now the difficulty was to determine on which Christ had suffered. What if the gallows of a brigand was consecrated instead of the cross of Christ! But at this time there was no lack of miracles. A funeral procession is passing. The corpse is touched by two of the crosses without result; contact with the third makes the dead arise, and gives him the opportunity of mixing with the spectators. Here evidently is the true cross! A narrative represents it to have been recognised by the writing which Pilate had put on it. According to others, on the contrary, no writing was on the cross when found. The legend then goes back into the East with additions and variations. According to the historian Socrates, it is on a woman long sick and reduced to extremity that the miracle was attempted under the advice of the Bishop of Jerusalem. The two first crosses prove powerless, as might be expected, but at the touch of the third, the disease is radically removed. Independently of the three crosses and the writing, legend discovers also the three nails which pierced the hands and feet of Christ. They were put into Constantine's helmet and the bit of his horse. There are inferior details. Jewish Rabbis were compelled to disclose the place where the true cross was interred. The nature of the wood is particularised. According to these the wood came from a tree in paradise; according to others it was of four kinds,—palm, cypress, olive and cedar. The wood of the cross has been multiplied indefinitely, and dispersed over the world. There are few Catholic churches that do not fancy they possess a portion. Veritable worship is paid to it. As connected with the discovery of the cross, we must add the winding-sheet of Christ, which several churches pretend to possess; the imprint of his feet on the Mount of Olives left at the moment of his ascension; Veronica's handkerchief; the portrait of Jesus, discovered in the sixth century at Edessa, whither it had been sent to King Abgarus. In imitation of Helena the Western Christians who visited Palestine, had nothing more at heart than to search for holy relics, and as they paid a good price for them, the orientals were too wise not to furnish them according to their wishes. They had merely to find some remains of human bodies, to feign a revelation to work miracles—a task always easy with superstitious spectators. Thus, about the year 415, a priest named Lucian, having discovered near a village twenty miles from Jerusalem four coffins containing human bones, made them into the relics of Stephen, the first martyr, Nicodemus, Gamaliel, and Gamaliel's son. The three last were left to the church of the village; but the relics of Stephen were transferred with great pomp to the Church of Zion. Lucian, however, keeps some parcels, some of which he gives to Avitus, a Spanish priest, who was then in Palestine. Avitus confides the precious gift to Orosius, to carry to the Bishop of Brague, in Spain. Orosius not being able to land in this last-mentioned country, remains sometime at Mahon, in the isle of Minorca, where Stephen's relics signalise themselves by a crowd of miracles. Some monks of Uzala, in Africa, having heard speak of them, succeed, one knows not how, in procuring relics of the same saint, namely, a phial of his blood, and some small fragments of his bones. Calamus and other African cities have equally relics of Stephen. These relics of Uzala, Calamus, and other cities perform miracles as much as those of Orosius.

The reputed body of Stephen, which was first transferred to Jerusalem, passed afterwards to Constantinople under the reign of Theodosius the Younger. But could Rome endure that such a treasure remained in the possession of its rival? A legend soon tells that Eudoxia, daughter of Theodosius, was tormented by the devil, and could not be cured except Stephen's body went to Rome. It is agreed to exchange it for that of Laurentius. On the arrival of the remains of the first martyr, the two bodies are put in presence of each other; Laurentius pushes himself into a corner of his tomb in order to make room for Stephen. The Greeks, according to the agreement, wish to carry away the body of Laurentius. The latter obstinately refuses to be removed. Thus Rome keeps the two saints, whose union took place in 425.

But divers parts are wanting in the body of Stephen. At the time of the translation the right arm had been given to the inhabitants of Capua. The Church of Besançon prides itself on having an arm of Stephen. It is not said whether it is the right or the left. A number of other cities glorify themselves also in possessing relics of this same saint.

The discovery of the head of John the Baptist is not less celebrated. This head is discovered for the first time in the year 393 by Theodosius the Great, in a village near Chalcedon, whither it had been brought in the time of the emperor Valens. Sixty years later it is again found at Emesa in Phenicia, in a cavern near which some monks had settled. The discovery is made by their Abbot, who deposits the relic in a church which the monastery built on that occasion. Since then you hear no more said of the head discovered by Theodosius; the monks carry the day over the emperor. However the head of the Saint travels in the sequel and is multiplied. A legend makes it come into Gaul in the reign ot Pepin; at present different churches possess each a head of John the Baptist, which they carefully preserve. After the head of the precursor his body could not be neglected. According to the legend it was buried by his disciples at Sebaste in Palestine, where it performed many miracles. In the time of the emperor Julian, the bones were dispersed, then burnt by the Gentiles, and the ashes thrown to the winds. But while they got together the bones to burn them, some monks secretly took possession of some of them which they brought to the bishop of Jerusalem. These bones were then transferred to Alexandria, and placed in the temple of Serapis, turned into a church of Saint John. Thence they passed to Genoa in the middle ages. The finger which anointed Christ was in the number of the bones thrown into the fire by the Gentiles, but the flames could not consume it and the monks preserved it. This same finger was, it is said, carried by Saint Thecla into Europe, into the Alps according to some, into Normandie according to others. Among the discoveries and transferences effected in the ninth century those of Mark and James the elder hold prominence. The preaching of Mark at Alexandria is a pure legend, we have said. But even those by whom it is admitted agree that all that is most reported of that evangelist is uncertain and fabulous. Nothing is known of the nature and place of his death, nor of the place of his interment. Eutychius even reports that his body was burned. None the less his body had a tomb at Alexandria Under the reign of Leo the Armenian (813-20), some Venetian merchants, seducing the guardians by gifts and promises, obtained the saint's relics. Some declare that they received the body of an Egyptian instead of that of Mark But the identity of the evangelist was duly demonstrated by revelations and miracles, as well as by the sweet odour which exhaled from him as from all the sacred relics. The precious body is taken into Venice which constructs a basilica to receive it. Thus is it that Mark became the perpetual patron of that country whose inhabitants assert that he brought the gospel thither. About the same time, under the reign of Alphonso the Chaste (792-842) the relics of James the elder are found in Spain. Human remains having been found near Iria Flavia, on the frontiers of Galicia, a brilliant light reveals to the bishop of that city that it is the body of James, son of Zebedee. Miracles confirm the truth of the matter. The relics are transferred in pomp into the neighbouring city which receives the name of Compostella. How could the body of James, put to death at Jerusalem in the year 44, be buried at the extremity of Spain ? A legend undertakes to explain it. It recounts that the disciples being scattered after Stephen's death, (the disciples, yes, but not the twelve apostles), James goes into Spain to spread the gospel, (later on he is made to travel into Gaul, Britain, and Hibernia). The apostle getting little fruit from his preaching in Spanish lands, chooses nine disciples ; he leaves two of them in the country and returns into Judea with the remaining seven. When he has perished by order of Herod Agrippa, his disciples receive his body, and not daring to inter it from fear of the Jews, they put it on board a vessel which they abandon to the care of Providence. That vessel traverses the seas guided by an angel, and comes to land in Galicia where the body is buried, to be discovered in the ninth century, and to form the glory of Compostella, that vast reservoir of miracles for the use of the entire world. The instances of the discovery and transference of relics which we have given must suffice. We could recount many others, but with few exceptions they all resemble each other. The process does not change ; you find in some place human bodies or simply bones, either through chance or because you have previously placed them there. Visions reveal to you to what apostle or disciple, to what martyr, to what saint, belong these relics, which always announce themselves by a sweet odour, whether they are old or fresh ; then come a plenteous shower of miracles, attested by monks, old wives, fools, and rogues.

But it is not solely for the glory of relics that are produced visions, apparitions, predictions, prodigies, miracles. There are such phenomena for all circumstances and for all wants ; miracles of saints in paradise, miracles of saints on the earth, miracles of bishops, abbots, monks, hermits and nuns ; miracles for the confirmation of new superstitions, such as the intercession of the Virgin and the saints, purgatory, masses for the dead, the worship of images ; miracles for the foundation of churches and monasteries, for the glorification of monks ; miracles for donations to the clergy, for the exaltation of its benefactors and the punishment of its adversaries ; miracles for the Episcopal power, for the supremacy and temporal sovereignty of the popes ; miracles at every hour, for every object, in every place.

We enter on the middle ages.

Book the Third.

THE CHURCH OF THE MIDDLE AGES.

(891-1517.)

CHAPTER I.

FROM THE SCHISM OF PHOTIUS TO THE TERMINATION OF THE CRUSADES.—(891-1291.)

SUMMARY.—The Successors of Charles the Bald to the Empire—Dependence of the Popes—Their bad Characters—Theodora and her two Daughters—The Othos—Crescentius—Sylvester II.—Approaching end of the World—Conversion of the Hungarians—Henry III. (the Black)—Leo the IX.—Berenger—The Normans in Italy—Greco-Latin Schism, Michael Cerularius—Henry IV.—Rule for the Election of Popes—Gregory VII.—Celibacy of the Clergy—Investitures—Struggle of the Priesthood and the Empire—The Countess Matilda —Abjection of Henry IV.—Rodolph of Suabia—Henry vanquished, excommunicated, and deposed—The Anti-pope Guibert—Pretensions of Gregory VII. ; *Dictatus papæ*—Death of Gregory VII.—Urban II. Revolt of Conrad—The Crusades—The Saracens driven from Sicily— Capture of Toledo—the Cid—Fatimite Kalifs—Seldjukide Turks— Capture of Jerusalem—Revolt of Young Henry—Death of Henry IV. —William le Roux—Disagreements of Henry V. with the See of Rome —Agreement in Investitures—First General Council of the Lateran (the ninth Œcumenical of the Latins)—Innocent II. and Anacletus— Bernard, Abbot of Clairvaux—Second General Council of the Lateran (Tenth)—Arnold of Brescia—Abelard—Gilbert de la Porée—Conrad— Louis the Younger—Frederic Barbarossa—Alexander III.—Thomas Becket—Third General Council of the Lateran (Eleventh) ; Election of Popes—Saladin—Philip Augustus—Richard Cœur de Lion—Innocent III.—Philip of Suabia and Otho of Saxony—John Lackland— Latin Empire of Constantinople—Manicheans—Peter de Bruys— Henry—Vaudois—Crusades against the Albigenses—Fourth General Council of the Lateran (Twelfth) ; Begging Monks—Inquisition— Frederic II.—War of the Pope and the Emperor—First General Council of Lyons (Thirteenth)—Louis IX.—The Tartars—Charles of Anjou, King of Sicily—Conradin—Death of Louis IX.—Second General Council of Lyons (Fourteenth) ; union of the Greeks ; Conclave ; Begging Monks—Rodolph of Hapsburg—Sicilian Vespers—Loss of Palestine--End of the Crusades.

THE second book has retraced for us the struggles of Hellenism against the official Church, struggles followed by a kind of fusion, the everlasting debates of the Trinitarians one with another, the invasions of the barbarians of the north, the birth and conquests of Islamism, the empire of Charlemagne and its rapid decline, Rome finally separating itself from the Greeks, and profiting by the ignorance of the nations, to publish fraudulent writings which prepare the way for the spirit of domination; that spirit we shall see in operation in the course of the present book.

At the death of Charles the Bald (877), the imperial dignity was conferred by Pope John VIII., and by the princes of Italy, on Carloman, who dies in the year 880, then on Charles the Fat, whom the Germans depose in 888; these last elect for King of Germany, Arnoul, bastard of Carloman. The empire is a prey to general confusion. All is trouble in Germany, in France, in Italy. The lords make themselves independent. A crowd of petty tyrants seize power. The imperial crown falls to the strongest and the highest bidder. One by the name of Rodolph forms a kingdom in Upper Burgundy. Bosen, Count of Arles, obtains the title of King of Arles and Provence, which he transmits to his son Louis, aged ten years (890). Berenger, Duke of Friul, proclaims himself king in a part of Italy; Guy, Duke of Spoletto, in another. Conqueror of Berenger, Guy is consecrated emperor by Pope Formosus (892), and Lambert, his son, the following year. Arnoul King of Germany, passes the Alps, and puts his two rivals to flight. Formosus crowns him emperor at Rome (896). After the departure of that prince, Berenger resumes the upper hand, and makes himself master of Lombardy; the Italian nobility rising, invite Louis Boson, King of Arles (898). He is crowned emperor by Benedict IV. His competitor surprises him at Verona, and tears out his eyes and sends him back to Provence. Berenger receives in his turn the imperial diadem from John IX. in 904, and from John X. in 915; the great, whom he displeases, chose Rodolph II., King of Transjuran Burgundy. Berenger shuts himself up in Verona, where he dies, assassinated (924). Rodolph is then expelled by the Italians (926). They put on the throne Hugh, King of Arles, who reigns twenty years in Italy, or rather in Lombardy, his kingdom scarcely extending beyond that. Berenger II., or the Younger, becomes insurgent in 939. Compelled to retire into Germany, he returns with troops (941), and seizes a part of Italy. At the death of Lothaire, son and successor of Hugh, he takes the title of King. His tyranny makes him odious. In the midst of all these movements, we do not, despite the pretended donations of Constantine and of the French kings, see that the popes then possessed any temporal sovereignty. Lords more or less powerful reign around them, and under the name of patricians or consuls, govern Rome itself with the concurrence of the great and the people. The bishops of that city are at the mercy of factions which predominate in turn. They dispose of the See of Rome. Most frequently the occupation of it depends on violence, intrigue, simony, poison; it is occupied by false pontiffs, men of abandoned character, and sullied with crimes. The bishops and the other members of the clergy are not less unworthy; their depravity equals their ignorance.

Pope Formosus is succeeded by Boniface VI., who holds the office only a fortnight; then comes Stephen VI., a man capable of any daring (896-97). The latter brings Formosus before a council for having been translated from the See of Porto to that of Rome (this is the first instance of such a translation). The corpse of Formosus is exhumed, and placed in the middle of the assembly, clad in pontifical attire. A defender replies for him. The sentence being passed, he is stript of his sacred garments, three fingers and his head are cut off, and the body is thrown into the Tiber. Stephen VI. is soon deposed himself, put into prison, and strangled. Roman and Theodore II. only pass to the pontifical throne. The body of Formosus is recovered and placed in the burying-place of the popes by order of Theodore. At the death of the last, Rome is divided as to the choice of his successor (898). Some elect Sergius III., others John IX., whose party gets the upper hand. Sergius retires into Tuscany, under the protection of the Marquis of Adalbert. John IX. rehabilitates the memory of Formosus, and rejects

the council of Stephen VI. After him come successively
Benedict IV., who holds the post for four years (900-4);
Leo V., who is driven away at the end of two months;
Christophile, who maintains himself a little more than six;
Sergius III., who had been a refugee for seven years in
Tuscany, is recalled and consecrated (905-12). He holds
as intruders John IX. and the three popes who followed
him, declares himself against Formosus, and approves the
procedure of Stephen II. At the same time Rome is
governed by Theodora, a woman of impure life. Her two
daughters, Theodore the younger and Marozia, are equally
celebrated for their beauty, their intellectual talent, their
dissoluteness, and their crimes. The three exercise absolute
power. They make and unmake popes, as led by their
passions and caprices. To their influence Sergius III. owed
his restoration. He has intimate relations with Marozia,
who bears him a son named John. He will be pope in his
turn. After Sergius come first Anastasius III. and Landon
(913-15). Theodore the younger gets John, Archbishop of
Ravenna, her lover, elected pope, and he rules under the
name of John X. (915-28). Marozia marries Guy, son of
Adalbert, Marquis of Tuscany, although she has had by the
latter a son of the name of Alberic. The new couple rise
against John X., who dies in prison the following year.
Marozia makes John XI. pope (931-36), the son whom
she had had by Sergius. Widow of Guy, she marries King
Hugh, who makes himself master of Rome. But Alberic
drives him away, and shuts up in the Castle Santo Angelo
John XI. his uterine brother, and Marozia, their mother.
She perishes miserably. Alberic maintains himself in spite
of King Hugh, with whom he is reconciled, while marrying
his daughter. He governs Rome until his death (954) in
the quality of patrician. In the interval the see of that
city is occupied by Leo VII. (936), by Martin III. (943),
by Agapetus II. (946). Octavian, son of Alberic, inherits the
power and the dignity of his father, although a clergyman,
and still very young. At the decease of Agapetus II. (956)
he, when scarcely eighteen, makes himself pope, and takes
the name of John XII. (this is the first pope that changes

his name at his succession). In his hands the civil power unites with the spiritual power. Threatened by Berenger II., he implores aid from Otho I., called the Great, who then reigned in German lands.

From the time of Arnoul's expedition, the German kings had not taken any part in the affairs of Italy. Otho I., who succeeds Henry the Fowler, his father (936), at first sustains long wars both against external enemies, Hungarians, Danes, Bohemians, Sclaves, and the great lords of Germany, and even against his son and son-in-law. The Hungarians or Magyars, coming last of the emigrants from the depths of Scythia, appear in Europe about the year 889. They settle in Pannonia, and in the country of the Avares, whence they make excursions into the neighbouring countries. On different occasions they ravage upper Italy, Thuringia, Franconia, Saxony, the upper Rhine, and advance into Lorraine. Driven from Westphalia by Otho I. (936), they fall back on Franconia and upper Germany. The following year they penetrate into France by Champagne, and, traversing Burgundy, they go and sack Italy as far as Capua and Beneventum. Otho held these people in respect, but in the year 954 they are invited by his rebel children, and desolate all Germany. Conquered near Augsburg (955), they retire, and remain in peace in the regions where they are fixed, which then receive the name of Hungary.

The germs of Christianity cast in the preceding century in Sweden and Denmark had all but disappeared. The religion of Odin prevailed there. The Danes, conquered by Otho, find themselves compelled to receive the Christian worship. But the force which imposes it can alone maintain it. If an opportunity offers for throwing off the yoke forthwith they return to their ancient gods. It is not before the second half of the eleventh century that Christianity will be definitively established in the three Scandinavian kingdoms. After a war of fourteen years, Otho succeeds in subjecting Bohemia (950), a large part of the inhabitants embrace the faith of Christ. It is introduced into Poland by Duke Micislas (965). The Sclaves beyond the Elbe, converted by

Charlemagne, returned to their primitive worship. Otho compels them to come back to Christianity, which they will reject again in the following age. With these people obliged to yield to the conqueror, their ancient religion is the symbol of liberty. Otho I. had subdued all his enemies when he is invited over the Alps by Pope John XII. and the Lombard nobles. He penetrates into Italy without resistance (961), passes the winter in Pavia, and the year following goes to Rome, which receives him with great acclamations. The Pope takes an oath of obedience to him as well as the people and the nobility. He restores to the Roman Church the possessions which it claims in Italy, and confirms the pretended donations of Pepin and Charlemagne, but always with the final clause; saving in everything our power and that of our descendants. In a regulation made for the election of the Pope, it is said that there shall always be in Rome commissioners of the emperor, who shall every year report to him how justice is administered by the dukes and the judges, and shall remedy complaints if the Pope does not. Italy and Germany, with some regions of the North, form there the empire called the Western. John XII. soon becomes aware that he has given himself a master more powerful than Berenger II. As soon as the emperor is returned to Pavia he leagues with Adalbert, son of Berenger, whom he makes come to Rome. Otho marches against them; they take to flight. The Romans undertake, under the sanction of an oath, never to elect or ordain a pope without the consent of the emperor. A council of bishops assembles at Rome to try John XII. There is no lack of charges; ordained pope at eighteen, he gave himself up to the fury of his passions, keeping concubines in his palace, and taking the round of all the women on the outside, whether married, widows, or virgins, handsome or not, rich or poor; he was also accused of homicide, perjury, simony, sacrilege, the invocation of devils. John took care not to appear. The council deposes him and puts in his place Leo VIII. (964-65). After the departure of Otho, John XII. returns, re-enters Rome as master, and calls another council, which deposes Leo VIII., and his adherents.

Three months after, John is killed in a gallant adventure with a married woman. The Romans elect Benedict V. Otho brings back Leo VIII. Rome gives up the pope of its choice; he is degraded and exiled by a council held in presence of the emperor. That prince and his descendants are confirmed in the power to choose a successor for the kingdom of Italy, to establish the pope, and to give investiture to the bishops. Otho carries into Germany the antipope Benedict, who dies the following year at Hamburg. Leo VIII. having ceased to live, John XIII. succeeds him with the imperial approbation (965-972). He soon finds himself a butt for the attacks of the Roman nobility, who shut him up in the castle Saint Angelo, then banish him into Campania. He is recalled at the end of eleven months, at the approach of the emperor (966). Otho hangs twelve of the principal men of Rome, authors of the expulsion of the pope.

Otho II., already crowned by the Pope, succeeds to his father in 973. Benedict VI. (972-74), who has taken the place of John XIII., makes himself odious to the Romans.

The consul Crescentius, son of Theodora, and of Pope John X., imprisons him in the castle of Saint Angelo, where he is strangled. Boniface VII. takes possession of the seat. But another party ordains Benedict VII. (975-89). Boniface flees to the emperor of Constantinople. Otho II. passes the Alps (981), and enters into divided Rome. He combats the Saracens and the Greeks with divers results. The latter maintain themselves in Pouille and Calabria. Otho dies at Rome, after having got his son Otho III. elected emperor, aged four years (983).

Benedict VII. is succeeded by John XIV. (984). Boniface VII. hastens up from Constantinople. His faction gains the upper hand. John is deposed, and dies in the castle of Saint Angelo of hunger and wretchedness. Boniface perishes by a sudden death. His successor, John XV. (986-96), who holds for the emperor, is ill-treated by Crescentius, the new consul, grandson of John X. Otho III. passes into Italy. The chief men of Rome receive his orders for the election of a pope in place of John XV. who has just died. He designates Brunon, his nephew, a young man of twenty-four years, who is ordained under the name of Gregory V. (996-99). Otho III., consecrated emperor at Rome, pardons, at the request of Gregory, the consul Crescentius, whom he had resolved to banish. Scarcely has this prince quitted Italy when Gregory is driven away by Crescentius. A Greek of Calabria is put in his place, by name Philagathos, who takes the name of John XVI. Otho returns accompanied by Gregory V. Crescentius fortifies himself in the castle of Saint Angelo; John XVI. takes to flight. He is arrested; his nose and tongue are cut off; his eyes are torn out; and in this state he is led through the streets of Rome, seated on an ass with his face toward the tail of the beast; whose tail he holds in his hands. The castle of Saint Angelo still resisting, safety is promised to the council on the faith of an oath. Crescentius delivers himself up, and the emperor puts him to death (998.)

The same year, Gregory V. pronounces in a Council of Rome, an anathema against Robert, king of France, for marrying his cousin Bertha. This excommunication produces effects unknown in the first ages of the Church, and which recall the holy horror inspired, in the times of the Druids, by the persons who had been interdicted the sacrifices. All the world avoiding him, Robert finally separated from his cousin.

At the death of Gregory V., Otho caused one of the most illustrious men of the period to be elected, his preceptor, Gerbert, under the name of Sylvester II. (999-1004). An Aquitain by birth, Gerbert had been formed in the school of the Saracens of Spain. He possessed all the knowledge of his time, and gave himself principally to the mathematical sciences. The people accounted him a magician. He endeavours, during his pontificate, to revive in the West a taste for letters and the sciences. Italy, France, Germany, experience the impulse; students go for instruction to the Saracens of Africa and Spain, who at that time were the depositaries of science. In the tenth century, an opinion of the approaching end of the world was spread throughout the West. It was expected for the year one thousand, according to a passage in the Apocalypse (Rev. xx. 2). The consternation was general. The rich made immense liberalities to the ecclesiastics and the churches. Others, giving up their property to the monasteries, betake themselves to Palestine, where it was thought Christ would descend. The temples and the other edifices fall into ruins. But in the following century, the nations of France and Italy, restored to hope, will rebuild the churches in a style grander and more handsome; everything will be renewed—the cathedrals, the monasteries, even the chapels of the humblest villages. The idea of the deliverance of Jerusalem begins to assume prominence in men's minds. At his ascent of the papal seat, Sylvester II. writes in favour of the holy war. Otho III. dies in the vicinity of Rome (1002), poisoned, it is said, by the widow of Crescentius, whom he has made his mistress. Henry, duke of Bavaria, succeeds him in Germany under the name of Henry II., and gets himself crowned king of the Lombards at Pavia.

At the same time, the conversion of the Hungarians was accomplished by the efforts of their Duke Stephen, husband of Gisele, sister of Henry II. The Pope Sylvester erects Hungary into a kingdom. This conversion occasions great troubles. The idolaters, subjected by Stephen, rise after his death and upset the country. But king Andrew finally brings all his subjects to the Christian religion (1047). After Sylvester II., the papal chair is occupied by John XVII. (1003), John VIII. (1004), Sergius IV. (1009), all the three confirmed by the emperor. The election of Benedict VIII. (1012-24), is contested. He is driven from Rome, whither is brought Henry II., who makes himself be crowned emperor (1013). Benedict supports the struggles against the Saracens and the Greeks. The former are driven from Tuscany with great losses. The Greeks occupy a part of the province of Beneventum, and threaten Rome herself. The emperor, marching against them at the request of the pope, recovers the cities which they had seized (1022). Benedict VIII. has for successor his brother, who gets himself elected by means of money, and although a layman, sits in the chair under the name of John XIX. (1024-33). Driven away by the principal men of Rome, he is restored in 1033 by Conrad the Salique. At the death of John, the pontificate is purchased for his nephew, aged twelve years, who becomes Benedict IX. The dissolute life of this pope, his rapine and murders, cause him to be driven away in 1044. Sylvester III. by means of money, places himself in the Roman chair. Benedict takes possession of it again the same year; he falls into general contempt, and decides to sell his place to Gratian, a rich man, who occupies it under the name of Gregory VI. According to another version Benedict IX., Sylvester III., and Gregory IV., sharing among themselves the revenues of the Church, occupied the post simultaneously—the one at Saint-Peter's, the other at Sainte-Marie's the elder, and the third in the palace of the Lateran.

Henry III. called the Black, repairs to Italy in order to bring about the re-union of the Church. The three competitors are deposed in a council held at Sutri, near Rome (1046). His place is taken by a Saxon bishop who assumes the name of Clement. II. After having consecrated the empire, that pope follows him into Germany, where he dies at the end of nine months (1047). Benedict IX. is again restored and maintains himself three entire months. But he yields the place at the approach of Damasius II., the choice of whom is made by the emperor; the last pontiff dies the same year. Bruno, bishop of Toul, is elected a Worms and enthroned at Rome under the name of Leo IX (1049-54). He is the first of the popes who keeps his bishopric with that of Rome. Leo IX., inspired by the monk Hildebrand, occupies himself with the reform o abuses. Under pontiffs scandalous in their lives the other members of the clergy possess not the most edifying morals Leo holds divers councils in Italy, in France and in Germany where rigorous laws are published against the excesses then common among the clerics, such as sodomy, adultery simony, usurpations of Churches, exactions and use of arms Other enactments forbid them to marry in an absolute manner.

❦ The attention of the pope is soon called by the discussions which rise on the Sacrament of the Eucharist. The doctrine of the real presence, supported in the middle of the ninth century by Paschase Rathbert, and combatted by the most eminent men, John Scot among others, had remained in the shade since that period. No decision of pope or council having been given for or against, each one was at liberty to entertain his own opinion. But the ignorance of the time allowed few persons to rise to the conception of an oriental figure. The majority held to the positive and in some way material sense. Even its absurdity recommended it to gross minds. The more the thing seemed difficult to believe the more it appeared miraculous. Is not everything possible with God? it was asked. This is a mystery which we must revere. The eleventh century, with the love of studies, brought back the order of controversies. Leutheric, archbishop of Sens, asserts that the body of Christ is received in the supper only by communicants that are in a state of grace (1004). But prudent friends and the secular authority prevent the propagation of that doctrine.

The opinion of John Scot on the Eucharist finds a more resolute defender in Berenger, who brings it forward publicly in the year 1045. This doctor, born at Tours in the commencement of the century, was schoolmaster in the chapter of Saint Martin of that city. He was respected for the extent of his knowledge, his irreproachable character, and his sincere piety. Become archdeacon of Angers, he does not discontinue his teaching in Tours. One of his old disciples, named Bruno, who occupies the episcopal see of the first of those cities, protects him against the attacks of his enemies. The doctrines of Berenger, spreading in France, Italy and Germany, count among their partisans the most enlightened men, clerics and laics. There is, however, a diversity of sentiments among the Berengerians. All agree that the bread and wine are not essentially changed, but they differ for the most part. According to these there is in the Eucharist nothing of the body or the blood of our Lord; it is only a figure and a shadow. According to the others, the body and the blood of Christ are really contained there but hidden under a species of impanation. The writings of Berenger offer arguments for both systems. Certain persons, modifying his ideas, say that the bread and the wine are changed only in part. A third opinion, while admitting an entire transmutation, maintains that if unworthy people offer themselves at the Communion, the body and the blood become bread and wine again. The doctrines of Berenger wounded the beliefs of the crowd and of the greater number of the ecclesiastics. Ardent opposition soon breaks out. In a council at Rome, Leo IX. excommunicates the doctor and his opinions (April 1050). Some months later the same pope holds at Verceil another council at which Berenger does not appear although duly invited. The book of John Scot is there read publicly, condemned, and burnt, and the opinion of Berenger smitten with anathema. The king of France convokes shortly after a council at Paris. The archdeacon, summoned to attend, judges it more prudent to remain with the bishop of Angers. The council anathematises John Scot's book, and unanimously deciding against Berenger and his followers, declares that if they do not retract, the army of France, with the clergy at its head, shall go and besiege them until they submit or are punished with death. Nevertheless the controversy continues.

Some years after, the sub-deacon Hildebrand, come into France for the suppression of simony, presides with another legate over a council held at Tours, in which Lanfranc and Berenger are present (1055). The latter, not venturing to produce his thought, confesses the faith of the council, and is admitted to the communion. He attends in 1059 a council held at Rome, assembled by Nicholas II. Instead of defending himself there, Berenger requests that the faith that should be held be given him in writing. A profession of faith is drawn up, in which it is said, that "the bread and the wine become, after consecration, not a simple sacrament, but the true body and the blood of our Lord Jesus Christ, that they are touched and broken by the hand of the priest, masticated by the teeth of the faithful, not only as a sacrament, but in truth, as are other sensible and bodily objects." Berenger signs and promises all that is required, burning the books more or less suspected which he possesses. The pope, triumphant, dispatches the profession of faith into all lands. But scarcely does the archdeacon recover his liberty, than he reproduces his veritable sentiments. Lanfranc combats them in a book on the eucharist, where he definitively confines himself to saying (as does the Roman Church in our days) that it is a mystery which people must not be allowed to scrutinise.

Gregory VII., to put an end to the dispute, enjoins on Berenger to attend a council at Rome (1078). Then that pope, so absolute in spirit, shows himself full of regard and moderation towards the doctor. Abandoning the purely material confession of Nicholas II. and his council, he is satisfied with a simple declaration which says that "after the consecration the bread put on the altar becomes the true body of Jesus Christ, born of the Virgin, who suffered on the cross, and at present is seated at the right hand of the Father;" and that "the wine placed on the altar becomes the true blood which flowed from the side of Jesus Christ." This formula seemed equivocal to the adversaries of Berenger. The question is agitated afresh, he being present, in another council held in Rome (1079). Most of the bishops there assert that the bread and the wine are substantially changed into the body and blood of Jesus Christ. Some nevertheless declare with the doctor that it is a figure, and that the substantial body is seated at the right hand of the Father. But the majority carries the day. Berenger is reduced to confess that the bread and wine are changed into the body and the blood of Christ, not only as a sign and in virtue of the sacrament, but properly in nature and verity of substance. The pope loads him with testimonies of esteem and friendship, gives him letters of safe conduct, and writes to the Bishops of Tours and Angers that, as from him, they command Foulques, Count of Anjou, not to persecute him any more. Returning home the archdeacon retracts again, and publishes a refutation of the doctrine to which he had been constrained to subscribe. Gregory VII. appears neither astonished nor offended; he refuses to take any further step. It has been thought that the pontiff was not himself far from the sentiments of Berenger on the eucharist.

Whatever opinion he may have entertained, he was too able a man not to see what respect and what authority would be attracted to his caste by a dogma which, at the voice of the priest, makes the Deity descend from heaven on to the altar, and identifies him with the bread and the wine which they consecrate. In the eyes of the multitude they would appear as supernatural beings, in some way imprinted with divine qualities. In 1080, the doctor, now above eighty years of age, appears no more on the scene. Withdrawn into the isle of Como, near Tours, he dwells there until his death (1088), passing his days in prayer, and in the practice of the Christian virtues. His doctrine survives him, living through the ages, but always anathematised by the popes.

Let us resume the narrative of the events of the pontificate of Leo IX. The Normand princes who carried on war in Italy against the Saracens and the Greeks had received from the emperor Henry III. the investiture of La Pouille and Calabria, as well as a part of Beneventum (1048). They seized divers countries, the possession of which was claimed by Rome. Leo excommunicates them, and goes to beg assistance from the emperor. He brings back from Germany troops and numerous volunteers. The Normands offer to become vassals of the See of Rome, and by that title to hold what they have taken from the Church. Leo refuses, and resort is had to force. The Normands becoming conquerors, seize the person of the pope, and compel him to absolve them. After having been detained nearly nine months at Beneventum, he returns sick to Rome, where he dies the same year (1054). The differences of Leo IX. and the Normands had furnished to the Greek emperor an opportunity for making an attempt at an approximation between Rome and Constantinople,—an attempt which proved abortive, and ended in nothing but the consolidation of the schism.

Let us call to mind in a few words the anterior relations of the two Churches. Notwithstanding the opposition of the popes, the Greeks had maintained, after the fall of Photius, the ordinations which he had made, without that conduct producing a rupture with the See of Rome. In the difficulties which his four marriages had occasioned him, the Emperor Leo, the philosopher, has recourse to the pope, as well as to the other patriarchs. Without children by his three first wives, that prince had formed the design of espousing a fourth, of the name of Zoé, although among the Greeks four marriages were assimilated to polygamy (902). At first he is satisfied with a civil union; but a son having been born to him, he proposes to baptize him as a legitimate child. The patriarch Nicholas the Mystic, and the other bishops oppose it unless the emperor dismisses the mother. Leo promises to do so on oath. But three days after the baptism Zoé is declared empress, and the marriage is celebrated without the ministry of any priest. The clergy are indignant. It is requested that the affair should be submitted to the examination of a council. The emperor writes to that effect to Pope Sergius and all the patriarchs. In the interval a priest consecrates the union. That priest is deposed by Nicholas the Mystic, and the emperor is forbidden to enter a church. The legates of the pope, on their arrival, deciding for the confirmation of the marriage, the patriarch abstains from seeing them in public. He is sent into exile—he and the bishops of his opinion. The others unite with the council under the presidency of the legates. Nicholas is deposed, and Euthymius put in his place (907).

At the death of Leo, the empire passes over to the young Constantine his son, with whom is associated his uncle Alexander (911). The latter restores the patriarch Nicholas, and dies after a short interval. Constantine called Porphyrogenitus remains alone emperor, under the direction of Zoé his mother, and seven tutors appointed by Alexander, in the number of whom is the patriarch. Zoé soon removes him from court. Six years later, she is herself shut up in a monastery by Roman Lecapene, whose daughter Constantine has married. Roman, declared emperor by his son-in-law, is consecrated by the patriarch Nicholas. A decree of union for the church of Constantinople is issued, by which a fourth marriage is interdicted, and penance prescribed for the third. A deputation is sent to pope John X. to procure his assent to the decree. Harmony seems to reign from that time between the two courts. When the young Theophylact, son of Roman Lecapene, is promoted to the see of Constantinople, pope John XI. sends legates with a synodical letter to approve the ordination (933). In the year 968 the emperor Otho I. deputes to Constantinople Luitbrand, bishop of Cremona, with a mission to ask for his son the hand of Anne, daughter of Roman the younger. According to the relation of that bishop, the Greeks considered themselves still as the sovereigns of Rome; the Lombards, the Franks, the Saxons were in their eyes only barbarians. They demanded, to consent to the proposed alliance, that Otho should put into their hands Ravenna, Rome, and all southern Italy, and in order to live in friendship without yielding the princess, that he should leave Rome free and abandon the princess of Capua and Beneventum. Nicephorus, Phocas, having made Otranto into a bishopric, prescribed that in la Pouille and Calabria, of which he was possessor, the divine mysteries should be celebrated in Greek and not in Latin; he held the popes of that period as traffickers and simoniacal. The disagreements revive between the two churches under the patriarchs, Nicholas Chrysoberg, Sisinnius, and Sergius (980-1019). The cause of it doubtless lies in the wars which the Greeks then carried on in Italy against the Western emperors and the Roman pontiffs. Sisinnius again sends to the Eastern patriarchs the encyclic of Photius, pronouncing anathema on the Latins. The names of the popes are effaced from the Diptychs of the church from the year 1009.

This state of things is prolonged to the time of Michael Cerularius. That patriarch, condemning the usage of unleavened bread which was introduced among the Latins, had shut their churches in Constantinople, and sent away the abbots and the monks from their monasteries. But under the pontificate of Louis IX. the Greeks feel a desire to approach the court of Rome; the Norman princes carry on an unsparing war against them, and the conduct of the pope with those princes gave Constantinople the hope of obtaining by its influence assistance from the emperor of Germany against their common enemy. Michael Cerularius and the metropolitan, in a spirit of charity, they say, wrote to the bishop of Trani in Pouille, and through him to all the clergy of the Franks, the monks, the people, and the pope himself, concerning the unleavened bread and the Sabbath (1053). They maintain that Jesus Christ instituted the Supper not with unleavened bread but with leavened, the only true bread. They moreover reproach the Latins with fasting on Saturday, with eating strangled animals, and not singing the Halleluia in Lent. This letter is communicated to Leo IX., who makes a long reply in which, after having set forth what he calls the errors of the Greeks, he blames them with forbidding the Latins to follow the Roman customs. The emperor Constantine Monomachos on his side, testifies to the pope a strong desire to restore union between the two churches, and writes to him to that effect through the patriarch. Leo sends three legates to Constantinople with dispatches for the emperor and for the patriarch Michael. In his letter to Constantine he demands the restitution of the domains of the Church of Rome, situated in his states, and complains of the persecution of Cerularius against those who make use of unleavened bread, as well as his attempt to subject to himself the patriarchs of Alexandria and Antioch. In his letter to Michael, whom he qualifies as simply archbishop, he reproaches him with taking the title of universal patriarch, and with persecuting those who communicate with unleavened bread. The legates are well received by the emperor. But they show themselves haughty in regard to the patriarch, who accordingly abstains from seeing them and speaking to them. They publish a reply to the accusations of Cerularius and of the metropolitan of Bulgaria, and terminate it with invectives against the usages of the Greek Church. Michael persisting in refusing to deal with them, they repair to the church of Saint Sophia and there depose on the grand altar, in presence of the clergy and the people, an act of excommunication against that patriarch, the next day but one they quit Constantinople. The emperor recalls them and vainly attempts a reconciliation. After their definitive departure, Cerularius, in a decree signed by himself and twelve metropolitans as well as two archbishops anathematises the act of excommunication and its authors whom he describes as false legates. From this time the schism between the East and the West may be regarded as irrevocably accomplished. The Greek emperors will on different occasions make overtures of re-union, but they will be led to the offer by political interests, without their clergy or that of the Latins ever lending themselves to any approximation. The patriarch of Constantinople did not want a master, the pope of Rome did not want an equal.

At the time of their wars in Italy against the Othos and the popes of Rome, the Greeks succeed in securing in the north of Europe a conquest which was one day to compensate them for the losses to which Islamism had subjected them. The Muscovites, whose conversion had been attempted in the preceding century, embrace the Christian religion under the reign of the emperor Basil II. Wlodomir. their duke, having espoused Anne, sister of that prince, is induced by her to receive baptism, and his example leads his subjects to imitate him (989). On the death of Leo IX. the Romans ask the emperor Henry III. for a new pope. Since the Council of Sutri that prince disposed of the papacy as had been done by Theodora, Marozia, and the Othos, and as did the Greek emperor for the patriarch of Constantinople. The sub-deacon Hildebrand goes into Germany for that election. Gebehard, bishop of Eichestet a rich and powerful personage and near relation of the emperor is appointed ; he occupies the seat under the name of Victor II. (1055-57).

Henry IV., aged six years, succeeds his father the following year, under the regency of the empress Agnes. His minority furnished the Church of Rome an occasion for throwing off the Germanic domination. Stephen IX. (1057-58) is elected by the people and the clergy without reference being made to the imperial court. This pope was severe on the clergy who had not observed the continence prescribed by the constitution of Leo IX. After him, the principal men of Rome and the neighbouring lords elect as pope the bishop of Velletri, who takes the name of Benedict and holds his seat for ten entire months. Hildebrand, at the time of the election, was on an embassy to the empress; on his return, he puts himself at the head of the contrary party. The bishop of Florence is proclaimed under the name of Nicholas II. (1058-61). The choice is approved by Henry IV., and Benedict makes his submission. Hildebrand, under Nicholas II., as under Stephen IX., exercises the principal authority in the Church. A resolution is formed to free the papacy at once from the imperial power, the tyranny of neighbouring lords, and the turbulence of popular factions. With a view to success, he is prepared to constitute the Roman cardinals a kind of senate to whom shall be reserved the right to elect the sovereign pontiffs. The title of Cardinal was not at that time peculiar to the Church of Rome; it was, among the Latins, applied to the priests and deacons of the great Episcopal Churches. In the eleventh century, the dignity of the Cardinals of Rome begins to grow, and grows in the same proportion as the power of the pontiffs. They were divided into three classes—cardinal princes, cardinal priests, and cardinal deacons. The first are the seven bishops of the city and the province, to whom belongs the consecration of the pope. The others are the priests or the deacons of the parishes of the metropolis. But it was not an easy undertaking to remove the right of election from the people and the majority of the Roman clergy. Accordingly, at first a round about way was pursued. There is drawn up in a council held in the Lateran, a rule for the election of the popes. After declaring that it belongs to the clergy and the people of Rome, it is decided that the cardinal bishops shall first treat of the matter among themselves, that they shall then call in the cardinal priests, and that finally the rest of the clergy and the people shall give their consent. The cardinal bishops shall consecrate the pope who shall be taken in the Roman Church, or in default of a capable person, in another church, and it is added, " saving the honour due to King Henry, who shall be emperor, and to those of his successors to whom the Roman See shall grant the same right." These arrangements evidently tend to concentrate the election in the hands of the cardinal bishops and the cardinal priests, while it renders all but illusory the intervention of the lower clergy and the people. As to the right of the emperors to confirm the election, it is represented as a personal privilege which the holy see may concede or not concede to the reigning prince. In the next century, the college of cardinals will be complete by the addition of five other members of the superior clergy of Rome, seven palatine judges, and some cardinal deacons. However, it is not enough to pass decrees in a council, power is needed for their execution. The prince will not always be a minor. The nobles of Rome and of circumjacent places may also dispute the election with the cardinals. To obviate these difficulties, support was sought in the Norman princes who were then establishing themselves in Italy, and aimed to make themselves independent of the empire. Nicholas comes to an agreement with them on grounds of reciprocal advantage. The Normans acknowledge themselves vassals of the Church of Rome, and the pope confirms to Richard the principality of Capua, to Robert Guiscard, the duchy of Pouille and Calabria ; besides, he cedes to the latter his claims to Sicily, from which Robert was on the way to expel the Saracens. Such is the origin of the kingdom of Naples. This treaty consolidates the conquests of the Normans in Italy, and secures to the pope vassals powerful enough to beat down the petty lords of the neighbourhood and to protect him in need against the emperors of Germany. The struggle between the church and the empire begins at the death of Nicholas II. Hildebrand, in concert with the cardinals and the Roman nobility, elect Alexander II., who is supported by Robert Guiscard (1061-73). The empress and the Lombard bishops combine in favour of Candalous, bishop of Parma, who is proclaimed under the name of Honorius II. The pretender suddenly arrives under the walls of Rome with troops, and gains an advantage in the first combat ; but Godefroy, duke of Tuscany, soon compels him to return to Parma. Meanwhile the Germans take from the empress her son and the regency. She is reproached with weaknesses for the archbishop of Augsburg, her minister. She flees to Rome to take the veil. The education of the young king and the government of the State are put into the hands of the bishops. The latter hold in Saxony a council in which Candalous is deposed. He, however, maintains himself with the aid of the duke of Tuscany, whom he has had the skill to attract to himself. On the demand of the bishops of Germany, a council assembles at Mantua. Alexander II. there clears himself by oath of the reproaches made against him, and comes to a reconciliation with the Lombard bishops. Candalous is condemned as guilty of simony. Far from yielding, he introduces himself secretly into Rome, and, supported by the troops, he by night seizes the church of St Peter. The soldiers having abandoned him, Censius, son of the prefect, gives him an asylum in the Castle Saint Angelo ; after a seige of two years, he forces him to buy himself off in order to leave. Candalous continues the part of pope until his death, and always preserves some adherents.

On the decease of Alexander II., Hildebrand is elected with the unanimous consent of the clergy, and amid the acclamations of the people : he takes the name of Gregory VII. (1073-85). To king Henry, who complains that he has not been consulted, he writes that violence was put upon him, but that his consecration has been deferred till his approbation is given. The prince, satisfied with this reply, confirms the choice, and the new pope is consecrated at the age of sixty. The ascent of Gregory VII. does not, to say the truth, bring a change of direction in the conduct of the Court of Rome. He perseveres in the conduct of preceding reigns, of which he had been the principal mover ; but he follows it with more vigour, and to its last limits.

His first care is to suppress the incontinence of the clergy and simony, against which Leo IX. and his successors had taken severe measures. In a council held in Rome, he decreed that the ecclesiastics who live in concubinage (which comprises even a legitimate alliance) shall not [be able to celebrate mass, or serve at the altar ; that those who shall have been ordained by simony, shall, for the future, be excluded from every function, and that the churches shall be taken from those who shall have obtained them by money (March 1074). The libertinism of the clergy was notorious A crowd of ecclesiastics kept concubines in their homes or elsewhere; the priests, the abbots, the monks dissipated the goods of the churches and the convents in the support of their mistresses and the education of their bastards Had the suppression of disorders been the limit, nothing would have been more worthy of praise. But the object was surpassed when the marriage of priests was interdicted Then a sacrifice was made to the predominance of celibacy supported by the monkish spirit, and strengthened by the example of the Manichaeans who begun to spread in the west. Gregory VII. doubtless understood what aid for the accomplishment of his designs would come from men free from all family ties, and subject unrestrictedly to the absolute will of their head. However this may be, the decree enjoining celibacy, which is published with an injunction on bishops and princes to give it their support, encounter strong opposition from all parts. A number of ecclesiastic prefer losing their benefices to separating from their wives The pope is taxed with heresy; his partizans receive the name of Patarins or Manichaeans, the puritans of the see abstaining from marriage; the will of Gregory and his successors will end by triumphing over the recalcitrant, who are not supported by general opinion. Are the clerics the more continent? was there no reason to regret the canon of the Council of Nice? Whatever violates the order of nature is perilous in its consequences.

The execution of the decree against simony gives occasion to the gravest troubles, to long and bloody wars which convulse state and church. The simony with which western Europe was infected came specially from the excessive riches of the clergy. Ecclesiastical dignities were obtained by money; the criminal alleging in self-disculpation that payment was not for the benediction which comes from the Holy Spirit, but for the enjoyment of the property and possessions of the church or the bishopric. In mo cases princes and kings were accomplices of the fact which was thus complicated by a question of public right. When lands subject to the rendering of faith and homage were given to bishops, abbots, or other ecclesiastics, neither they nor their successors could take possession until they had received investiture from the sovereign lord—investiture, which in the beginning took place for clerics as well as laics, by means of diplomas and the touching of a wand. Hence it arose, to the prejudice of ecclesiastical elections, that the princes often arrogated to themselves the right of appointment to bishoprics and abbeys, and even to sell them. The clergy, to put an obstacle to this abuse, hastened, on the death of a bishop or an abbot, to elect his successor, and to consecrate him forthwith, an act which rendered the election irrevocable; the benefice could no longer be given or sold to another. But in the time of Otho I., the sovereign lords, in order to foil the calculation, ordered that on the death of a prelate, his cross and his ring, without which consecration was impossible, should be brought to them. From that time the election could not take effect except with the concurrence of the lay power. In this state of things Gregory complained, not without an appearance of reason, that the princes disposed entirely of the right of election to ecclesiastical dignities; it was moreover, he said, a profanation to confide to lay hands the cross and the ring, holy things which none but clergymen have the right to touch. The suzerains replied not less pertinently that the bishops and abbots exercising, in the character of temporal lords, a portion of the public power, could not take possession thereof without having been accepted by the prince, and done homage to him. The evil arose from the prelates possessing landed property, and from the pope's aspiring to supremacy over all Christian states. Gregory then, for the execution of his decrees, sends legates into Germany. They are well received by Henry, who endeavours to humour them; but the clergy absolutely oppose the assembling of a council for inquiring into simony. They return with presents from the king, and a letter in which that prince asks counsel of the pope for the reparation of the disorders, while maintaining his right to investiture by the cross and the ring.

The pontiff, irritated, suspends several bishops of Lombardy and Germany, and excommunicates five domestics of the king, who had excited him to sell the churches (Feb, 1075). Other legates go and intimate to Henry himself an order to repair to Rome to reply to accusations made against him. The prince drives them away ignominiously and assembles at Worms the bishops and abbots of Germany. In this assembly Gregory is deposed, as much on account of irregularity of election as for certain misdeeds and severities (Jan. 10, 1076). The Bishops of Lombardy and the Marches of Ancona subscribe to the condemnation. Henry IV. writes to the clergy and the people of Rome to stir them up against Hildebrand.

Gregory VII., at this same time, convoked a new council at Rome. The very day of its opening he receives, while sitting in the assembly, Henry's letters, and the decrees of the assembly at Worms. Then the pope, invoking Saint Peter, Mary, the Mother of God, Saint Paul, and all the saints, excommunicates the king in their name, forbids him to govern the Teutonic kingdom of Italy,—frees his subjects from their oath of fidelity, and orders them to refuse him all service; he equally hurls excommunication on several bishops of Italy and France, and on the bishops of Lombardy, who have conspired against the holy see. This is the first time that a pope loosened subjects from their oath of fidelity toward their sovereign. The decree is addressed to all the faithful; and Gregory takes pains in his letters to prove that he has the right to excommunicate and depose princes. The Lombard bishops, in an assembly held at Pavia, pronounce a new excommunication against Hildebrand. Minds in Italy and Germany are divided between the pope and the king. Some, relying on the false decretals, declare that the pope cannot be judged and excommunicated; others, more faithful to ancient right assert that he has no power to excommunicate and depose kings.

While the Lombards and the bishops of Germany oppose

Gregory's designs, he succeeds on his side in raising against the emperor the nobles of Germany, and principally those of Saxony and Suabia. At his instigation they assemble near Mayence to advise on measures to be taken for the good of the state and of religion (October 1076). Two legates are present. After several days of debate and deliberation, it is determined to defer to the judgment of the pope. Notice is given to Henry that he must get absolved from the excommunication before a year and a day; if he does not, he will be deprived of the kingdom. The prince does not endeavour to resist; but instead of waiting for the pope in Germany, he goes to meet him in Italy. The Lombard bishops and lords welcome him with great honour, under the idea that he comes to depose Gregory; in a few days a numerous army assembles round his person.

At the same time the pope directed his steps toward Germany, accompanied by Matilda, Countess of Tuscany, who testified great affection for him, and honoured him as a father and a lord. Henry asks him for absolution. After long resistance the pontiff consents to receive him. The prince enters alone into the fortress, and remains all day in the second enclosure, barefooted, clad in wool next the skin, in vain seeking for the pope's orders. The same takes place the second and the third day. At length, on the fourth, Gregory admits him to his presence, and deigns to absolve him on the following conditions: the king shall submit to the pope's judgment on the accusations put forward by the German nobles, and until the decision of the cause, he shall abstain from wearing the insignia of royalty, and exercising its functions; if he justifies himself, and if he is maintained as king, he shall always be subject and obedient to the holy see. At this price the king is relieved of his excommunication. At the news of this pusillanimity, the Lombards, in their indignation, prepare to reject Henry, and to recognise his son, still a child. The king, to appease them, at the end of a fortnight, breaks his ignominious engagement. Sometime after, he projects seizing the pope and the Countess Matilda. The latter, informed of his design, take shelter in fortified mountains where they remain together during three months. Evil reports are spread among the enemies of the pontiff, especially among the clerics whose marriage he condemns. During this retreat, Matilda bestows on the holy see all her states, reserving merely the usufruct of them until her death.

The nobles of Germany, informed of the rupture of the treaty, appoint an assembly at Forsheim in Franconia for the 13th of March 1077. The pope summons Henry to attend to be definitively judged. The prince asks for a longer interval. Two legates entreat the assembly of Forsheim to defer the nomination of a new king until the arrival of the pope. But it proceeds to business and elect Randolph of Suabia, who is consecrated some time after. War is declared between the two competitors : all the empire is on fire. Gregory announces that he will go into Germany to decide with the council of the clerics and the laics, to which the crown belongs. He thus makes himself the arbitrator and his arbitration is accepted. In two councils held at Rome the ambassadors of Rodolph and Henry swear in the name of these princes that they will submit in all things to the legates who shall be sent into Germany. These same councils forbid clerics to receive investiture to a bishopric or a church from the hand of a prince or any other laic (1078-79).

But the legates take their journey in vain, they are unable to hold a conference. The war continues with more fury between the two parties. Henry is beaten by Rodolph and the Saxons. The news reaches Gregory in his seventh council (March 1080). All hesitation then ceases ; and addressing himself as before to Saint Peter and Saint Paul he hurls excommunication against Henry and his supporters declaring them to have forfeited the kingdom of Germany and Italy. He gives to Rodolph the teutonic kingdom, and to his partisans the absolution of their sins and the benediction of the apostles.

Henry, who has no longer any reason for managemen convokes in the Tyrol the bishops attached to his party they depose Hildebrand and call to his seat Guibert, arch bishop of Ravenna, who becomes Clement III. (June 1080

During his struggles with Henry IV. Gregory does not lose from view the other countries of the Latin language. If he intends to subject even the empire to his domination, with greater reason does he wish to dictate laws in the secondary kingdoms and principalities. According to him all temporal powers depend on the pope. He excepts moreover individual rights on each of the Western states. He claims as either possessions of the holy see or at least as its tributaries Spain, Sardinia, Sicily, France, England, Denmark, Poland, Hungary, Bohemia, Dalmatia, and even Russia.

In his letters you find, under the title of *Dictatus papæ* (the Pope's Dictates), twenty-seven articles in which are consigned the different pretensions of the Roman Church. Whoever drew them up, the maxims announced in them seem to have been taken from divers passages in Gregory's letters. You there, besides other things, see that the name pope should be used alone of the Roman pontiff; that the pope, canonically elected, becomes holy without doubt; that he is the only person whose feet all kings kiss; that he alone has the right to wear the imperial ornaments, and to make new laws according to the necessity of the times; that the Roman Church can never err; that the pope can be judged by no one; that he has the power to depose bishops without a council, to transfer or restore them, as also to form new bishoprics; to separate or unite old ones; that he is able to depose emperors and to set subjects free from their oath of fidelity; that no one has the right to retract the sentence of the pope, and that he is able to retract that of every other person; that no one can condemn another by appeal to the holy see; that no one whatever is permitted to remain in the same abode as those who have been excommunicated.

These theories consecrate as a whole the most absolute despotism, in temporal as well as spiritual matters, over the princes of the world, over councils and bishops, over the conscience of all men. They are now and till now unheard of pretensions.

Some of these maxims are drawn from the false decretals, the others flow from these more or less directly. The pretensions of the pope to universal monarchy date from the publication of the work ascribed to Isidore Mercator. John VIII. already compared himself to Moses, and the cardinal priests of Rome to the seventy elders that judged the people of Israel. During the feudal anarchy, as under the government of the Othos and their successors, these doctrines were compelled to sleep; they reappear with Gregory VII. supported on one side by the false decretals, and on the other by the fear of excommunication, so terrible in the eyes of the populations of the West, who have not yet laid aside Druidic ideas. The pope in attacking the emperor assaulted in its front the principal difficulty of his enterprise. Once established in regard to that prince, his pretensions would be easily recognised in other states, of which the emperor was in sort considered as the chief. Nevertheless Gregory does not neglect to make trials in the different countries, and carries his efforts more or less far according to circumstances. Thus Philip, king of France, being accounted more than any other inclined to simony in the sale of churches, the pontiff writes to different bishops of the kingdom to employ all their efforts to correct him: "Either the king," he says, "will renounce simony, or the French, smitten with general anathema, will refuse to obey him, unless they prefer to renounce Christianity" (1073). The next year, he addresses another letter to the Episcopate, in which he depicts the disorders which reign in the provinces, the cause of which he attributes to the weakness of the government and the bad examples given by king Philip; he enjoins on the bishops to give him warning, and if he does not listen to them, to excommunicate him, and to put France under an interdict, and that if censure produces no effect, he declares that with God's aid he will use all his efforts to deliver France from oppression. These letters seem not to have had much effect; accordingly, in the council of Rome of the year 1075, the king of France is threatened with excommunication unless he gives an assurance of amendment. Notwithstanding this menace Philip prevents the pope's legates from holding councils in the countries under his sway, and, as far as depends on him, in the lands which hold of his crown.

England was then under the laws of William the Conqueror. After the great Alfred (901) that country had fallen into barbarism. At the death of Edward the Confessor, the last of the Anglo-Saxon kings (1060). William, duke of Normandy, assuming to be the heir, subjects all the country to his power. He introduces the manners of France, more polished than those of his new subjects. The ancient laws are confirmed, principally those which concern the Church. Peter's pence continue to be paid. Three legates sent by the pope crown William afresh, to strengthen his authority. Langfranc, having become archbishop of Canterbury, restores religion in England. Gregory VII., in the early days of his pontificate, writes to king William that he holds him in high esteem. But at a later day he bids him by a legate to take the oath of fidelity to the holy see, and to be more careful in sending Peter's penny. On the last point William gives satisfaction; but he refuses the oath, which he has not promised, he says, and which none of his predecessors have taken to the predecessors of Gregory. The pope, in a rage, replies through his legate that money is with him a small matter compared with honour (1079) he complains that William prevents his bishops from going to Rome, and threatens him with Saint Peter's indignation, unless he is more moderate.

Robert Guiscard, Duke of Pouille, Calabria, and Sicily, had seized some lands of the Church in Campania, although he owned himself a vassal of the holy See. The pope fulminates an excommunication against him and his adherents in the first Council of Rome (1074). He renews it in two others (1075-77), and pronounces the penalty of deposition against the bishops and the priests who should serve them with mass.

Directing his attention to the most distant churches, the pontiff writes to the Kings of Norway and Denmark to send to Rome sons of their nobility to be instructed in the law of God, that they may carry back home the orders of the Holy See (1078). He sends to the King of Sweden, requesting him to depute to Rome a bishop and another clergyman, who shall give him information of the morals of their nation, and then take charge of his orders for the king (1082).

At the same time he occupies himself with the last wreck of the Church of Africa. It had decreased daily under the Moslem rule, and tended to entirely disappear. In the time of Louis IX. it had only five bishops; in 1076 there remains but one. Gregory consecrates a second, and orders that a worthy person may be sent to him that he may lay hands also on him, so that there may be three bishops in Africa, who might ordain a fourth.

In his idea of universal rule, the pontiff succeeds, not without difficulty, in substituting in Aragon and the rest of Spain the Roman liturgy for the Mosarabic, which had been employed till then (1074-78).

With a similar aim he refuses the Bohemians leave to celebrate the office in the vulgar tongue (1080). From that time it becomes the rule to employ exclusively the Latin language in the worship of the Church of Rome. The letter of Gregory VII. gives as the reason that God has not intended that the Scripture should be clear to all the world, lest it should be despised, and lead into error. However, at the moment when he solemnly deposes Henry IV., Gregory feels the need of putting himself on friendly relations with the other princes, whether in order that they may not take part against him, or that they might lend him aid in the grave conflict which is about to take place. He specially seeks to conciliate William the Conqueror and Robert Guiscard. He writes to the King of England in a very different style to that which he had formerly employed in regard to him. He speaks to him of his constant friendship, and his confidence in him against the enemies of the Church; letters are also addressed to Queen Matilda and prince Robert, their son (April 1080). In Italy the pope enters into conference with Robert Guiscard and the other Norman lords, whom he has more than once excommunicated; he receives them into favour under promise of their support. He gives to Robert Guiscard the investitures of the lands which had been conceded to him by popes Nicholas and Alexander, and leaves open the right to the possession which he accuses him with having usurped from the holy See. At the news of the election of Guibert by the Council of Brixen, Gregory allies himself more intimately still with Robert Guiscard; he reckons on the troops of the Normans, and on the vassals of the Countess Matilda for attacking the anti-pope in Ravenna (July 1080). Unforeseen events suddenly change the face of things. Robert loses his life in a sanguinary battle (Oct. 1080). The same day the troops of Matilda are vanquished in Lombardy. The majority advise the pope to come to a reconciliation with Henry IV. Far from that, he thinks of strengthening himself in Germany by the election of a new king, and prepares for the elected man a form of oath by which he will promise, as vassal of Holy Peter, fidelity and obedience to the See of Rome. His cares redouble in order to keep in good humour William of England, who seems to hesitate between the two popes; and he inquires, with not less solicitude, whether he may reckon on Robert Guiscard.

Henry passes into Italy, and prepares to march on Rome (1081). The pope holds there an eighth council, in which he excommunicates him afresh, as well as all his partizans. The king encamps before the city with his pope, Clement III. But the Romans defend themselves, and the prince is constrained to return, after having ravaged the country. Robert Guiscard at this time was carrying on a successful war with the Emperor Alexis Comnene (1081). The pope, in the name of Saint Peter, exhorts him rather to defend the states of the Church. Notwithstanding the election of Herman of Luxemburg by the Saxons and their allies (1081), Henry returns into Italy and besieges Rome again during several months (1082). The heat obliging him to return into Lombardy, he leaves the command of his troops to the anti-pope, who continues the war all the summer, and devastates the surrounding country.

Henry also presents himself before Rome the following year, while manifesting a desire for peace. The Romans urge the pope to conclude it. He replies that he will voluntarily absolve and crown Henry, if he is willing to satisfy God and the Church, otherwise, no. The calling of a council to decide the question of the kingdom is agreed upon. At the appointed time Henry fixes himself near Rome, and arrests on their way the deputies of the German nobility and the bishops most devoted to the pontiff. In this council (the ninth of Rome) Gregory with great pain abstains to renew the excommunication against the king by name, but he pronounces it against whosoever has hindered persons coming to Rome. The people end by allowing themselves to be seduced, and leave entrance into the city open to Henry, whom the anti-pope crowns as emperor (March 1084). The nobility is faithful to Gregory. He retires into the castle of Saint Angelo.

Robert Guiscard, yielding at length to the persistent urgency of the pope, leaves to his son the care of continuing the war against the Greeks, and returns into Italy. At his approach, Henry, not in a condition to resist, returns into the Lombard provinces. Robert enters Rome, pillages and burns a large portion of the city. The pope, replaced in possession of the palace of the Lateran, holds his tenth council, and renews the excommunication against the antipope, the emperor, and their adherents. A little time after, he quits Rome, where he is no longer safe, to repair to Solerno, which he inhabits till his death, supported by the Abbot of Mount Casino. Feeling his end draw near, he absolves and blesses all those who recognise his power, except king Henry, the anti-pope Guibert, and his principal supporters. His last words are : "I have loved righteousness and hated iniquity, and therefore I die in exile ? (1085). Was that language sincere ? Did Gregory really believe in his omnipotence for temporal matters as well as spiritual ? Did the false decretals of Isidore Mercator dazzle that domineering spirit to the extent of leading him, by way of inference, to the system of universal monarchy, a system of which his predecessors had a glimpse, and which he pursued with so much persistence ? It is impossible not to see in Hildebrand a vast and prolific genius, an inflexible character, a courage proof against all difficulties. This superior man has deeply sunk an imprint of himself on the pontifical church. But to justly appreciate his enterprise in itself, we must ask if it was in harmony with the rights of nations, and the word of the Christ whose supreme minister he represented himself. In his time, the feudal anarchy was coming to an end. Otho the great, and his successors, had, during a hundred years, been restoring the imperial authority in Germany and Italy; the Normand royalty was establishing itself in the south of the Peninsula; the Capetian dynasty was consolidating itself in France; William the Conqueror held the sceptre of England with a firm hand; the Spaniards had reconquered more than half of their territory. The love of study had spread under the impulse of Sylvester II.; ignorance tended every day to become less deep. It only required the popes to second the civilising movement. No one in the Latin Church contested their spiritual supremacy. The faith of the people was ardent, and their oppression without limits. If the see of Rome had been animated by a truly evangelical spirit, if no suspicion of personal interest had enfeebled the authority of its word, it would, without any temporal power, have exercised the in world an irresistible influence on the peace and the amelioration of Christian society; but, in aspiring to the empire of the earth, it everywhere provoked resistance, sowed treason, discord, and hate, convulsed the world during long ages, until at last the nations become less credulous, have thrown off the yoke and annihilated the pretensions of the Roman priesthood. Moreover, it does not appear that Gregory VII. ever took pains to ameliorate the condition of the humbler classes. The clergy, possessors of lordships like the nobility, had the same interest as it in keeping the people in subjection; the serfs were no better treated by one caste than by the other. The decrees of the pontiff tended only to fashion the people for religious servitude, the infallible preparation for political servitude. Thus he ordered that they should address God in the Latin tongue, in order that, not comprehending the meaning of their prayers, they may have no other communication with heaven than through the priest. Thus also he forbade the gospel to be read in the vernacular, as if Christ, sent for the salvation of men, had not used a language known to all his hearers; Rome rather feared his words would be too well known, and that men would find in them the condemnation of its doctrines and its ambitious projects. The only thing that Hildebrand in reality proposed to himself, the one thought of his life, the constant object of his efforts, was the absolute monarchy of the popes in temporal matters as well as spiritual. Now, this idea of domination was in flagrant contradiction with the teachings of Christ; it was not then in the new law that he had to seek his point of support. To such designs the Old Testament lent itself with less difficulty. The pontiff and the cardinals were found in Moses and the council of the elders, supreme directors of the holy nation; kings and princes were nothing more than the heads of the tribes of Israel. The papacy, in the course of the ages, becomes imbued with the despotic spirit and the barbarous traditions of the Israelite priesthood. All those who resist its will are for it Amalekites, Amorites, Midianites, whom it exterminates with fire and sword. Its vengeance is all the more implacable that it defends not only its authority but also its wealth, its territorial possessions, its absolute supremacy over the powers and the princes of this world; copious rivers of blood mark its way in all places through the successive generations.

After the death of Gregory VII., the see remains vacant nearly a year. At last, the cardinals elect, in spite of himself, the Abbot of Mount Cassino, whom they designate by the name of Victor III. (1086). A few days after, the new pope lays down his insignia, and withdraws into his abbey, where he remains a long time without allowing himself to be overcome. At length, yielding to general urgency he is conducted into Rome by Jourdan, Prince of Capua (March 1087). He is consecrated in the Church of Saint Peter, after having driven the anti-pope Clement away. Victor III. possesses that part of Rome which is on the right bank of the river, the Castle Saint Angelo, the basilica of St Peter, and the island of the Tiber. The two parties fiercely dispute with each other; the church of Saint Peter, taken and retaken, it finally remains in the hands o Victor. In a council held at Beneventum (1087), tha pope excommunicates every emperor who shall give the investiture of the ecclesiastical dignities, and every member of the clergy who shall receive it from them. The same anathema shall be renewed in all the councils which shall be held until the end of the dispute about investitures (1123).

Urban II. (1088-99) commences by declaring that he shall tread in the footsteps of Gregory VII. The civil war is losing its ardour in Germany. Hermann, abandoned by the Saxons, retires into Lorraine, where he dies shortly after (1088).

Henry IV., returning into Italy, defeats the troops of the Countess Matilda, and renders himself master of the city of Mantua (1091). His cause is on the point of triumphing, when his son Conrad, revolting against him at the solicitation of the pope, in his defection takes with him the greater part of the army (1093). Milan, Lodi, Cremona, and Plaisance form a league of twenty years against the emperor; he is reduced to take refuge in a fortress. Urban holds at Plaisance a council, in which are renewed the decrees against the marriage of priests, and against the investiture by the cross and the ring (1095). Ambassadors of Alexis Comnene come to the council to ask assistance against the Moslems, who advance to the walls of Constantinople. The pope exhorts the faithful to that enterprise, without, nevertheless, preaching a crusade to the peoples of Germany and Italy, who have enough to do in the war of the priesthood and the empire. He repairs to Cremona, where King Conrad takes an oath of fidelity to him. The pontiff, on his return, promises him aid and counsel to obtain the imperial crown as the price of renouncing investitures. Urban passes by sea into France. After visiting the monastery of Cluny, of which he had been monk and prior, he presides at Clermont over a council held in the open air, at which are present two hundred and five prelates, the majority Frenchmen, four thousand ecclesiastics, and three hundred thousand laymen (Nov. 1095).

In this council the pope renews the excommunication already hurled against Philip, King of France, who, leaving

the queen Bertha under pretext of kinship, had married
Bertrade, his mistress. This last marriage had been celebrated publicly by the Bishop of Senlis, and with the consent of the Roman legate. But complaints had arisen, another legate came who excommunicated Philip and Bertrade (1094) without obtaining any satisfaction. The great wrong of Philip, in the eyes of the pope, was doubtless the maintenance of his right for investiture.

The most famous act of the Council of Clermont is the publication of the Crusade.

The idea of war against the infidels, conceived by Sylvester II., had been warmly embraced by Gregory VII., whom circumstances prevented from carrying it into effect. It was reserved for Urban II. to carry it into execution.

In those times a hermit of the diocese of Amiens, named Peter, having gone to Jerusalem from religious considerations, was painfully impressed with the sad condition of the holy places. He returns into Europe with letters from the patriarch and Christians for the Pope of Rome. Well received by the pontiff, Peter traverses Italy, passes the Alps, and goes from court to court soliciting all the princes for the deliverance of Palestine and the Christians of the East; he is in some sort the precursor of the Council of Clermont. In that assembly the pope exhorts all Christians to take part in the sacred work; to those who take up arms, he grants remission of their sins, and his protection for their persons and their property. Those that were present shouted, "God wills it! God wills it!" Those who make a vow to undertake the task wear on their garments the figure of the cross. As chiefs of the expedition Adhemar, Bishop of Puy; and Raymond, Count of Toulouse, are designated.

Urban traverses the provinces of France in the south of the Loire, preaching the holy war everywhere. He fixes the fifteenth of August 1096 for the departure of the crusaders. Arrived at Nimes, he there holds a council in which king Philip is absorbed on the promise of quitting Bertrade, which nevertheless he re-takes shortly after. The pope returns triumphantly to Rome with the aid of the Countess

Matilda. The Guibertins now occupy only the castle of Saint Angelo; the greater part of the city had submitted to Urban at the approach of numerous crusaders. At the same time the troops of Matilda force the emperor Henry IV. to quit Lombardy in order to retire into Germany. During the pontificate of Urban II., Count Roger, brother of Robert Guiscard, completes the expulsion of the Saracens from Sicily (1090), where they have ruled for more than two centuries. By a bull of the 5th of July 1098, the pope undertakes not to place in that island any legate contrary to the will of Roger or his successors, conceding to them the right to do what the legate would have done; whence the Sicilians pretend that their king is the born legate of the holy see, a right which they name the monarchy of Sicily, but which is contested by the Court of Rome. Before speaking of the events of the crusades, let us report the situation of the Moslem powers in the east and in the west. In Spain, the Christian kingdoms are always at war either against the Saracens, or with one another. Sanche the Great, king of Navarre (1000-35) makes himself master of Castille and the kingdom of Leon. At his death his states are divided among his children. Ferdinand, his second son, surnamed the Great, is the first king of Castille. He adds to it the kingdoms of Leon and Navarre, wars against the Moors, and pushes his conquest to the middle of Portugal. But, like his father, he commits the error of dividing his states between his sons (1065). Alphonso the sixth unites the kingdoms of Leon and Castille. In a reign of thirty-six years, he extends his conquest over the Moors, and lifts up Christianity in Spain. He captures Toledo (1085) after a memorable siege directed by the Cid, whose reputation had attracted thither a crowd of princes and knights from France and Italy. Magnificently endowed by Alphonso, the church of Toledo sees its archbishop become the primate of all Spain (1088). The Cid subjugates on his own behalf the kingdom of Valentia. Peter the first, king of Arragon (1094-1104) gains a great battle over the Moslems (1096), and takes possession of Huesca. Despite all these advantages, the infidels continue to occupy the moiety of the Spanish provinces. Supported by the Moors of Africa, they are able to maintain themselves, yet a long while, in consequence of the division of their adversaries. In the east the family of Touloun no longer governs Egypt, which at the beginning of the tenth century had fallen under the power of the Caliphs of Bagdad. But about the same time the civil power escapes from the hands of those Caliphs; they are no longer anything but the chiefs of religion. The governors of the provinces render themselves independent, Egypt and Syria have a master; another rules in Arabia, another in Mesopotamia, and so with the rest. Even Bagdad, the residence of the Caliphs, obeys another prince called the Emir of the Emirs. The name of the Caliphs is still seen on the coin, and is uttered in the public prayers: they give investiture to those who rise to power, without ever refusing it to the strongest.

However, a new religious chief, the Caliph of the Fatimites, offers himself as their rival, and takes away from their supremacy a great part of the Moslem countries. This sect had been founded in the first years of the tenth century by Mohammed surnamed Obeidalla, who claimed to be a descendant of Ali and Fatima, the prophet's daughter. Coming from Irak, he went into Africa, where he was recognised as Emir Almumenin (prince of the faithful). His powers passed to his descendants. Moëzlidinilla, his great grandson, seizes the Egyptian provinces and is proclaimed Caliph there. Prayer is no longer made in the name of the Caliph of Bagdad. Hence a schism among the Moslems; the Fatimite Caliphs are of the sect of Ali; those of Bagdad hold for the Tonna. Moez builds grand Cairo. His successors subject Syria and a considerable part of the Arabian provinces; but they soon find themselves in presence of the new rulers who adhere to the Caliph of Bagdad, the Seldjukides Turks.

These people begin to be powerful about the middle of the eleventh century. Togrulbek, grandson of Seldjuk, occupies all Khorasan. Sent for by the Caliph of Bagdad, he soon becomes the master of that city (1055). Olub-Arselan, his successor, (1063) conquers Mesopotamia, Armenia, and extending his power over Syria, captures Jerusalem from the Fatimites. He then penetrates into Asia Minor, advances to Caesarea in Cappadocia, invades Phrygia, beats the Greek army, and captures the Roman Emperor Diogenes, with whom he concludes a treaty of peace. Under Melek Shah, who reigns after Arselan, Soliman, son of Katlumich retakes Antioch (1084), of which Nicephorus Phocas had possessed himself some years before; he found in Natolia the third dynasty of the Seldjukides, that of Rum. Konieh is his capital; his troops threaten Constantinople. Melek Shah dies in the year 1092; the first years of the reign of his son are troubled by civil wars which last down to the appearance of the Crusaders in the East. The first crusade is all French. The entire population of that kingdom takes part in it—lords, priests, monks, hermits, common people, women and children. From the month of March 1096 to the month of October an immense multitude puts itself in movement. The first division, composed of walkers, is led by Gautier sans Avoir. Peter the hermit soon follows him at the head of forty thousand men. Another body is under a German priest, named Godescalk. A troop of about two hundred thousand footmen follows without leaders to guide and control it. These undisciplined bands wend their way through Germany, giving themselves up to all excesses. They massacre the Jews at Cologne, Mayence, Spires, and Treves; terror goes before them. In Germany, Hungary, and Thrace they devastate, plunder, and slay. The population being exasperated, exterminate a large part of them. There reigns more order in the bodies commanded by the nobility. Godefroy de Bouillon and Baldwin, his brother, lead through Germany and Hungary eighty thousand chosen men, cavaliers and infantry. The division of the Count of Toulouse passes through Sclavonia, Hughes of France, Robert of Normandy, Robert of Flanders, Stephen of Blois embark with their forces at Brindisium or Tarentum. Boemond, prince of Tarentum, follows them with seven thousand picked men. The Greeks are justly alarmed at the advent of so many myriads of Franks. Alexis Comnene fears specially the Normands of Italy. He hastens to make these hordes pass the Hellespont, who devastate beyond it as they have done in the neighbourhood of Constantinople. The French lords, who have set out the one after the other assemble in Asia and lay siege to Nice (1097). They count, it is said, one hundred thousand horsemen, and six hundred thousand people on foot, comprising women. The Emperor Alexis was obliged to aid them with his troops, and to furnish them with provisions; the Crusaders, on their part, are to put into his hands the places of the empire that they shall take from the infidels, or hold them of him under the title of vasselage.' Nice surrenders at the end of a month of siege, and the emperor takes possession of it. But as he keeps his promises badly, according to what the Crusaders say, they refuse to yield to him the other places which they take in Asia Minor. After the conquest of Cilicia, Baldwin separates from the army; conducted by an Armenian noble, he penetrates to the Euphrates through Christian populations, which surrender to him, seizes Edessa, and founds a powerful state in those regions. The Crusaders, always victorious in pitched battle, had lost many lives by famine and sickness; their army, considerably reduced, penetrates into Syria, takes Antioch at the end of a siege of nine months, and massacres there all the Moslems (1098). Three days after it finds itself besieged by innumerable troops. Provisions fail; the Christians, reduced to despair, rush upon the enemy, put him to flight, and get possession of his camp. Their courage had been singularly stimulated by the discovery of a lance which was said to be that which had pierced the side of Christ. But after the battle, doubts arise in this matter among the Crusaders themselves. Divine service is restored at Antioch with the Greek patriarch. Boemond receives the principality of the country. When the Crusaders arrived in Syria, the Egyptian Caliph put himself into relations with them in the hope that they would aid him to repel the Turks. He takes Jerusalem under the impression produced by their victories, and announces to the Franks that he will allow them to visit it in full security provided that they come unarmed, and at the most not more than three hundred at a time. To this derisive offer the

Crusaders reply that they will go in force. They in effect arrive, reduced to twenty thousand footmen and fifteen hundred horse. The city passed for holding forty thousand well-armed men. It is nevertheless taken at the end of five weeks (15th July 1099). A horrible massacre of the Moslems ensues. Godefroy de Bouillon is elected the King of Jerusalem, and of the countries which depend on it. The cities under his sway are few in number, separated by hostile places, and threatened by the infidels who occupy all the open country. After the departure of the other lords, Godefroy has with him only three hundred horsemen and two thousand foot for the defence of his kingdom. The Crusaders had also founded a county of Tripoli, of which Raymond, Count of Toulouse, becomes the lord. Urban II. did not survive the capture of Jerusalem more than some days. He is succeeded by Pascal II. (1099-1118).

The anti-Pope Clement III. having died the following year, is followed by Albeat, whom the partisans of Pascal seize the very day of his election; then by Theodoric, whom they remove at the end of three months; and finally by Maginulfe, who perishes in exile. The death of the young king Conrad, which took place in the year 1100, does not restore peace to the empire. Pascal II., in a council held in Rome (1102), confirms the excommunication pronounced against Henry IV. by Gregory and by Urban.

The emperor, intending to visit the holy sepulchre, appoints for king his other son Henry. The young prince, seduced by Pascal, revolts against his father, and marches to encounter him (1104). The two armies remain in presence of each other three days, not far from Ratisbon. The principal lords of the father's army allowing themselves to be won over, Henry IV. escapes with a small following. He is surprised and forced to renounce the crown in favour of his son, who is again proclaimed under the title of Henry the Fifth (1106). The emperor gets away and recommences the war, which is terminated by his death shortly after. Henry IV. is first buried in the church of Liege, but almost immediately he is disinterred as an ex-communicated person. His body is carried to Spires where it remains five .years in a stone coffin. Not in the empire only did differences arise on the investiture and enjoymen of temporal lordships and other properties of the church Analogous pretensions were produced in other countries.

In England when a bishop or an abbot died, the king William Rufus, took possession of the property of the bishopric or the abbey to enjoy it during its being vacant which he prolonged indefinitely. On the decease of Lang franc (1089), the See of Canterbury remains thus vacan during four years, until, in a dangerous illness, Willian permits the appointment to it of the learned Anselm, abbo of Bec. A good understanding does not subsist lon between them. With the king's permission, the archbisho goes to Rome to consult the Pope (1097), Urban II., wh welcomes him with the greatest regard, and opposes hi resolution to renounce the Episcopate. After attendin the Councils of Bari (1098) and Rome (1099), the prelat returns to Lyons, which he determines to inhabit. Fror the time of his departure the property of the Church was i the hands of the king, who received its revenues despite th warnings of the Pope. The death of William permits th archbishop to return into England (1100). On his arriva he is required to do homage to the new monarch, and t receive from him the investiture of the archbishopric. Thi was the constant usage of the country. But Anselm ha learnt at Rome that it is forbidden, under pain of excom munication, for laymen to give investiture, and fo ecclesiastics to receive it at their hands. He refuses th homage and declares that if the king will not cômply wit these regulations, he shall abstain from communion wit him. Henry V. refers to the Pope, who rejects hi demand. The prince persists in his resolution to force th archbishop to do him homage, and to consecrate those t whom he shall give bishoprics and abbeys. Anselm resists They send in common new deputies to Rome. These, o their return, differ as to the reply made by the sovereig pontiffs. Anselm, at the request of Henry, goes himself t the papal city with a king's envoy (1103). The ponti yields to the prince some usages of his predecessors, bu

he absolutely forbids to give investiture. In repassing
through Lyons, the envoy signifies to the archbishop that
he will not be received in England except on condition of
acting with the king according to the usage of his predecessors. Anselm remains at Lyons eighteen months.
He is then reconciled to Henry. They again send deputies
to Rome. The Pope overlooks the past, and rules that for
the future the archbishop shall ordain those who shall have
received bishoprics or abbeys without investiture, although
they have done homage to the king. Anselm returns into
England. Agreeably with the decision of the Pope, a
council meeting in London grants homage to the king while
forbidding him investiture by the cross and the ring (1107).
Investitures give occasion in France to no trouble. King
Philip upholds his right. The wisest bishops say, with
Yves de Chartres, that it is of small consequence for investiture to be given with the cross and the ring, if thereby the
prince intends to confer not the spiritual power but only the
seignorial right. Then the Pope does not insist. But Philip
is again prosecuted on account of his connection with
Bertrade, whom he has taken back despite his promises.
Pascal II. sends legates, who excommunicate him on that
ground in a council at Poitiers (9th Nov. 1100). The
same council passes a canon against investitures, which does
not seem to have had much effect. The excommunication
of Philip is taken off by a legate in a council held in Paris
(1104). That prince and Bertrade renounce being together
unless in presence of witnesses. But in reality they continue to live together without being disquieted by the
Church. The Pope, in his struggle with the emperor, had
need to humour France.

The question of investitures is reproduced with the young
king Henry V. Pascal II. judges it prudent to debate it in
France rather than in Germany. A council is held at Chalons
sur Maine without result, the ambassadors of Henry maintaining his right to invest with the regalia and the envoys
of the pope taxing with sacrilege the investiture with the
cross and the ring (1107). Henry V. forms the resolution
of marching into Italy with a large army to receive the im-

perial crown and make his right of investiture acknowledged (1110). He traverses Lombardy as master, and from Florence sends deputies to Rome to regulate the conditions of his coronation.

It is agreed that the emperor shall renounce in writing all investitures, leaving to the churches the oblations and the domains which have never belonged to the crown, and that the pope shall renounce the regalia, that is to say, the cities, duchies, marquisates, counties, monies, marshes, and lands which depended on the crown before being in possession of the church; that he will order the bishops to make the same requisition and forbid them by writing to usurp the regalia. The king goes into Saint Peter's church. But, when the question of the respective renunciations comes up, the bishops exclaim against the cession of the regalia. In the midst of the difficulties which ensue Henry arrests the pope and keeps him for two months a prisoner out of Rome. At last an agreement is concluded between them, by which Pascal consents that the king shall give investiture of the cross and the ring to the bishops and abbots of his kingdom, who shall have been elected freely and without simony. Henry is then crowned emperor in the Church of Saint Peter. Then he withdraws into his camp, and Pascal returns into Rome (April 1111). Henry V. on returning into Germany gives in virtue of the pope's permission a magnificent funeral to his father, whose body had remained till then without ecclesiastical sepulture. The treaty accepted by Pascal II. calls forth in Rome general condemnation. He is solicited to annul his Bull. A schism is on the point of breaking out.

The pontiff assembles in the church of the Lateran a council which condemns and annuls the privilege extorted by king Henry (1112). The pope nevertheless abstains from pronouncing anathema; but particular councils going further do not fear to excommunicate the prince. Even an attempt is made to set in opposition to him the nobles of Germany (1115). The Countess Matilda dying during these events, Henry passes into Italy to receive his succession without paying attention to the donations made to the church. He sends at the same time deputies to the pope, with a view of terminating their differences. Pascal convenes a council in the Lateran in which he confesses that he has failed, and condemns under a perpetual anathema the agreement made by him with the emperor. He renews the prohibition pronounced by Gregory VII., under pain of excommunication, to give or receive investiture. The assembly even approves the excommunications already uttered against Henry by divers provincial councils (1116). The emperor comes to Rome at the head of an army (1117). The great place themselves at his side. After vain attempts to conclude the peace, he removes on account of the summer heat, promising to return when the inauspicious season is over. The pope, who had retired to Beneventum returns to Rome after his departure, and dies there the 18th of January 1118. Henry comes back in haste, and seizing the church of St Peter, demands of the new pope Gelasius II. (1118-19) if he will observe Pascal's treaty, if not another pontiff will be chosen. Gelasius, escaping by sea, retires to Gaeta, where he remains until Easter. Henry causes a new pope to be elected, who receives the name of Gregory VIII. Gelasius excommunicates both. The prince is a second time crowned emperor by his pope; then he returns into Germany. France and most Christian lands are for Gelasius II. He returns to Rome after the departure of the emperor. Driven away by a sedition, he retires into France and dies at Cluny. The archbishop of Vienna succeeds him under the name of Calixtus II. (1119-24). This pope holds at Toulouse a council in which are condemned, in a general manner, those who disallow the sacrament of the body and blood of Jesus Christ, the baptism of children, the priesthood, legitimate marriages. This was done in view of Manichaeans who were spread in the Western regions and other dissidents who sprang up in different places. Calixtus II. assembles a council at Rheims to promote the union of the church. The emperor Henry V. and the antipope Gregory are there solemnly excommunicated, with lighted wax candles (October 1119). The pontiff enters Rome the year following. The antipope took refuge in Sutri; the papal army besieges the church and Gregory is delivered up by the inhabitants. He is imprisoned till the end of his days. The civil war being rekindled in Germany, prudent noblemen interpose. Conditions of peace are regulated and a general council is asked of the pope. Calixtus sends three cardinal legates. In a diet held at Worms an agreement is drawn up in the following terms; the elections of bishops and abbots of the teutonic kingdom shall take place in the presence of the king or his delegate, without violence and without simony; the person elected shall receive from the king the regalia and the sceptre, and perform to him the duties which are his right; the king renounces all investiture by the cross and the ring; the emperor Henry and his adherents are absolved and reconciled to the church (September 1122).

Thus is settled that quarrel on investitures which convulsed the church and the empire for nearly half a century. But this was only an episode in their struggle for the universal monarchy; we shall soon see them recommence the war.

Calixtus II. holds at Rome a general council, the first of the Lateran (which the Latin Church counts for the ninth œcumenical (1123). The convention of Worms is confirmed there. Numerous complaints arise afterwards in the council against the monks which possess, it is said, churches, lands, castles, tithes, oblations of the living and the dead, a canon is drawn up which forbids the Abbots and the monks to assign public penance, to visit the sick, to say public mass; they are restricted to receiving from the diocesan bishops, the holy oils, the consecration of altars, the ordination of clerics.

The pontificate of the successor of Calixtus, Honorius II, (1124-40), offers nothing remarkable; but his death becomes the occasion of a schism in the Latin Church. A party of the cardinals elects Innocent II. (1130-43), the others name Pierre de Leon (Anacletus II.)

The latter is the more powerful in Rome. Innocent, constrained to quit it with his followers, retires to Pisa and thence to France.

Anacletus is acknowledged in Italy by Roger, Duke of Calabria and Count of Sicily, to whom he concedes the principality of Capua, the lordship of Naples, and the title of King of Sicily. Louis le Gros, King of France, pronounces in favour of Innocent, according to the advice of Bernard, Abbot of Clairvaux, whom his eloquence and his reputation for sanctity cause to be regarded as an oracle. The same pontiff is supported by the King of England and by Lothaire II., who reigns in Germany from the death of Henry V. (1125); but Lothaire has for competitor for the empire, Conrad, Duke of Franconia, of the house of Suabia (Hohenstauffen), who unites his cause to that of Anacletus. Innocent returns into Italy, accompanied by Bernard (1132), King Lothaire goes to meet him, and conducts him to Rome, where that prince is crowned emperor by the Pope, who, after an oath, concedes to him the usufruct of the domains of the Countess Matilda. Anacletus II. then occupied the castle Saint Angelo, St Peter's Church, and a number of fortified places. Lothaire, who is not strong enough to dispossess him, resumes the road to Germany after a sojourn of seven weeks. Innocent II. again retires to Pisa. He there holds a council, which is attended by Bernard de Clairvaux (1134). The latter then visits Milan and several cities of Lombardy, in the design of pacifying the country. Returning into France, he goes in Aquitania at the legate's request, and induces the duke of that country to be reconciled with Pope Innocent.

' The emperor Lothaire, whom Conrad had at last recognised, re-enters Italy with a numerous army, and directing his steps toward the southern provinces, which hold for Anacletus, seizes Beneventum, Capua, La Pouille, and penetrates into Campania. He re-establishes the Pope in Rome, and at his return dies at the foot of the Alps (1137). Roger, King of Sicily, re-takes Beneventum and most of the cities of La Pouille. Lothaire II. has for successor, under the name of Conrad III., that same Duke of Franconia, who had disputed the empire with him. Henry, Duke of Bavaria, protests against that election. Hence a war which gave occasion to the names Guelphs and Ghibelines, the last designating the partizans of the emperor, the former, those of his adversary.

The death of Anacletus changes the state of affairs at Rome (1138). A successor is given to him under the name of Victor; but at the end of two months Victor and his cardinals make their submission to Innocent II., who resumes authority in the city.

The pontiff convenes there, the 18th of July 1139, a a general council—The Second Council of the Lateran, the tenth œcumenic of the Latins. The members declare null the ordinations made by Anacletus and the other schismatics. The Pope publicly strips of the episcopal insignia those of their bishops who are present. The canon of the council held at Toulouse by Calixtus II. against the new Manichaeans is reproduced, and the opinions of Arnaud of Brescia, a former disciple of Abelard, are condemned.

Arnaud (Arnold), after having long studied in France, had returned into Italy where, in the dress of a monk, he declaimed against the Pope, the bishops, the clerics, and the monks, reproaching them with possessing lordships and other immovable property. "All these goods," he said, "belong to the prince, who can confer them only on laymen; clerics ought to live frugally on the gifts and oblations of the people." He also, it is added, published heterodox sentiments on the eucharist and on baptism. He is brought before the council of the Lateran, when the Pope imposes silence on him. Arnaud flees to Zurich, continues to teach his doctrines, and spreads them widely abroad.

The resumption of studies from the beginning of the eleventh century, had given minds an activity which exercised itself principally on religious matters. There existed among the Moslems of Spain several books of Aristotle's, brought from the East, where they were introduced at the time of the Nestorian and Eutychian controversies. These works soon circulate in the Latin countries, who are pleased with the doctrines of the philosopher of Stagira, well or ill explained. Thence proceeds the scholastic philosophy or the application of dialectics to theology. Among its adepts are two archbishops of Canterbury, Langfranc and his successor Anselm. The latter, not less celebrated by his talents in dialectics than by his eminent virtues, is considered as the first author of Christian metaphysics, which, without quitting the circle of the revealed faith, proposes to develop the science of divine things according to the principles of reason. But a schism is soon produced among the new disciples of Aristotle, on occasion of what were called universals or ideas of kind, species, difference, property, and accident. Some assert that these are realities, others regard them as simply denominations. The two parties are designated under the names of realists and nominalists. The question which divides them, all but futile in itself, acquires importance by its mixture with theological conceptions. The trinity, for instance, ends in Sabellianism in one of the systems, and in the other, turns into tritheism. The new method of philosophy triumphs in the schools whence comes its name of scholastic. But numerous and zealous contradictions arise among the ancient theologians. At their head is Bernard de Clairvaux, whose credit prevails more and more in the Church. He becomes an adversary of the new doctrine, and denounces, as suspected of heresy, Abelard, and other doctors of the schools.

Peter Abelard, born near Nantes the year 1079, had studied under Roscelin of Compiegne, the first head of the Nominalists, under William of Champeaux and divers others. He opens in Paris a school of logic and theology, whither flock numerous disciples. His amours with Heloïse, and their unfortunate consequences, interrupt the course of his lessons. He enters the monastery of St Denis, and then holds another school in the priory of Deuil. A book which he composes on the trinity is laid before a council at Soissons, and brings on him condemnation to perpetual seclusion in a monastery of that city. He is taken thence a few days after to be sent to St Denis. He continues to teach theology during eighteen years. But about the year 1140, one of his books is indicated as containing different errors on the trinity, the incarnation, freewill, the Eucharist, original sin. It was in reality difficult that in entering on these matters according to the principles of sound reason, theologians, even without hostile intention, should not be led to more or less shake the scaffold of religious theories that had been built by the official church. A council assembles at Sens. Bernard produces the book, and cites the passages which he intends to incriminate. The author, abstaining from a reply, appeals to the Holy See. Bernard writes on the subject to the Pope and the principal prelates of the Court of Rome, to whom he denounces Arnaud de Brescia, then living in Zurich. The Pope imposes perpetual silence on Abelard; he enjoins on the archbishops of Sens and Rheims to imprison them separately in monasteries, Arnaud and Abelard, and to burn the books which contain their errors. Meanwhile Abelard had put himself on his way to Rome to support his appeal. On his arrival at Cluny he there finds the Abbot of Citeaux, who reconciles him with Bernard, when the decision of the Pope is known. Abelard desists from his appeal, and forms the resolution of passing the rest of his days in the monastery of Cluny, where he lives two years in absolute seclusion.

Gilbert de la Poree, bishop of Poitiers, a man of earnest character and deep knowledge is, in his turn, accused by Bernard of uttering ill-sounding opinions on the trinity and the incarnation. They appear first before a council in Paris presided over by the Pope (1147), and then before a council held at Rheims, where the doctrine of Gilbert is condemned.

But among the ancient theologians some sought to conciliate the rival systems. After the example of Langfranc and Anselm, they rested on sacred Scripture and the decisions of antiquity, without disdaining philosophical discussions. The most illustrious of them is the bishop of Paris, Peter Lombard. In the middle of the twelfth century, he publishes his book of *Sentences*, a compilation of passages from the fathers, which forms a veritable course of theology. Received with universal applause, this work is soon the only one that is explained in the schools; its author is called the *Master of the Sentences*.

About the same epoch the study of civil law and canonical right commenced.

Under the reign of the emperor Lothaire II. a copy of the Pandects is discovered, it is said, in the ruins of Amalfi in Pouille (1137). Forthwith the civil right of the Romans is restored to honour. It is taught at Bologna and in the other schools of Latin Europe. The tribunals conform to it in their judgments. The Salic laws, the Burgundian, the Lombard and others of barbarous origin, lose all their credit. From the schools of civil right will proceed all those legists who in future will be the firmest support of princes against the pontifical pretensions. The Court of Rome by a kind of presentiment of the danger which threatens it, judges it opportune to oppose the study of canonical right to that of civil right. A monk of Saint Benedict, named Gratian, makes a new collection of Canons which he entitles the *Concordance of the Discordant Canons*. This collection comprises decisions of councils ancient and modern, the False Decretals of Isidore Mercator, diverse other Decretals, and passages extracted from some fathers of the church. There are consecrated on every point the pretended right which popes arrogate in virtue of the False decretals. They indeed are outdone, for it is said without any proof that the sovereign pontiff gives their authority to the canons, but is not bound by them. Pope Eugenius III. approves this work and orders it to be taught at Bologna. It is, so to say, the sole canonical right that the Latins have known since then. The work of Gratian, designated simply under the name of decree, has been followed in all their schools, and until the end of the twelfth century, passed for the purest discipline of the church. The ecclesiastical right of Rome was completed afterwards by the addition of five books of decretals compiled by Gregory IX. of a sixth book published by Boniface VIII., the Clementines (of Clement V.) the Extravagants, without reckoning the glosses, the rules of the chancellery and of the rota, the bullarium, &c., all things conceived in the same spirit as the decree of the monk Gratian.

Pope Innocent II. had also excommunicated, in the general council of the Lateran, the king Roger, who still supported the schism. Scarcely is the council closed than that prince comes to Salerno and invades the Pouille. The pontiff advances with troops as far as the foot of Mount Cassino. Negotiations are undertaken, in the interval, Innocent is made prisoner by the king's son. Peace is concluded on condition that the Court of Rome grants Roger the kingdom of Sicily, to one of his sons the duchy of Pouille, and to the other the principality of Capua. The pope repairs to Beneventum, where he is received with the greatest honours. When free, he refuses to break the treaty which he has just made. During the different phases of the struggle between the priesthood and the empire, Italy of the north had taken a new face. After the example of Venice, Genoa, Pisa, the majority of its cities were erected into republics, while keeping themselves under the patronage of the empire and the papacy. This form of government reigned at Florence, Sienna, Bologna, Milan, Pavia, and in the other Lombard cities. Rome found itself drawn in the same direction by the memories of its history. Insurgent against the pope, it re-established the senate which had been long abolished (1143). Innocent II. dies after a short interval without being able to regain the temporal power. He has for successors Celestin II. who rules only five months, and Lucius II. who deceases at the end of eleven. The Romans pursue their enterprise. With their senate they have a Patrician on whom they confer the regalian rights, saying the pope ought, as the ancient bishops, to be satisfied with the tithes and the oblations. The Romans on their side, send to that prince that they hold for him against the pope and the king of Sicily. At the time of the promotion of Eugenius III. (1145-53), they wish to constrain that pontiff to confirm their senate. Eugenius goes to be consecrated in the monastery of Farse and retires to Viterbo. Arnaud of Brescia goes then to Rome. He proposes to rebuild the capitol, to re-establish the dignity of the senate, and the order of the Chevaliers. The Romans abolish the office of the prefect of Rome, constrain the principal men of the city to submit to their Patrician, beat down the towers of some of the grandees, and fortify the church of Saint Peter. The pope Eugenius excommunicates the Patrician and his partisans, and with the aid of the inhabitants of Tibur, compels the Romans to beg for peace. The patriciate is abolished, the prefect restored, the senators submit to the pope. The pontiff enters Rome amid general acclamations (Christmas 1145), but he is almost forthwith obliged to retire beyond the Tiber into the castle Saint Angelo. Fatigued with these troubles, he passes into France, where he intends to press the execution of a crusade necessitated by the state of the East (1147). Godefroy de Bouillon, who died after the reign of a year, left the throne of Jerusalem to his brother Baldwin, Count of Edessa. The narratives respecting the first crusade moving people's minds in Europe, fifty thousand crusaders leave Lombardy in the year 1101, and arrive at Nicomedia at the beginning of the following year. At the same time some French nobles, among others William, duke of Aquitaine, Hugues of France, and Stephen of Blois, of whom the two last had abandoned the first crusade at Antioch, put themselves on the road with thirty thousand men. At Constantinople they meet Raymond, Count of Toulouse, whom they choose for their chief. These Crusaders of France and Italy traverse Asia Minor in two separate bodies. Some get entangled in mountain defiles whence only a small number escape; the others assemble at Antioch, and thence direct their steps toward Jerusalem (1103). The duke of Aquitaine soon returns into his estates. The crusaders that remain in the East perish for the most part in a battle fought with the infidels by king Baldwin. The Latin Church soon takes the place of the Greek Church in the countries occupied by the Franks. A Latin patriarch sits in Jerusalem, another at Antioch; after the capture of Tyre an archbishopric of the Roman rite is established there (1124). Two military orders are founded in Palestine, the Templars and the Chevaliers of the hospital of Saint John of Jerusalem. The Templars devote themselves to the service of God, undertaking to live in chastity, obedience, and poverty, their first duty is to guard the high roads against robbers and thieves, for the safety of the pilgrims who go to Jerusalem. The order of the crusaders of Saint John of Jerusalem, or Hospitallers, is divided into three classes; that of chevaliers of illustrious birth, who bear arms for the defence of the faith; that of priests, who officiate in the churches of the order; that of brother servants or soldiers of common origin. A certain number of the order take care, in the hospital of Saint John, of the poor and sick pilgrims. On the death of Baldwin I. (1118) the kingdom of Jerusalem passes to Baldwin II. who is succeeded by his son-in-law Foulques of Angers (1131). Foulques has for successor his young son Baldwin III. (1142).

In December 1144 the city of Edessa is taken after a siege of two years, by Atabeck Zenguy (Sanguin) a powerful priest of the East; a great massacre of the inhabitants who were all Christians takes place on the occasion. Succours are instantly called for in Europe. Eugenius III. writes thereon to the king of France. In a Parliament held at Vezelay, Bernard preaches a crusade by the express order of the pope. Louis VII. and his spouse, Alienor de Guyenne, take the cross in Germany and induce the king Conrad to follow their example.

The German crusaders sail for Spain, which also entreated reinforcements. Arrived in Galicia they aid the king Alphonso Henriquez to capture Lisbon; the city remains to the king, the booty to the crusaders. Conrad sets out with his nephew Frederic of Suabia, directing his steps to Constantinople (1147). That prince advances into Natolia under infidel guides, who lead him into sterile and impracticable places. He is assailed by the Turks and loses three-fourths of his army. Escaped from the massacre, he meets at Nice Louis VII. who has just passed the strait. The French crusaders defeat the Turks on the borders of the Meander. But the rear guard of Louis is afterwards cut to pieces and destroyed. He arrives with the rest of his troops at Antioch and thence at Jerusalem. Conrad goes by sea to the port of Acre. They besiege Damascus without success. Then Conrad returns home. The king of France remains in the East till the spring of the year 1149. Nevertheless pope Eugenius, after a short sojourn at Clairvaux, in which he had been a monk under the direction of Bernard, returns into Italy and proceeds to Rome (1148). Frederic of Suabia, surnamed Barbarossa, who has succeeded Conrad his uncle (1122), engages toward the holy see to make neither peace nor truce without his consent, either with the Romans, or with Roger, king of Sicily, to defend against all the dignity of the pope and the rights of Saint Peter. Eugènius III. promises in return to give the king the imperial crown when he shall come to receive it, and to aid him to maintain and augment his dignity. Eugenius III. is succeeded by Anastasius IV. (1153) then by Hadrian IV. (1154-59). The pope then resided in the Leonine city; Arnaud of Brescia still bore sway in Rome. The inhabitants drive him away at the approach of Frederic Barbarossa (1155).

Arnaud falls into the hands of that prince, who delivers him to the pope; an ecclesiastical verdict condemns him to the fire, his ashes are cast into the Tiber. Frederic returns into Germany after his coronation, notwithstanding the urgency of the pope and the Greek Emperor Manuel, who urge him to make war on the King of Sicily, their common enemy. After the death of Roger, first king of that country (1154), Pope Hadrian refuses William his son the confirmation of his kingdom. That prince invades the lands of the Roman Church. The pope excommunicates him and makes war on him (1155). But the following year Hadrian IV., besieged in Beneventum, is reduced to make peace on disadvantageous conditions. The emperor returns into Italy in the year 1158 with a formidable army; he assembles a meeting of bishops and nobles of Lombardy. Judges and doctors there determine what are the regalian rights; and Frederic resumes those of his rights which are possessed without valid reason by the bishops or nobles of the country. Hadrian IV., dissatisfied with this measure, exchanges with the prince bitter-sweet letters full of threats. Meanwhile he excites the Milanais to revolt, and dies shortly after.

A schism breaks out for the nomination of his successor. Alexander III. is elected by the majority of the cardinals (1159-81). Three opposers proclaim Octavian, one of them under the name of Victor III. A council convened by Frederic at Pavia pronounces in favour of Victor, who is acknowledged equally by Hungary, Denmark, and Norway;

on the contrary France, England, Sicily, Spain, and Palestine hold for Alexander. Victor is master of Rome by his family and by the protection of the emperor. Alexander, retiring into France, establishes himself in the city of Sens whence he discharges the affairs of the Church, from the month of October 1163.

In the midst of these divisions the cities of Lombardy raised the standard of liberty (1161). Milan is taken by the emperor and razed to its foundations (1162); several of the other cities are dismantled; all lose their privileges. Frederic installed in each of them a podestat by whom he is represented. Alexander III. offers himself as the defender of Italian liberty. He excommunicates the emperor and sets his subjects free from their oath of fidelity. All the cities of Lombardy combine for their common defence. The names of Guelphs and Ghibilines become current in the Peninsula to designate the partizans of the pope and those of the emperor. Victor has for successor Pascal III. (1164). But the affairs of Frederic go on badly in Italy; he is driven away by the Lombards. Then the Roman people approach Alexander III., who sets out for France in the course of 1165, and returns to Rome the 21st of November. Frederic repasses the Alps, followed by considerable forces (1166). He lays siege to Ancona, which the Greeks had seized, and after the capture of that city, he directs his steps on Rome. The Pope Alexander retires to Beneventum and the people submit. But the maladies which decimate his army oblige the emperor to return. In his retreat he is attacked by the Lombards. Alexander III. takes from him nearly all Italy, excommunicates and deposes him. It is with much difficulty that the prince succeeds in regaining Germany in passing through Burgundy (1168). The Antipope Pascal, who dies this same year, is replaced by Calixtus III.

England at this time was agitated by violent quarrels between the king and the Archbishop of Canterbury.

Stephen, the last Normand King of England, had for successor Henry Plantagenet, his nephew, son of Geoffroy, Count of Anjou (1154). Henry II. becomes the most powerful prince of the west by his marriage with Alienor de Guyenne, at first spouse of Louis VII. Independently of England, he has possessions in France, Normandy, Anjou, Touraine, Maine, Aquitaine, and Poitou, to which Britain unites itself. Moreover Ireland is given him by Pope Hadrian IV. So many states do not shelter him from intestine dissensions.

That prince chose for Archbishop of Canterbury his chancellor Thomas Becket, in whom he had entire confidence. From the day of his consecration the new archbishop changing his manner of life, affects great austerity in the practices of religion, gives himself assiduously to the study of sacred things, and carefully seeks for the property usurped from his church. Division arises between him and his prince. Their principal difference ensues in connection with the ecclesiastical jurisdiction. Henry II. wished that having been degraded according to the canons, clerics should be subject to the secular judge for ordinary misdeeds; while, according to Becket, they ought to be answerable only before ecclesiastical tribunals, even for acts of that nature. Henry, in an assembly held at Clarendon, presents the customs of his kingdom in sixteen articles, and asks the prelates to approve them (1164). At first they consent; but after the complete exhibition of those customs, the archbishop refuses to affix his seal to the document. The pope consulted declares in favour of Thomas, while recommending to him great circumspection in consequence of the difficult circumstances in which the holy see finds itself owing to the schism. The king, who holds to his customs, has the clerics accused of robbery, homicide, or other crimes of the same nature to be tried before the secular tribunals. The other bishops submit, but Becket resists obstinately. He is cited to Northampton before an assembly of all the prelates and nobles of the kingdom; pecuniary fines are pronounced against him; he is declared a perjurer and a traitor. The bishops alarmed think of calling for his deposition. The archbishop appeals to the pope, and withdraws in the midst of the insults of the courtiers. On the outside an immense crowd press around him to receive his benediction. He escapes during the night and succeeds in finding a refuge in France. The pope, annulling the sentence passed at Northampton, assigns to the prelate the abbey of Pontigny for his place of retreat. Henry II. confiscates the property of the archbishop, banishes his relatives, his domestics, his friends, and threatens Alexander III. to renounce obedience to him. After his return to Rome, the pope creates the archbishop of Canterbury his legate for all England, the diocese of York excepted (December 1165). Thomas forthwith notifies his appointment in the country. He addresses to the king a letter full of mildness for the first admonition; he afterwards writes to him another in which he threatens him with the wrath of God. The king appeals to the holy see. Thomas excommunicates de Vezelay, several of his adversaries by name, and in general all those who in future shall lay hands on the property of his church (June 1166). He invites Henry to do penance under threat of anathema; he condemns the alleged customs of England, declaring excommunicated those who shall profit by them, and discharging the bishops from the promise which they had made to observe them. The bishops in a council held in London equally appeal to Rome against the measures taken by the prelate. Two legates *a latere* sent by the pope do not succeed in conciliating the parties; but they forbid Thomas to issue any interdict or excommunication until both sides appear in the Court of Rome. After divers fruitless attempts the pope bids the king to be reconciled with the archbishop before the 18th February 1170; he removes the suspense of Thomas in the case that satisfaction has not•been given at that date. Finally peace is concluded under menace of an interdict. Henry undertakes to restore his favour to the archbishop, and to restore to him the church of Canterbury, and the lands which depend on it. The pope addresses to the prelate powers for all possibilities, except the excommunication of the king and his family. Thomas returns into England after seven years of exile (November 1170). A multitude of people welcome him on the shore; they press upon him all along his road: entire parishes go to meet him in processions. He directs his steps to London; the citizens pour forth to salute him, but the civil authority interposes, and stops the manifestation of enthusiasm. When the king learns the conduct of Thomas, he in his anger curses all those whom he has laden with his benefits, and of whom no one avenges him, on a priest who troubles his kingdom. Four chevaliers of his chamber pass into England, penetrate into the church in which the archbishop is officiating, and put him to death at the foot of the altar (29th December 1170). The friends of the prelate demand vengeance from Rome. The king, who fears an excommunication, swears through his deputies that he will submit to the orders of the holy see. Alexander excommunicates the murderers of the archbishop, their accomplices, as well as those who shall give them refuge and protection (March 1171), he confirms the interdict hurled by his legate on the king's territories beyond the sea. Legates are sent into Normandy. Henry swears publicly by their hands that he is a stranger to the murder of the archbishop. But acknowledging that his animosity may have given occasion to it, he binds himself to send to Jerusalem two hundred chevaliers, to support them there during a year, and to take the cross himself for three years. He abrogates the illicit customs which he has established in his states, permits appeals freely to the holy See, and engages to restore all the property of the church of Canterbury.

Thomas Becket is solemnly canonised by the Pope and put into the rank of martyrs (1173). He was in reality a martyr to the doctrine of the papal autocracy. This is the first example of a saint created in virtue of the exclusive right which the Roman pontiffs take to themselves. Down to the ninth century Paradise was opened by the superstitious fancy of the multitude or by the astuteness of the priests and the monks, who people it with names known or unknown, sometimes the creatures of the imagination. To obviate this inconvenience, the councils of the ninth century decree that no one shall be held for a saint before the bishop has decided it in a provincial council, in presence of the people. The intervention of the Pope was not absolutely requisite; but already the custom was establishing itself of his confirming the decisions of councils and bishops. However they do not proceed to a revision of what was done before. The celestial *statu quo* is maintained for the anterior saints, whether of good or bad alloy. Rome proposes only to regulate things better in the future. We shall see it ceaselessly place in heaven, before all others, the zealous defenders of its omnipotence, the visionary fanatics, and the good people who give their property to the churches and the monasteries. However the schism and the war continued in Italy; the Milanese had rebuilt their city. After divers vicissitudes, Frederic finally resolves to conclude a peace. By the treaty of Venice, which the peace of Constance follows, he acknowledges Pope Alexander, and consecrates the independence of the Lombard republics (1177). But the imperial right is maintained and the Podestats receive the command of the military forces. The emperor and his partisans are absolved and reconciled. The pontiff re-enters Rome. Calixtus himself makes his submission to Alexander III., who welcomes him favourably and always treats him well in the sequel. To obviate the danger of a new schism, the Pope convokes a general council for the 5th of March 1179; it is the third of the Lateran and the eleventh œcumenical of the Latins. The assembly passes a canon which confers the election of the popes on the cardinals, without any concurrence with the clergy or the people, and requires the union of two-thirds of the voices. The prescriptions on the celibacy of priests are renewed, as well as the anathemas against heretics and their supporters. At the death of Alexander, the new decree is followed for the election of Lucius III. (1181-85). The cardinals find themselves invested for ever with the right of appointing the Pope, to the exclusion of the people and the other members of the clergy. Driven from Rome by an insurrection (1183), Lucius retires to Verona, where he dwells until his death. Urban III. (1185-87) has at first some differences with the Emperor Frederic. He is dissatisfied with the marriage of Henry, son of the emperor, with Constance, inheritrix of William II., King of Sicily. But the German Bishops interpose and reconcile them.

Disastrous news arrive from Palestine. Since the ill success of the crusade of Conrad and Louis VII. (1149), the situation of the Christians had become worse and worse daily. Baldwin III., King of Jerusalem, had had for successor his son, Amaury, whose forces were exhausted in attempting the conquest of Egypt (1162). He leaves the crown to his young son, Baldwin IV., a prince of infirm health (1173). The advent of Saladin to power is baneful to Christianity. A Kurd by nature, Saladin (Sàlah-Eddin) had become the vizier of the Fatimite Caliph Aded. At the death of that prince (1171), he takes the title of Sultan, and receives investiture from the Caliph of Bagdad, whose name he replaces in the public prayers. Master of Egypt, he extends his power into Syria, takes possession of Damascus, and unites under himself the Moslem forces. He at first loses a great battle against the young king, Baldwin IV. (1177), but the crusaders are afterwards beaten near Sidon (1179). Baldwin seeks for succour in Europe. Chevaliers leave France with a multitude of people on foot. England is more prodigal of promises than performances. Baldwin IV. is succeeded by his nephew, Baldwin V. (1185), and Baldwin V. by Guy de Lusignan (1186). The war with Saladin is rekindled. He possesses Egypt, Arabia, Syria, and Mesopotamia. He takes the city of Tiberias, the castle of which continues to resist. A bloody battle, which lasts two days, ends with the complete defeat of the Christians. The king and the principal chiefs remain prisoners. The pretended wood of the true cross falls into the hands of the Moslems. Saladin takes possession of Jaffa, Nablus, Sebaste, Nazareth, Cæsarea, Sidon, Berytus, and other places. Ascalon becomes the price of the ransom of Guy de Lusignan. Jerusalem capitulates after a siege of fourteen days (October 1187). No more remains to the Latins than Antioch, Tyr, and Tripolis.

Pope Urban III. falls under these disasters. Gregory VIII. sits only two months. Clement III. (1187-91) eagerly exhorts the faithful to reconquer the Holy Land. The kings of France and England take the cross (1188). Whoever does not do so in these two kingdoms is made to pay the tenth of his income (Saladin tithe). The emperor also crosses himself, with his son Frederic, and the principal nobles of the empire. Frederic Barbarossa sets out in the spring of the year 1189. He traverses Hungary and Bulgaria, takes possession of Philipopolis, and passes the winter at Adrianople. The year following he crosses the Hellespont, twice beats the Turks, and ends by drowning himself in a small river of Cilicia. His son, who takes the command of the army, perishes before Acre (1191). The kings of France and England set out at the same time, Philip Augustus from Genoa, and Richard Cœur de Lion from Marseilles (1190). They pass the winter at Messina. Philip is under the walls of Acre in April 1191. Richard, thrown by a tempest on the isle of Cyprus, takes it from the Greeks. At his arrival before Acre, this siege is pressed, and the city surrenders. During the siege the order of teutonic chevaliers is founded to defend religion in the Holy Land, and to succour the poor and the sick ; it consists solely of Germans of noble origin.

Philip Augustus, sick and discontented with Richard, returns into his estates, leaving the crusaders of his nation under the leadership of the Duke of Burgundy. After his departure, the King of England defeats Saladin near Arsuf, although with very inferior forces. But troubles caused by his absence call him back into his kingdom. He concludes with the Sultan a truce of three years ; Jaffa, Caesarea Arsuf, Hiffa, and Acre remain with the Christians (1192). Richard on his return is shipwrecked in the gulf of Venice. He is arrested on the lands of the Duke of Austria, and given up to the emperor, who detains him for a whole year.

After the death of Frederic Barbarossa, his father, King Henry VI., came into Italy to take the imperial crown, and support the rights of his wife over the kingdom of Sicily. Crowned by Celestin III. (1191-98), he, to the great displeasure of the pontiff, hastens to attack Tancred, who has reigned in Sicily from the death of William III. (1189). Several places fall under his power, among others Salerno, in which he leaves the Empress Constance. The maladies which waste his army oblige him to retire. Tancred retakes the majority of the places. The empress is delivered up to him and he sends her into Sicily. But that prince soon dies, leaving as his heir only a son yet a child (1194). The emperor returns and is crowned in Palermo. He carries into Germany the widow and the son of Tancred, whom he keeps in perpetual prison, after having plucked out the eyes of the young prince. This union of Sicily with the states of the house of Suabia, which appeared likely to make the emperors all powerful in Italy, has for result to secure to the popes the alliance of the Lombard cities, which fear for their liberty. The antagonism of the Guelphs and the Ghibilines is consolidated for many generations.

A new crusade is preached at the death of Saladin (1193). Division having arisen among the children of his brother, the occasion seemed propitious for the re-taking of Jerusalem. The German form three armies; the first goes by land to Constantinople; the second, embarking in Germany, coasts along France and Spain and proceeds to Acre by the straits; the third sails for Italy, and arrives at the port of Acre in September 1196. The crusaders are scandalized at the lives of the Templars and the Latin lords of Palestine; those Levantines kept much more to the coast, of which the territory is fertile, than at Jerusalem and the Holy Sepulchre. The Germans gain some advantage over the infidels; but the death of Henry VI. recalls them home almost immediately. That emperor had died at Messina (1197), the kingdom of Sicily passes to his son Frederic, under the tutelage of Philip of Suabia. The latter is himself elected King of the Romans by higher Germany and the states of Sicily; lower Germany makes choice of Otho of Saxony; thence arise troubles in the empire and the church. Innocent III., called to the Holy See at the age of thirty-seven years, shows himself the worthy imitator of Gregory VII. (1198-1216). His first care is to exact an oath of fidelity to the prefect of Rome, who till then took it to the emperor.

Constance, widow of Henry VI., obtains from the pontiff the investiture of the kingdom of Sicily for her and her son, but in renouncing the concessions made to William I. for the elections, appeals, legations, and councils. That princess dies the same year, after having conferred the regency of the kingdom on the pope.

War was kindled in Germany between the two competitors for the empire. Innocent, from opposition to the house of Suabia, of whose power in Italy he is afraid, declares for Otho (1201), and makes himself arbiter of kings and bestower of the imperial crown. Philip protests; his cause gathers strength daily. Otho, beaten not far from Cologne (1206) passes into England to the side of John his uncle. The pope interposes to obtain a truce. During the negociation Philip perishes a victim of individual revenge (1208). Otho, recognised throughout the world, marries the daughter of Philip, and is crowned emperor at Rome (1209). But the good understanding does not subsist long between the pope and him. Otho refuses to give up the lands of the Countess Matilda; he wishes to take possession of la Pouille and other countries which he regards as imperial possessions. Innocent excommunicates him, and foments a revolt in Germany. The young King of Sicily, Frederic, is elected King of the Romans. Otho retires into Saxony, then to Cologne; he is abandoned by everybody. The authority of Innocent III., which troubles Germany, does not make itself less felt in other countries. He confers the royal dignity on Primislas, Duke of Bohemia, on Joannice, prince of the Bulgarians, who has separated from the Greek Church to join the Latin. He consecrates at Rome Peter II. King of Aragon, whose states become tributary to the Holy See. An excommunication, followed by an interdict, constrains Alphonso King of Leon, to separate from Berengere, daughter of Alphonso IX. of Castille, whom he had espoused, although his father's cousin-german. An interdict hurled on France compels Philip Augustus to take back Ingerburge, from whom he had separated under the plea of unjustifiable kinship. In England specially does the policy of Innocent III. triumph. The See of Canterbury becoming vacant, a double election is made by the monks. King John speaks strongly for one of the elected. The affair is carried before the pope. He annuls both elections, and appoints a third person by means of the monks that are at Rome. John refusing to recognise the new choice, the pope throws a general interdict on his kingdom, and next year excommunicates him himself. Far from yielding, the king persecutes the ecclesiastics who oppose him. His subjects are then set free from their oath of fidelity by a papal sentence, and all relations with him are forbidden under pain of excommunication. Finally Innocent deposes him (1212) and transfers his kingdom to Philip Augustus, who makes arrangements for invading it. John had made himself odious by his cruelties, his exactions, and his debauches; he could not reckon on his people. In the threatening danger he comes to the resolution of giving to the Church of Rome his kingdoms of England and Ireland. A charter is drawn up by which the king engages to hold them as a vassal of the pope, and to do liege homage to him for them (1213). In consequence of this gift the pope takes off the interdict which had been lying on England for six years. But the barons rising against John compel him to grant a charter confirmative of their liberties (1215). Innocent breaks and annuls it. The barons continue the war despite the excommunication fulminated against them. They bestow the crown on Louis, son of Philip Augustus, whose spouse is King John's niece. However, in the midst of all the cares which occupy him, the crusade and the extirpation of heresy are the two things which Innocent III. has most at heart.

In the early days of his pontificate, he exhorts the peoples of France, England, Hungary, and Sicily, to enter on a crusade (1198). Two cardinals take the cross as an encouragement. The clergy tax themselves to the fortieth of their revenues, the cardinals and the Pope to a tenth. Legates are sent to Venice, Lombardy, and France.

The French crusaders repair to Venice to embark (1202). There not finding themselves in a condition to pay all the sum promised for their transport, they agree to free themselves from the surplus by putting under the power of the Venetians the city of Zara, which the King of Hungary had taken from them. In effect, they capture it, notwithstanding the prohibitions of the Pope, and pass the winter there.

While these things are going on, the young Alexis, the Angel, brother-in-law of Philip of Suabia, proposes to them to drive his uncle Alexis from the throne of Constantinople.

This leads us to take up our narrative somewhat in the rear. From the time of Michael of Cerularius down to the crusades the relations between the Greeks and the Latins had been very few. Nevertheless Pope Alexander sends a legate to Constantinople (1072), and the year following, two deputies of the Emperor Michael Paripanace solicit from Gregory VI. aid against the Saracens, who have ravaged to the very gates of his capital. Gregory, on this occasion, has the thought of a holy war, of which he would be the head; but circumstances do not allow him to pass to the execution of the plan. Alexis Comnene endeavours to maintain friendly relations with the Latins, whose assistance is necessary to him. He sends ambassadors to the Council of Plaisance (1095), precursor of that of Clermont, in which the first crusade is published. At a later time, despite his griefs against the crusaders, he none the less persists in remaining in communion with the Church of Rome. The emperors Calo-John and Manuel pursue the same policy. At the time of the schism which follows the death of Hadrian IV. (1159), Manuel sends into France two deputies to Alexander III., whom he acknowledges for the true Pope. A good understanding does not cease to reign between that pontiff and him. During the disagreements with the empire of Germany, Manuel offers to the Court of Rome all sorts of aid and the re-union of the two churches, on the condition that Alexander will secure him the imperial crown; this was to offer and ask more than the two could perform. The Greek emperor even sends the metropolitan of Corfu to assist at the third general council of the Lateran (1179). But this prelate falls ill at Otranto and does not recover till after the close of the council. The favourable proceedings of the Comnene in regard to the popes of Rome are explained by the needs of their policy, without any thought of concession having existed in either one or the other church. The grounds of disagreement between them had, on the contrary, increased and been aggravated. The Greeks said with reason that the Pope was an emperor and not a bishop; they gave the Latins the name of Azymites, and held them as excommunicated on account of the addition made to the creed. They did not receive the decrees of the pretended œcumenical councils of the Lateran, to which they were not invited. Add to this the subjects of discontent against the crusaders, who respected nothing in their passage through the provinces of the lower empire, and finally the substitution of Latin Churches for the Greek Churches in oriental countries. It was not then without vexation and anger that the Hellenic populations saw the relations of the Comnene with the popes, and the favour enjoyed by the Latins established in Constantinople. On the death of the Emperor Manuel, public hate soon explodes. A conspiracy is spun under the direction of Andronicus. The soldiers and the multitude of Constantinople, led by the priests and the monks, fall on the Latins and burn their quarter (1182). Four thousand of them are sold as slaves to the infidels. But a great number of others compromised in advance, embark with their families on vessels and gallies. In the way of reprisals they traverse the Hellespont, make descents on the cities and other places, kill the monks and the priests, burn the monasteries. The same ravages are reproduced on the coasts of Thessaly and other maritime provinces. The Latins succeed in getting together a considerable fleet.

Andronicus is proclaimed emperor with the young son of Manuel, whom he kills some days after (1183). At the instigation of a relative of the Comnene, William II., King of Sicily, undertakes the conquest of the Greek empire, he takes possession of Thessalonica and marches on Constantinople. Andronicus is massacred by the multitude (1185). Isaac the Angel, his successor, repels the Sicilians, and after a reign of ten years, is dethroned by his brother Alexis, who plucks out his eyes and puts him into prison. It is in this state of things that the young Alexis, son of Isaac, comes to implore the aid of the crusaders against the emperor, his uncle. They welcome his request, on condition that his brother-in-law Philip the Suabian shall aid them to recover the holy land. The enterprise is carried into effect, notwithstanding the opposition of the pope. Constantinople is carried by assault (18th July 1202). Isaac the angel reascends the throne which he divides with his son. But the young Alexis eluding his promises in regard to the Crusaders, hostilities soon break out between them and him. A revolution in the palace puts an end to his life and raises to power another Alexis surnamed Murchufle (1204). The war only becomes more embittered; the crusaders take Constantinople by scaling; Baldwin, count of Flanders, is proclaimed emperor. But his possessions comprise with Constantinople only Thrace and Moesia. The Venetians adjudge to themselves Peloponesus, Crete, and several cities of Phrygia. The Marquis de Montferrat obtains Thessaly as his share. Feudality installs itself in the Hellenic countries. Innocent III. resolves to approve the establishment of the new empire. He believes, or wishes others to believe, that it will be a point of support for the conquest of Palestine. An illusion of short duration! The emperor Baldwin and his feeble successors, out of condition to undertake anything abroad, succeed in maintaining themselves to the year 1261 only with the aid of the succours, which they go to beg for in every place. The West has the Greeks to combat in addition to the Moslems; the crusades for Constantinople injure those of the Holy Land. But the popes find in the new conquest occasion to gratify their old grudge against a rival See. In place of the Greek patriarch who had fled, Innocent of his full power names a Latin patriarch, and establishes bishops of the same rite in the other regions of the new empire. He promises the crusade indulgences to all those who shall aid it, in the view of facilitating the conquest of the Holy Land. He soon sees, to his great displeasure, arrive in the Bosphorus unexpected defenders. At the report of the taking of Constantinople, nearly all the Latins, clerics and laics, natives or foreigners, abandon Palestine for the Hellenic provinces. The Holy Land lacks men and money; the legates of the pope have themselves quitted it. The king Aimery de Lusignan and his son being dead, as well as the patriarch of Jerusalem, there no longer remains anyone for the temporal and spiritual government of the country (1205). The Count of Tripolis and a petty Armenian king, who is subject to the pope, dispute, arms in hand, the principality of Antioch. At the death of Isabella, widow in the fourth marriage of Aimery de Lusignan, her right to the royalty passes to Mary her oldest daughter, whom John de Brienne has lately married (1209). He is called the king of Acre, because in effect his kingdom goes little beyond, and his city is itself threatened by Moslems. In this extreme necessity, Innocent III. addresses all Christian nations (1213), a Bull which revokes in favour of Palestine the indulgences previously granted for the crusades against the Moors of Spain and against the heretics of Provence and Languedoc. Nothing less than the imminent peril of the Holy Land could have relaxed the war of extermination that had been pursued for many years against the latter, known under the name of Albigenses. It was one of Innocent's first enterprises ; overflowed in all places by the dissidents, the Roman Church had decreed against them implacable measures. These dissidents were of two kinds, the one of foreign origin, the other born in the bosom of the Latin Church. The first were derived from the Manichæans or Paulicians, who had been transported from the East into Thrace and Bulgaria. From these provinces a great number of them soon pass into Sclavonia, Lombardy, France, England, Germany. They are commonly called Manichæans, Cathari (Puritans), Patarins, Poblicans (Paulicians). As the Manichæans old or new they recognise a good principle and a bad one, make Christ descend into Mary's womb, clad with a celestial body, disdain the sacraments or explain them symbolically, reject the Old Testament to hold to the New, especially the Gospels. Their discipline is severe ; they rigorously practise fasting and abstinence, deny themselves wine and flesh, and exalt celibacy above marriage. They are divided into two classes, the perfect or consoled, and the confederates. These live as bachelors and in extreme mortification ; the others are not bound to certain observances, but they receive consolation before they die. Wherever these sectaries are discovered they are rigorously persecuted and most frequently burnt alive. Not less rapid is their progress, principally in Italy and in Southern France. The people are won over by their pious ardour, their austere practices, their pure morals, which contrast so favourably with the cupidity, the display, and the dissolution of the Latin clergy. Moreover there exists more than one affinity between the dogmas and the institutions of the two churches; both are governed by a supreme head, a superior council, and bishops; on both sides celibacy is lauded. The perfect observe it among the Manichæans. Rome imposes it on its clergy and on monks; in the Latin Church lay persons in dying love to muffle themselves up in a monkish dress, a sort of consolation similar to that of the Manichæan sect. Moreover, the devil plays a great part in the beliefs and legends of the middle ages; he gives so many occasions to the Virgin and the saints for defeating his evil designs, that one may easily be led to regard him as an evil principle almost equal to the good principle. In regard to the heresies bred in the Western Church, they are produced in great number during the twelfth century. We have already spoken of the speculations more or less hazardous of the scholastic doctors, of the declamations and enterprises of Arnaud of Brescia against the opulence of the clergy and the temporal sovereignty of the popes. We shall point out other sectaries of the same period.

A person named Tranchelme or Tranquelin preaches at Anvers and its environs a doctrine which rejects the pope, the bishop, and all the clergy, gives to the churches the name of places of prostitution, and to the sacraments that of profanation, and forbids the payment of tithe. This preacher is slain by a priest; but his opinions survive him. Peter de Bruys condemns the baptism of infants, the worship of images, and the wood of the cross, the pretended sacrifice of the mass, prayers for the dead, and the monastic if e. After preaching for twenty years in Dauphiny, his country, in Provence and in Languedoc, he is seized and burnt by the Roman Catholics of Saint Gilles (1147). Henry, disciple of Peter de Bruys, continues his teachings; but with some modifications. A pope's legate, and Bernard de Clairvaux come to Toulouse to oppose him, him and his adherents. At their approach Henry takes to flight. He is arrested, and he dies in the bishop's prisons.

The Petrobrusians and the Henricians multiply in the southern provinces. They abound specially at Albi, whence comes their name of Albigenses. More numerous still and more renowned, the sect of the Vaudois commences at Lyons about the year 1100. They are also called the poor of Lyons or Leonists from the place of their origin, as well as sabbaté's or insabbaté's from sabots or wooden shoes worn by their doctors.

Peter Valdo, a rich merchant of Lyons, having got the Gospels and other books of Scripture translated, discovers by reading them how much the Roman Church differs from that of Jesus. He distributes his goods to the poor and begins to teach what he regards as the true doctrine. In vain do the clergy of Lyons oppose his undertaking. The piety of the Vaudois, their contempt of riches and honours, bring new disciples over every day. According to another version, their doctrine existed from the earliest ages in the vallies of Piedmont where it was preserved pure of any mixture. The name Vaudois comes from vaux (vallies), and Peter received the surname of Valdo from having embraced their opinions. The Vaudois, rising against the tyranny, the superstitions, and the traditions of the Church of Rome, which they called Babylon and mother of all confusion, aspire to bring back the government of the primitive church. They translate the Scripture into the vulgar tongue, and explain it by themselves or in supporting themselves on the opinion of the ancient Fathers. Every good Christian has, according to them, power to instruct others; nothing obliges us to confess to a priest; God alone can forgive sins. They deny the existence of purgatory and the efficacy of prayers for the dead. Their morality is rigid, their characters very pure. They have bishops, priests, deacons, but they must be without fortune and live on the exercise of some profession. The laics are divided into *perfect* and *imperfect*, according as they are more or less austere and disinterested. The Vaudois are spread in Languedoc, the south of France, and in some other regions.

There also exist at that time several less considerable dissidences, such as those of the Apostolics, who propose to imitate the life of the Apostles, without possessing anything in this world, and that of the Passaginians, who attempt to follow the law of Moses, and regard Jesus Christ as a pure man. The sects that appeared in the west are a living Protestantism against the tyranny and the ambition of the popes, against the cupidity and the corruption of the clergy, against idolatry and the superstition of the Roman Church. The Manichæans thinking the same in this regard, all the dissidents of the south of France, whatever their number and their origin, despite the diversity of their beliefs, are designated under the general name of Albigenses. The extension of these heresies calls forth so much the more disquietude in the Roman pontiffs, since they attack their supremacy and their temporal power; they survey them with anxiety and stimulate the vigilance of the bishops.

In a council held at Toulouse by pope Calixtus II., condemnation is pronounced in a general manner on those who disapprove the sacrament of the body and blood of Jesus Christ, the baptism of infants, the priesthood, legitimate marriages (1119).

A council at Rheims, presided over by Eugenius III., forbids all and sundry to receive or protect the heretics of Gascony and Provence, under pain of excommunication against the persons and interdict on the lands (1148).

Another council, assembled at Tours by Alexander IV., enjoins on bishops and priests to keep their eye on the Manichæans, on the Catholic nobles, to put down their conventicles, to confiscate their goods, and to forbid any and all to give them refuge and to have commerce with them, under pain of excommunication (1163). Notwithstanding these measures, heresy continues to gather strength at Toulouse and its vicinity. It extends to churchmen. The most illustrious men of the country second it, and draw a great multitude with them. The kings of France and England send learned doctors to convert the country (1178). Raymond V., Count of Toulouse, the Viscount of Turenne, and others, are charged with applying force. Three years later, a legate of the pope leads an army against the Albigenses. He takes the castle of Lavaur, and compels Roger de Beziers and other lords to renounce the heresy. The doctors of the sect abjure equally; but as constraint alone made them act, they return to their opinions as soon as it has ceased. In the council of Verona, at which were the Pope Lucius III. and the Emperor Frederic Barbarossa, anathema is pronounced against the heretics, and notably against the Cathari and Patarins, the humiliated or poor of Lyons, the Passagins, the Josephins, the Arnaudists, and against those who give them shelter or protection (1184). The decree prescribes measures to be taken for the extirpation of heresy, measures which seem to be the origin of the Inquisition; among other things you find there the concurrence of the two powers for the suppression of heretics and persons suspected of heresy, and penalties of different kinds for the convinced, the penitents, and the relapsed.

But the Manichæans, the Petrobrusians, the Vaudois are not the less propagated in all the country. Other sects arise, who, despite their divergences, proclaim like them, that the Roman Church is an assemblage of errors and superstitions, and the power of the popes a tyrannical usurpation. Dissidents of all kinds swarm especially in Provence, Languedoc, Gascony, and the neighbouring countries. In the first year of his pontificate, Innocent III. charges two monks to make in these regions a search after heretics, to convert them or to excommunicate them, and to punish them if they are obstinate. The Albigenses nevertheless do not cease to prosper with the aid or by the toleration of the nobles, among others Raymond VI., Count of Toulouse and Provence, and Roger, Count de Foix. The pope sends, with the title of legates, Peter de Castelnau and another monk, to whom another was added afterwards, and gives them full power in the provinces of Aix, Arles, Narbonne, and in the circumjacent dioceses (1204). Their preaching does not obtain great success. Objection is made to them of the opulence and disorderly morals of the clergy, also the pomp with which they surround themselves. The bishop of Osma in Castille advises them to go on foot like the apostles ; and giving the example himself, he mixes in their labours with one of his canons named Dominic (1206). The last remains ten years attached to the mission of Languedoc, of which he becomes chief, and founds at Toulouse the order of Preaching Brothers or Dominicans (1216). In this first mission, the legates, Dominic and their companions are charged with the search after and the conversion of heretics ; but they have not the power to judge them. They seem to have been only the precursors of the tribunal of the Inquisition, which will be established under Gregory IX. Peter de Castelnau is assassinated in Provence, at the moment when he stirred up the nobility of the country against Raymond, Count of Toulouse, whom he has just excommunicated (1208). The pope enjoins on the bishops to anathematise the murderer and his accomplices. The excommunication of the Count of Toulouse is renewed ; his subjects are set free from the oaths they have taken to him ; every Catholic is permitted to pursue his person and seize his property. A plenary indulgence is granted by Innocent to those who shall take up the cross against the heretics of Languedoc. Alarmed at these preparations, Raymond submits to the will of the legate. He gives up seven castles which he possesses in Provence ; the consuls of Nimes and Avignon become guarantees for him. He is absolved before the gate of the Church of Saint Gilles, stript to his shirt, after he had taken the required oath ; he is permitted to take the cross with two of his chevaliers.

The crusaders unite at Lyons, to the number, it is said, of five hundred thousand (1209). Raymond goes to wait for them at Valence, and marches with them against his former friends and his own subjects. Beziers, a city of more than sixty thousand souls, is taken at a blow, reduced to ashes, and all the inhabitants massacred without distinction of age or sex, catholics or dissidents ; the legate cried out, " kill, kill ! God knows who are his." The inhabitants of Carcasonne obtain a compromise, on condition of abandoning everything and to go out into public in their shirts. Simon, Count of Montfort, proclaimed chief of the crusade, receives the lordship of the conquered lands. The majority of the baronial crusaders retire shortly after. Raymond VI. is ceaselessly exposed to the vexations of the legates; they are resolved at any cost to despoil him of his provinces for the benefit of Montfort, whose pitiless sword does the work of the Church so well. In vain the Count of Toulouse goes to supplicate Innocent III.; the concessions which he succeeded in obtaining are soon revoked on the protests of the legates and bishops. Simon pursues the course of his exploits on the subjects of the Count of Toulouse and his vassals. The expeditions are renewed every year. The crusaders, engaging themselves only for six weeks, return home at the expiration of that delay. After their departure revolts become frequent. In the years 1210, 1211, 1212, the war recommences with all its horrors, combats, sacking of cities, devastations, massacres, and here and there some hundreds of men burned alive for the greater glory of the Roman Church. Raymond, whom the legates excommunicated again under the pretext that he had not kept his word, is beaten by Montfort in divers rencontres, and finally finds himself reduced to the cities of Toulouse and Montauban. He seeks a refuge with his family by the side of the king of Aragon, his brother-in-law. That prince, after having vainly interceded at Rome in his favour, takes up arms to protect him, and has just sat down before the castle of Muret. But he is conquered by Montfort, and perishes in the battle (1213). A number of lords submit, delivering up their fortresses. Everything yields to the conqueror in Quercy, Agenois, Perigord, Lemousin, Rouergue.

Louis, son of Philip Augustus, to accomplish the vow he had taken to enter on a crusade, marches into Languedoc at the head of an army (1215). Toulouse, Narbonne, and other places press forward to make peace with the legate; the walls of Toulouse are beaten down. Montfort is entrusted with the guard of all the conquests until the general council which Innocent III. had convened (1213). This council (the twelfth œcumenical of the Latins, the fourteenth of the Lateran) meets on the 11th of November 1215. There are to be seen ambassadors of Frederic II. of the Latin emperor of Constantinople, of the kings of France, England, Hungary, Jerusalem, Cyprus, Aragon, and of divers other princes. Its convocation had two principal objects: the recovery of the holy land and the reformation of the universal church by the correction of morals and the extirpation of heresy. At the head of the decrees of the council is an exposition of faith made in view of the dissidents. The term transubstantiation appears there for the first time; a new word, a new thing. The assembly anathematises all heresies, whatever their name. Heretics are handed over to the secular powers, the property of laics being confiscated, that of clerics applied to the churches. Those who are suspected of heresy, if they do not exculpate themselves, will be excommunicated, and a year after, in default of absolution, condemned as heretics. The lords shall drive heretics out of their lands, under pain of excommunication, and if, after a year, they have not given satisfaction, their vassals shall be set free from their oath of fidelity, and their lands given up to the conquest of catholics. The followers, the concealers, the patrons of the heretics shall be excommunicated and deprived of their civil rights. The obligation of sacramental confession is decreed in these terms: " Every Christian arrived at the age of discretion shall confess alone to his own priest at least once a year, and shall receive, at least at Easter, the sacrament of the eucharist." This is the first canon that commands auricular confession. Until then people were at liberty to confess mentally to God, or, if they wished, to some spiritual director. This requirement directed against heresy, has always since been maintained in the Roman Church; the man's conscience is bound by the priest's will; this is one of the principal bases of the sacerdotal power. Another canon, in the same spirit, requires medical men, under pain of excommunication, to exhort before all things the sick to send for a confessor. A special decree of the council condemns a treatise which Joachim, abbot of Flora, had written against

Peter Lombard, touching the trinity. This abbot, it is supposed, had run into tritheism. The other decrees contain a number of regulations on discipline which have served as a foundation to that which since then has been observed in the pontifical church. We shall cite some of these regulations: All the clerics shall live in continence and chastity under the penalties laid down by the canons ; they shall be applied more severely to those who, following the usage of their country, have contracted marriage and are at liberty to use it.

Clerics shall not carry on any secular business ; they shall not be present at spectacles of mimes, buffoons, and players; they shall not play at games of chance.

They are forbidden to pronounce a judgment involving the shedding of blood, to carry any such into effect, or to be present at the time. Those who have the right to elect to a bishopric or to an abbey shall proceed to it within three months, if not, the election devolves on the immediate superior.

The children of canons, especially bastards, cannot be canons in the same church. Tithes must be paid to the churches. Ancient relics must not be exposed for sale, or shown out of their receptacles ; veneration must not be shown to new relics before the Pope's approbation.

The last commands of the general council concern the Jews.

During the middle ages that people is ceaselessly exposed to persecutions in the different countries of the Latin Church. Odious as the offspring of the murderers of Christ, the Jews are not less so for their immoderate usuries and their immense riches. Blind fanaticism and stupid ignorance gave credence to the monstrous excesses and sacrilegious horrors of which they are accused. The multitude is ever ready to rush upon them, and princes to banish them, in order to possess their spoils. At the commencement of the eleventh century (1010), the Moslems of Egypt having destroyed the temple of the holy sepulchre, the act is ascribed to instigation on the part of the Jews. They are everywhere run down ; some are massacred or drowned ;

others hide themselves in divers places, during five years. At the time of the first crusade it is alleged that they informed the Saracens of the projected expedition. The crusaders cut their throats wherever they meet with them, especially at Cologne, Mayence, Spires, Worms, and Treves. Certain preachers of the second crusade excite the populations against them. A great number of them perish in several cities of France and Germany, despite the efforts of Bernard de Clairvaux, who opposes this false zeal. Philip Augustus, in the early years of his reign, drives them out of his estates, confiscating their immoveable property, and discharging his Christian subjects from their debts, of which he reserves one-fifth for his own benefit. The Jews enter France a little later. Then they are accused of crucifying or cutting the throat of a child on Saint Thursday, or another day of the same week. These imputations become very frequent. It is an easy pretext for authorising their banishment and spoliation. It would occupy too much space to enumerate all the popular or legal persecutions which these constant victims of public aversion undergo.

The general council of Innocent III., yielding to the common prejudice, bids princes put a stop to the usuries of the Jews. It commands the Jews to wear a particular dress by which they may be at first sight distinguished from Christians, and not to appear in public on the anniversaries of the Redeemer's passion. It orders due punishment to be inflicted on the blasphemers of the crucified Christ. Such directions were not of a nature to dispose people's minds less unfavourably toward the people of Israel. But what mercy can be expected from a Church which massacres and burns Christians by hundreds of thousands, because they reject some of its superstitions, and because they protest against the opulence and tyranny of its sacerdotal caste? After these regulations comes the decree for the new crusade, the meeting for which is fixed for the 1st of June 1217. Innocent III., with the approbation of the assembly, pronounces a sentence by which Raymond, Count of Toulouse, is despoiled and banished from his states: Toulouse, Montauban, and all the countries which the crusades have taken from him beyond the Rhine are adjudged to Simon, Count of Montfort; the lands which Raymond possessed in Provence are guarded under the orders of the Church, to be given in all or in part to his only son, if he renders himself worthy when he is of age. At the end of the council the Pope confirms the election of Frederic II. to the kingdom of Germany; that prince had previously engaged to transmit, when he received the imperial crown, the kingdom of Sicily to his son Henry, who would hold it of the Roman Church. In this general council the existence of the two first orders of religious beggars is recognised and consecrated. They are established in a totally new spirit. The riches and the corruption of the clergy gave, as it is said, great force to the preachings of the dissidents, whose criticism did not spare the monks more than the seculars; the monasteries swam in opulence, and the abbeys rivalled the pomp of the bishops. A young man, twenty-five years of age, Francis d'Assisi, forms the design of living in evangelical poverty, like the apostles. He makes some disciples. Clad in coarse garments, they and he, living on alms, go out to simply preach the Saviour's words. Innocent III., at first ill-disposed toward them, restricts himself to confirming their rule by a vocal utterance (1210). The new order makes rapid progress. At the Council of the Lateran, the Pope recognises the approbation which he had given without a bull. The brethren, designated by the name of Minor Brethren, or Franciscans, spread through all the provinces of the west. In the first general chapter of the order they amount to more than five thousand (1219). There is also established near Assisi, under the direction of Francis, an order of poor women, called the order of Saint Clara, from the name of its foundress, who governs it forty-two years. Afterwards Francis institutes a third order for those who, without quitting the world and its goods, wish to be united to the number of his disciples. He vocally prescribes a less rigorous rule which will be reduced to writing under the pontificate of Nicholas IV.

The brother preachers, collected by Dominic, had not yet given themselves a rule. The Pope orders them, in the general council, to choose one among those which are approved. Dominic adopts that of St Augustin, adding to it more austere practices. The order has its first church and its first cloister at Toulouse (1216), the brothers are sixteen in number. At the first, the Dominicans are not beggars. While renouncing earthly property, they preserve the revenues. But in the first general chapter a resolution is formed to live in complete poverty (1220).

Honorius III. will, by a Bull, confirm these two begging orders. Innocent barely survived the close of the general council. The news of Louis de France passing into England, being invited by the barons, transports him with fury. He falls ill and dies in the midst of the measures which he prepares against that prince and Philip Augustus, his father (16th July 1216). Provence soon rises in favour of the young Raymond. While efforts are made to put down that movement, Raymond, the father, repassing the Pyrenees, establishes himself in the city of Toulouse (1217). Montfort wishes to drive him away, and perishes in the siege; the enterpise is abandoned by his son Amaury. From that moment the Albigenses begin to rise; the elder Raymond remains in possession of Toulouse until his death (1222). His son for some time continues the war; the indulgence granted to those who shall march against the Albigenses is revoked for a time. Two years later the young Raymond is excommunicated afresh. His lands are handed over to King Louis VIII., to whom Amaury de Montfort and Guy, his uncle, ceded all rights. Louis comes to Lyons at the head of an army. He takes possession of Avignon, and advances into Languedoc. The cities, the castles, the fortresses are surrendered to him as far as four leagues from Toulouse. On his return from the campaign, he dies at Auvergne (1226). A new army moves in the name of King Louis IX. and devastates the neighbourhood of Toulouse. Finally, peace is concluded in 1229. Raymond preserves, merely for his life, the half of the diocese of Toulouse, Agenois, and Rouergue (at a later day Provence is abandoned to him under the same condition), he undertakes the obligation of driving from his territories heretics and hangers on, to restore to the churches their property and their tithes, to pay the costs of former wars, to support at Toulouse, during ten years, four doctors in theology and in canon right, six masters of the liberal arts and two of grammar (this is the origin of the University of Toulouse). His only daughter is to be put into the hands of the king, who will marry her to one of his brothers, and will leave him the diocese of Toulouse. After the death of Raymond, his lands belong to the husband of his daughter and to their children ; if he does not leave them, they will return to the king (an eventuality which realised itself in 1270).

The clergy only become more ardent to continue the persecutions. A council at Toulouse draws up rules for the search after heretics (Sept. 1227). Some years later, Pope Gregory IX. discharges the bishops from the care of discovering and judging them ; he gives that commission to the brother preachers, with an order to the bishops to aid them with their advice (1233). The Councils of Narbonne (1235) and of Beziers (1246) draw up rules, the substance of which follows :—

The inquisitor on his arrival summons those who feel themselves culpable, or know others in that condition, to declare it within a time called the term of grace ; they are admitted to adjure in promising to discover heretics. After the term of grace, citation is given to those who are not presented ; lacking a valid defence and confession of their sins, they are condemned without mercy. Confirmed or concealed heretics are secretly examined: if mildness cannot convert them, they are made to confess their errors publicly ; after having condemned, they deliver them to the secular power. The relapsed, the fugitives who return, those who return only after the term of grace, or who have suppressed the truth, are condemned to perpetual imprisonment and confined in separate cells. Those who are not shut up wear two yellow crosses on their dress, are present at the public services on the Sunday and festivals, and are beaten with rods by the priest. The property of heretics condemned or imprisoned is confiscated. Laymen are forbidden to possess books of theology even in Latin, and ecclesiastics to have any in the vernacular. The office of the inquisition is delegated exclusively to the preaching brothers and the minor brothers, especially to the former, who exercise it with greater rigour.

In the canons approved by Gregory IX. on the method of the Inquisition, it is prescribed : That heretics or persons suspected of heresy be denounced to the inquisitors, even by their nearest relatives, whether their son or their father, under pain of excommunication ;—that they be put into a severe prison open to none but the inquisitors ;—that they be forced to the canonical purgation, which requires several witnesses ;—that every testimony be admitted against them ;—that on the deposition of two witnesses, or even one, they be compelled to confess by torture ;—that their goods be handed over to the public treasury ;—that if their pardon has been promised them, even on oath, none the less are they to be punished, because the penalties suffered by the heretics are favours ;—that any one who has given heretics shelter shall be punished as a heretic. In the thirteenth century the tribunal of the inquisition is set up in most countries. The Albigenses and the Vaudois suffer the most cruel punishments at Rome and in other countries of Italy, France, Navarre, and Aragon. Abuses of power committed by the inquisitors excite troubles in Toulouse, Florence, Plaisance, Genoa, and otherwheres. But the authority of the popes wins the day ; kings and princes are forced to acknowledge those tribunals under pain of being branded with heresy. The office of the inquisition increases also in the following centuries. The secular judge has no longer any part in the jurisdiction, not even for the sequestration or confiscation of property. Inquisitors have prisons of their own for keeping or punishing the accused. In doubtful cases frequently perpetual incarceration is inflicted. Besides manifest and impenitent heretics, this tribunal has charge of such as are suspected of heresy even without proof ; those who brought before the judge constantly deny their crime ; those who lend their home to heretics or give them refuge or council ; those who do not aid with all their power the ministers of the inquisition. The confiscation of goods extends to children and children's children, unless their parents are denounced by them. The bodily punishments are perpetual imprisonment and death by fire or sword. Every testimony is admitted against the accused : two testimonies suffice for the proof. Lacking witnesses, indication, or admission, the suspected are subjected to torture. No one is exempt from the jurisdiction of the holy office.

While new troubles were agitating Languedoc, the emperor Otho died (1218). The same year a diet recognised Frederic II. for king of the Romans. A little later he confers the same title on his son Henry, still a child (1220). Pope Honorius III. (1216-27) disapproves this election, which unites Sicily to the empire: but none the less he gives the crown to Frederic; the emperor forthwith takes the cross and obliges him to set out the following year. Different causes keep him back, but in testimony of his zeal, he publishes very rigorous laws against heretics (1224). The situation of the Holy Land has not ceased to be very precarious. Honorius succeeds but little in his efforts to set in activity the crusade decreed by the general council of the Lateran. In the year 1217 a multitude of crusaders go by sea into Palestine, under the leadership of Andrew, king of Hungary, and Leopold of Austria. Circumstances do not improve. Andrew returns at the end of three months, regarding his vow as accomplished; Leopold remains. The resolution is formed to attack Egypt, in view, it is said, of securing a march on Jerusalem. The Christians besiege Damietta under the orders of King John of Brienne (1218). But a papal legate comes up with new crusaders, and claims the command ; thence arises division in the army. The city is at last captured (1219). The lordship is given to John of Brienne as an addition to his kingdom. He soon retires in consequence of a misunderstanding with the legate. At a later time he is recalled (1121). An expedition against Cairo is attempted, but so badly conducted that they are almost reduced to capitulate. A truce of eight years is concluded on the condition that Damietta shall be given back to the Sultan, who, on his part, will restore the wood of the true cross and all his Christian captives.

At the news of these events, Honorius urges the sending of fresh succours. In a conference held in Campania, at which John of Brienne is present, the emperor swears to pass into the holy land on the 24th of June 1225, and forms an engagement to marry Yolande, daughter of the king of Jerusalem. After the marriage he constrains his father-in-law to yield to him the kingdom, the domain of Yolande, and makes himself acknowledged as its sovereign. John of Brienne withdraws into France. In the year 1226 the emperor holds a solemn court at Verona. The cities of Lombardy, alarmed at his coming, form a league and refuse to receive him. Their liberty seems the more in peril because King Henry, ordered by his father, advances toward Italy with a considerable army. The Veronese march to meet him and oblige him to return. Frederic declares enemies of the empire the cities which form part of the confederation. The pope Honorius succeeds in arranging an agreement between the two parties (1227). Gregory IX. occupies the pontifical chair (1227-41) when the crusaders unite at Brindisium. The greater part of the army is carried off by sickness. The emperor, ready to set out with what remains, falls ill himself and cannot travel. The pope, believing nothing as to the illness, excommunicates that prince, and interdicts all the places where he is. Frederic preparing to set sail, the pope writes to him that he must not presume to pass the sea as a crusader, without being absolved from the ecclesiastical censures. The emperor disregards the communication. He reaches the holy land but with insufficient forces, and concludes with the Sultan of Egypt a truce of ten years, of which the principal point is that Jerusalem shall be restored to him, except the temple of Solomon of which the Moslems are to remain possessors (February 1229). He then repairs to the holy city where he remains only a single day. The death of the empress Yolande occasions the kingdom to pass to their young son Conrad. Frederic embarks secretly on the first of May 1229. He takes back into Europe the teutonic chevaliers, who soon undertake the conversion of the Prussians, and after fifty years of cruel war, succeed in subjecting them and in founding a powerful state in those regions.

The emperor hastens to return into Italy, where the pope makes war on him advantageously. After his departure Gregory IX. collected an army under the command of John of Brienne, and seized a great number of places in the kingdom of Sicily. Frederic, on his return, easily recovers what he had lost. John of Brienne quits Italy to reign at Constantinople. Gregory is only the more animated against the emperor. He repeats his excommunication, and at last obliges that prince to make a peace, the conditions of which are regulated by the court of Rome (1230). Notwithstanding this treaty, the emperor continues none the less to foment the rebellion of the Romans against the pope, who, on his side, applies himself to reconcile the Lombard cities in order that they may be in a state to withstand Frederic. That prince, passing the Alps, makes war vigorously on them (1236). He is recalled into Germany by a revolt of the Duke of Austria whom he soon defeats and despoils of his states. Returning into Italy, he gains a great victory over the Milanese and seizes Lodi. Hents or Henry, his natural son, occupies Sardinia by his orders, and makes himself king thereof (1238). The pope, who regards it as a possession of his See, excommunicates the emperor. They write one against the other, and return insults for insults. Frederic drives from the kingdom of Sicily the Dominicans and the Franciscans. Excommunication is renewed against him and against his son Hents who has made himself master of the marshes of Ancona (1239). The emperor makes his way to Rome. The pope then offers the empire to the French, who refuse it. The princes of Germany, whom he invites to make a new election, reply to him that he has not the right to create an emperor, but solely to crown him. Gregory convokes a council at Rome. The emperor opposes it, and carries on the war with vigour. His fleet defeats the fleet of the Genoese which was conveying bishops to the council (1241). The prelates are retained prisoners, excepting those of France, which the persistence of Louis IX. sets at liberty. The imperial army encamps in the neighbourhood of Rome, where the death of Gregory takes place (Aug. 1241). Celestin IV. holds the see only six days. After an interval of about twenty months, the pontifical chair passes to Innocent IV. (1243-54). Negociations are carried on with the emperor. The pope, who fears to be arrested, flees by sea to Genoa with seven cardinals (1244). Louis IX. refuses to receive him. The kings of Aragon and England do the same. Innocent goes to reside at Lyons, a neutral city governed by his archbishop.

A general council meets on the 24th of June 1245 (the thirteenth œcumenical of the Latins, the first of Lyons). Among those present are ambassadors of Frederic II., envoys of the king of France, of England, and other princes, as well as Raymond Count of Toulouse, and Baldwin emperor of Constantinople. The principal object of this council is to proceed against the emperor, Frederic II. The accusations are produced, his ambassadors defend him. He did intend to present himself, but, informed of what is going on in the assembly, he remains at Turin. In the last session, the pope pronounces against him, with lighted wax candles, a sentence of deposition from the empire and from the kingdom of Sicily, with absolution from their oath of his subjects and excommunication for whosoever should give him aid and counsel. Against this sentence, Frederic writes to Germany, France, England, and other countries. He proposes to take the king of France for arbitrator. Louis IX. with a conciliatory view, uselessly holds conferences with the pope in the abbey of Cluny.

Innocent IV. invites the princes of Germany to choose another king of the Romans. The secular lords refuse ; but the archbishops of Mayence and Cologne with some laymen elect Henry, landgrave of Thuringen, whom his adversaries name king of the priests. The excommunication of Frederic is again published in Germany ; the lands of those who obey that prince are put under an interdict. It is the same in the kingdom of Sicily, where a conspiracy is formed among his own servants. The pope was thinking of giving the imperial crown to king Henry, when that prince is beaten by Conrad, son of Frederic (1246). He dies of vexation the next year. Innocent IV., pursuing his courses, published a crusade against Frederic, and gets William of Holland elected king of the Romans, a young prince twenty years of age who is supported by great alliances (1247). Censures are launched against several princes of Germany who hold for Frederic. That emperor passes from la Pouille into Germany at the head of a great army, intending to go to Lyons. But an insurrection of the Parmisans obliges him to besiege their city during winter. He fails and retires (1248). The crusade preached against him raises great troubles in Germany. William of Holland makes himself to be crowned king of the Romans at Aix-la Chapelle (Nov. 1248).

Hents, king of Sardinia, is taken in an ambuscade by the Bolonese (1249), who keep him in prison until his death. A natural son of Frederic perishes in la Pouille. This prince is himself afflicted with the malady called the Sacred Fire. Beaten down by so many reverses, he offers reasonable conditions of peace, which are rejected by the Court of Rome. The emperor expires in December 1250. Innocent IV. eagerly exhorts the people and the nobility of Sicily to return into the bosom of the Roman Church. Before leaving Lyons, he repeats the excommunication against the memory of Frederic as well as against Conrad, and confirms the election of William of Holland (1251). After some stay at Genoa and Milan, he passes the rest of the year at Perusia. King Conrad entering Italy in the month of May, beats the partizans of the pope, who has a crusade preached against him with indulgences greater than those of the holy land. None the less, that prince pursues his success in la Pouille, when he is overtaken by death (1254). Conrad or Conradin, his son, aged two years, is placed under the protection of the holy see. The pope promises to defend him, on condition of his being put into possession of the kingdom of Sicily until the majority of the young prince. A legate proceeds thither with an army of ample powers. Mainfroy, bastard of Frederic II., and tutor of Conradin, at first opposes no resistance; but soon perceiving from the legate's conduct that Rome intends to appropriate the kingdom, he collects an army, defeats the pope's troops and drives him out of la Pouille (Sept. 1254). The holy land necessarily felt the struggles between the pope and the emperor Frederic II. ; after the departure of that prince, discord was fomented among the Latins by the patriarch of Jerusalem. But Gregory IX., after his reconciliation with Frederic, attempted to put an end to the troubles, and to raise the imperial authority in Palestine. A new crusade is published in Europe by the Dominicans and the Franciscans. The agents of the pope amass in a short time great sums, the use of which was not known. The zeal of the people for the enterprise sensibly grew cold. The crusaders assemble at Lyons in the year 1240. But then the pope and the emperor are at war one with another. Gregory forbids them to proceed ; Frederic directs them not to set out until he is at their head. The crusaders know not what part to take. Some return home ; others embark at Marseilles ; among the last, the majority remain in Sicily or repair to Brindisium. Richard of Cornwall, brother of the king of England, who had embarked at Marseilles, continues his voyage, and arrives in Palestine in the month of October 1240. In November he concludes a truce with the Sultan of Egypt. In 1244 the holy land is a prey to extreme desolation. The Khorasmians, driven from Persia by an invasion of Tartars, obtain from the Sultan of Egypt permission to settle in Palestine. They fix themselves there, capture Jerusalem, massacre the Christians, ravage the holy places, and defeat the Latins of the coast. But discord soon breaks out between the Khorasmians and the Sultan of Cairo, who destroys them in two battles. The news of their invasion arrives in Italy in the spring of the year 1245. About the same time, Louis IX., in a serious malady, takes up the pilgrim's cross. A legate comes into France at his request. In a grand parliament held in Paris, a certain number of prelates and barons cross themselves, at the solicitation of the prince and the legate. The king fixes the departure for 24th June 1248. His mother and the grandees of the realm press him in vain to commute his vow. Louis persists, smitten from that moment with the monomania of the crusades, which will never leave him. He embarks at Aigues Mortes (1248) and goes to pass the winter in Cyprus with Lusignan, king of the island, on whom the pope had conferred the crown of Jerusalem after the condemnation of Frederic II., and of his son. During his sojourn in Cyprus, the king of France receives an embassade from a king or chief of the Tartars, people who had reached the highest degree of power under Gengis Khan and his successors. Gengis having made himself master of Turkistan (1202) had rapidly extended his conquests over all northern Asia, from China to Muscovy. After his death (1226) the Tartars advance in all directions. In Europe they subdue Russia, ravage Poland, attack Bohemia, invade Hungary (1241), which they devastate during three years. In Asia they extend their dominion over all China, take possession of Persia, and threaten the neighbouring countries. The pope sends two Dominicans on a mission to the Tartars of the north, and two Franciscans to those who occupy Persia (1245). From the last country an embassy had gone to Louis IX. The Tartars, ready to attack the Caliph of Bagdad, sought to come to an understanding with the Christians, enemies like themselves of the Moslems. According to rumours which found belief then, the religion of Christ was more or less spread among those peoples. Those reports doubtless came from travellers misled by the numerous resemblances between the Roman Church and the worship of Buddha, observed by the Tartars. Louis embarks for Egypt (1249), takes Damietta and marches on Cairo. But a French corps is annihilated at Massura (1250). The army wastes away by sickness and the want of provisions. The Saracens attack it in force; the king who is ill is taken prisoner. A treaty is concluded, by which he binds himself to restore Damietta, as well as pay his ransom, and that of the other captives. Become free, he sends from Acre vessels to bring back the prisoners, the arms, the machines of war. But the machines have been burnt, the sick killed; the Egyptians at first give up only four hundred prisoners out of more than twelve thousand. In the sequel, all the captives which they had taken during twenty years are rescued from their hands.

After fortifying, at his own expense, Acre, Caesarea,

Joppa, Sidon, Louis IX. embarks and returns to France in 1254 ; but he does not give up the cross, and considers himself as always bound by his vow. William of Holland, King of the Romans, having miserably perished in a war against the Frisons (1256), Pope Alexander IV. (1254-61), for fear that the kingdom of Sicily should be reunited to the empire, forbids the electors, under pain of excommunication, to choose the young Conradin, the last Scion of the house of Suabia. They divide into two parties : these name Richard, brother of the King of England ; those Alphonso, King of Castille. Richard is crowned at Aix la Chapelle (1257). Alphonso remains in Spain. Each of them requests from Rome the confirmation of its election. Alexander, quite inclining for Richard, defers to decide between them. A popular movement obliges that pontiff to retire to Viterbo (1257). The people of Rome set up a senator, to whom an oath is taken. Excommunications fail of effect, the Romans asserting their privilege to be exempt from them. Mainfroy allies himself with them. Master of la Pouille, Sicily, Naples, and Capua, he gets himself crowned king at Palermo (1258). The Pope excommunicates him ; but the Lombards account him the legitimate king. He marries Constance, his only daughter, to Peter, eldest son of James, King of Aragon (1262). At the same time a spirit of superstitious devotion gives birth to the sect of flagellants (1259). It begins in Perusia, passes to Rome, and into all Italy, whence it spreads into Germany, Poland, and several other regions. Persons of both sexes, of every condition, and every age, uniting by hundreds, by thousands, by tens of thousands, traverse the cities and the rural districts, with the upper part of their bodies naked to the waist, the head and face covered, under the guidance of priests with crosses and banners. These fanatics walk two and two in procession, hold in their hands a whip of stripes of leather, with which they lacerate their shoulders, with many tears and cries, to implore God's mercy and the aid of the Virgin. But the secular power becomes uneasy at this foolish superstition, and takes measures to put an end to it. It will be sure to re-appear several times in posterior ages.

Without regard for the rights of the young Conradin, Pope Alexander offers the kingdom of Sicily to Edmund, son of the King of England. Urban IV. (1261-64) offers it to Louis IX. for one of his sons, and on the king's refusal, to his brother Charles, Count of Anjou and Provence. In the interval, Mainfroy attracts to him nearly all Tuscany, and penetrates into the Marshes of Ancona. The kingdom of Sicily is put under an interdict (1263). Clement IV. (1265-68) terminates the negociation commenced with Charles of Anjou, to whom a Bull concedes the Sicilian States. That prince arrives at Rome with a thousand chevaliers, going before the army procured for him by a crusade preached against Mainfroy and the Saracens of Nocera. Crowned by five delegated cardinals (1266), he immediately enters the field, and near Beneventum defeats the army of Mainfroy, who is killed on the spot. Conradin, aged fifteen years, takes the title of King of Sicily, and advances into Italy, whither he is invited by the Ghibelins. His march is not arrested by an excommunication and an interdict. The people of Rome welcome, with transport, that grandson of Frederic II. But in Pouille he is conquered by Charles of Anjou in the sanguinary battle of Tagliacozzo, and remains prisoner with the Duke of Austria, his cousin, and Henry of Castille, senator of Rome (1268). They are conducted to Naples and condemned to death as guilty of treason and enemies of the Church. The young Conradin, Frederic of Austria, and some others are beheaded in the market-place (26th October). In Conradin ended that house of Suabia which the simultaneous possession of the empire and the kingdom of Sicily had rendered so odious to the Roman Court. It has been believed that the execution of that prince was recommended, if not commanded, to Charles of Anjou by Pope Clement IV. At the death of that pontiff, the See of Rome remains vacant for three years; then they elect Gregory X. who was in Palestine at the time (1271-76). He arrives at Viterbo in 1272. One of his first acts is to convoke a general council at Lyons for the 1st of May 1274 (the fourteenth of the Latins, the second of Lyons). One of the two princes that contended for the title of King of the Romans, Richard of England, had died during the vacancy of the papal chair (1271). Notwithstanding the unfortunate state of things occasioned by a long competition, the pontiffs had always put off pronouncing for one or the other. The death of Richard puts Gregory X. under the obligation of taking a part. He rejects the pretensions of Alphonso of Castille. A new election takes place, Rodolph of Hapsburg is chosen unanimously, and crowned at Aix la Chapelle (1273). He was a new man, to whom the protection of the popes was necessary for his support.

During the interregnum, Denmark, Poland, Hungary, and the kingdom of Arles were separated from the empire. The German aristocracy had become consolidated; the cities had made a league for their defence; seven princes had taken to themselves the exclusive right to elect the emperors, a right which will be regulated by the *Golden Bull* in 1356.

The Pope goes to Lyons in the month of November; the general council opens on the 7th of May 1274.

Three principal objects led to its convocation: the succours to be sent to the Holy Land, the extinction of the schism of the Greeks, the reformation of the vices and errors which are multiplying in the Church. Everything declined in Palestine since the departure of Louis IX. The Christians, reduced to a small number, are at each instant threatened with losing their last possessions. The Venetians and the Pisans carry on war with the Genoese, as in the other countries. Their fleets fight several battles. The Venetians take possession of the port of Acre (1257). At the same epoch, a furious quarrel breaks out between the templars and the hospitallers, who massacre one another even to extinction. Meanwhile the Mamelukes, new tyrants of Egypt, do not cease their attacks. They ravage all the country up to the gates of Acre, raze the Church of Nazareth, demolish that of Mount Tabor (1263), ruin Cæsarea, and take the castle of Arsuf (1265). The environs of Acre are devastated (1266). Jaffa falls into their power (1268). They penetrate, without fighting, into

Antioch, whence, weary of massacring, they carry off a hundred thousand slaves, a disaster which that city never got over. In 1271 they seize the castles of Crack and of Montfort, and, after having made a truce with the Count of Tripolis, present themselves under the walls of Acre. The Pope writes letters on letters to the Christian princes to claim succours. The clergy of France tax themselves to raise pecuniary aid. The Dominicans and the Franciscans promote the crusade (1265). But at the same time a crowd of others are preached, which injure each other; independently of that of the Holy Land, there is in France the crusade against Mainfroy and the Saracens of Nocera; in Aragon and in Castile, the crusade against the Moors of Africa; in Hungary, in Bohemia, in Poland, in Austria, in Carinthia, in Brandenburg, a crusade against the Tartars, and another for the teutonic chevaliers, and the faithful of Livonia, Prussia, and Curlande; in England, the crusade against the lords which make war upon the king.

The king of France is the only one who has the affair of Palestine at heart. In a Parliament held at Paris, he crosses himself with three of his sons and a considerable number of nobles (1267). They embark on the first of July 1270. The fleet assembles at Cagliari. But instead of going to the East, Louis IX. repairs first to Tunis, the king and people of which he hopes to convert, or at least to force them to pay tribute to the king of Sicily, his brother. On the land of Africa sickness decimates the army. One of the king's sons perishes; Philip his eldest son falls sick; Louis IX., himself seized with a fever, expires the 25th of August. A truce of ten years is concluded with the king of France. Edward, eldest son of the king of England, who survives the events, condemns the truce, but none the less he follows the French into Sicily. A tempest occasions the loss of four thousand lives near Trapani. Thibaut king of Navarre dies in that city. King Philip passes the lighthouse of Messina and returns into France by land.

Edward of England embarks in the spring of 1271, and lands at Acre with a thousand chosen men. He remains a year and a half in that city, whence he attempts several excursions without much effect; finally he returns after having made a truce of ten years with the Mamelukes. During the sojourn of Edward in Palestine, Gregory X. led by devotion into those parts receives the news of his election to the See of Rome.

One of his first cares in the general council is to get conceded by all the prelates for the needs of the crusade a tenth of the ecclesiastical revenues during six years, commencing with the 24th of June 1274. The extinction of the Græco-Latin schism was another of the pontiff's objects. The hope had been suggested by the Greek emperors who sought to conciliate the good graces of the court of Rome. Propositions as early as the year 1232 had come from John Vatace, emperor of Nice, who feared to see an army of crusaders arrive in Constantinople; conferences had been held between the Greek clergy and four begging brothers sent by the pope, but without more result than from anterior attempts. After the recapture of Constantinople by the troops of Michael Paleologos (1261) the emperor Baldwin II. succeeded in finding safety in Italy, the Latin nobles still possessed the principalities of Achaia, Morea and the neighbouring islands. Urban IV. caused to be preached in France a crusade against Michael, with the same indulgences as those of the Holy Land (1262). That prince then sends ambassadors with many presents for the pope and the cardinals, asking for the peace and reunion of the churches. None the less he carries on war against William de Ville Hardouin, prince of Achaia, and the other Latins of the country. Urban deputes to him four Minorites in the quality of Nuncios (1263). Paleologos draws up with them some articles for union, and submits them to Clement IV. with his profession of faith. During the negotiation, the emperor Baldwin II. makes, in the presence of the pope, a treaty with Charles of Anjou, king of Sicily (1267); the latter engages to give him in six years two thousand chevaliers to recover the empire of Constantinople; in return Baldwin yields to the kingdom of Sicily the direct lordship of the principality of Achaia and Morea, as well as the lands conceeded by the despot of Epirus to his daughter Helen in marrying her to Mainfroy, and the third of what the two thousand chevaliers might be able to conquer; it is also agreed upon that Baldwin's son shall marry the daughter of Charles, and that at their death, if they have no chidren, the rights of the empire of Constantinople shall pass to the kings of Sicily. Charles was already master of Canino in Epirus, of the isle of Corfu, and of the lands of Helen : he had thus free access into Romania. Become peaceful possessor of the throne of Sicily by the defeat of Conradin, he thinks of giving effect to the rights which the treaty concedes to him. Paleologos implores the pope to prevent the war, by undertaking to put an end to the schism. During the vacancy of the papacy he sends frequent embassies to the court of Rome. Gregory X. on his return from Syria informs him of his election. On the respectful reply of Michael, he deputes to him four Franciscans, inviting him, as well as the patriarch of Constantinople, to be present in the general council in person or by ambassadors (1272). The difficult point was for Michael to bring the patriarch and his clergy to ideas of union. His urgency remains without success. He none the less charges two Minorites to go and give testimony to the pope of his favourable dispositions; he then dispatches to the council five ambassadors, in the number of which is German, formerly patriarch of Constantinople. These last arrive at Lyons on the 24th of June. In a mass said by the pope in presence of all the prelates, the creed is solemnly sung in Latin and Greek, with the article—

Who *proceedeth from the Father and the Son.* Gregory causes to be read in the council before the ambassadors the three letters written by the Emperor Michael, his son Andronicus, and the prelates of the Greek Church; that of the emperor contains word for word, with his adhesion, the profession of faith which pope Clement sent to him in 1267; nevertheless Michael insists that the Greek Church shall continue to read the symbol as it has always done, and to observe its ancient usages. The bishops in their letter recognise the primacy of the holy see, adding that they will depose their patriarch if he does not come into their opinion.

One of the ambassadors, in the name of Michael Paleologos makes an oath that he abjures the schism, accepts the profession of faith of the Roman Church, and acknowledges its primacy. The pope chants the Te Deum ; they chant too the symbol with the addition *And of the Son* in Latin and in Greek. The union of the two churches seems thus an accomplished fact. We shall see the consequences of it.

As to the third object of the general council, the reformation of vices and errors, no decision was formed by the assembly, but the Pope declares that the fall of society ought to be attributed to the bad conduct of the bishops ; he warns those who are not free from reproach to correct themselves, if not, that he will act against them with rigour. After having made, on the occasion of the re-union of the Greeks, a profession of faith in which it is declared that the Holy Spirit proceeds from the Father and the Son, the council pronounces decrees on several points of discipline. Complementary measures are added to the preceding regulations for the holding of conclaves. Divers canons receive sanction relative to the election of bishops, the ordination of priests, conduct in the churches, the suppression of usury, and other objects. The twenty-third canon has for object to restrict the multitude of the religious orders, especially the begging orders. Rome, which had first hesitated to approve the orders of the Minors and the Preachers, had not delayed to recognise in them the most zealous defenders, and the most firm supports of the pontifical authority. The riches and the power of the clergy, and the old monastic orders, excite general envy, while the poverty of the begging orders procures for them the good will of the populations. The other monks, moreover, possessors of goods and lordships, depend always more or less on the public power, and attach themselves by divers bonds to the interests of their country ; but the begging orders, without fortune, without country, subject to chiefs residing in Rome, are at the bidding of the Pope in all things and against all persons. Accordingly, they are soon seen to be dear to the pontiffs, at the same time that they have the ear of kings and the confidence of their subjects. It is true that they justify those favours by their ardour for study, and by their incessant labours in the schools and the churches; they are regarded as the depositaries of all the sciences. Out of their bosom proceed the most eminent men of the time, among others Alexander Hales, Albert the Great, and above all, Thomas Aquinas, the *Angel of the Schools*, the first of the doctors who treated Christian philosophy according to the scientific method.

The rapid progress of the Dominicans and the Franciscans attracts the attention of the bishops and other superior ecclesiastics. Divers prelates attempt to subject them to their jurisdiction, like all the clergy of their dioceses. But on the complaints of the begging orders, these pretensions are put down by the bulls of the holy see (1231). Strong in its support the brothers entrench on all sides, and call forth great complaint. Their buildings, it is said, rise like palaces, and display priceless treasures; they are greedy of gain, extort secret wills, undertake the direction of consciences, and substitute themselves for the ordinary pastors with the rich and the great. The councils of kings and powerful men are open to them. They mingle with all classes; by them the extortions of the Pope are executed. The clergy of Germany state to Frederic II. (1243) that they see themselves supplanted by the beggars with princes and peoples, and become a public derision; that these brothers take to themselves penances, baptisms, the unction of the sick, the cemeteries, and by means of their fraternities, draw everybody into their churches, while those of the parishes are deserted, and priests thereby deprived of their tithes and oblations; that these beggars have built palaces supported by lofty columns, where they display their wealth and pomp. The same incriminations are uttered in England (1246). A bull from Innocent IV. justifies these complaints (1254), but the following month Alexander IV. revokes that bull and all similar ones. The same pope favours the Dominicans in a long quarrel which they have with the University of Paris, which finds itself obliged to yield to them (1252-60).

Among the other begging orders of this period we must place in the first rank the hermits of St Augustin and the

Carmelites. The former, of which there existed previously several societies, was reduced to one by Alexander IV. (1256), they are settled in Paris as early as 1259. The Carmelites were hermits established on Mount Carmel before the end of the twelfth century ; Louis IX. installed some of them in Paris on his return from the Holy Land. Despite the prohibition carried in the general council of 1215, the bodies of monks tended to multiply ceaselessly, and before all others, the beggars. To remedy the evil, the second general council of Lyons, in its twenty-third canon, forbids, and so far as there is need, revokes all the begging orders, which are not confirmed by the apostolic see ; as to those whom it has confirmed, they are forbidden to receive any one to profession, as also to acquire any house, or to alienate those which they possess ; their members are also forbidden to preach, confess, or to bury strangers. But the council expressly declares that this canon does not apply to the preaching or minor brothers, who are approved in consequence, it is said, of the evident utility drawn from them by the universal Church. In regard to the Carmelites and Hermits of Saint Augustin, whose institution is anterior to the council of 1215, they are permitted to remain in their actual state until it is otherwise ordered. After the conclusion of the general council, Gregory X. occupies himself with organising the crusade for the Holy Land ; the bishops are directed to preach it in their dioceses. The quarrel about the empire is terminated by the renunciation of Alphonso de Castille ; the pope obtains it from him by threats and censures, and by the concession of a tithe for the war against the Moors. Rodolph of Hapsburg, recognised as King of the Romans, takes at Lausanne, at the hands of the pontiff, an oath to conserve all the rights and the property of the Roman Church, and to defend its right to the kingdom of Sicily (1275). He crosses himself at the same time for the Holy Land, as well as the queen, his spouse, and nearly all the nobility which accompanies him. Gregory X. dies on his return into Italy (1276). He has for his first successors Innocent V., who occupies the chair only five months ; Hadrian V., who dies at the end of thirty days, without having been consecrated ; John XXI., who wears the tiara eight months. Nicholas III. (1277-80) obtains from Rudolph the confirmation of the donation made by the emperors to the Roman Church, and puts himself in possession of Romania. It is to the pretended donation of Constantine that he attaches his right of sovereignty over the city of Rome. The confirmatory charter of Rodolph distinctly separates the Italian provinces which depend on the pope from those which depend on the empire ; the states of the Church are from this time constituted within the limits which they have had down to our own times. Rodolph does not seek to exercise any power in Italy. He does not go to Rome to be crowned, and restricts himself to selling their liberty to the cities which consent to pay him their price.

Martin IV. (1281-85) forced at first to quit Rome troubled by factions, establishes there peace with the aid of Charles of Anjou. The pontiff shows himself better disposed toward that prince than was Nicholas III. Moreover he has divined the true designs of Michael Paleologos, and prepares to excommunicate him. What had taken place at Constantinople since the general council of Lyons ? After the departure of the Greek ambassadors for this council, the patriarch Joseph retired into a monastery to wait the result. The Emperor Michael, by urgency of threats, obtained from the clergy its consent to the primacy of the See of Rome, to the appeals, and the insertion of the pope's name in the prayers ; but they exacted from that prince an oath that he would oblige no one to add anything to the symbol. The ambassadors return with papal nuncios toward the end of 1274. The patriarch Joseph is deposed ; John Veccus takes his place ; Gregory X. is mentioned in the prayers, the Greek clergy ratify the union. But soon oppositions of various kinds manifest themselves among the people ; rebellions burst out. The violence of Michael exasperates minds ; a crowd of people disperse into countries where that prince is not recognised,—Morea, Achaia, Thessaly, Colchis. Michael sends new ambassadors to Rome to confirm the union (1277). They have besides the secret mission of learning the dispositions of Charles, King of Sicily, the principal object of the Greek emperor's solicitude. Charles, breathing out anger, incessantly entreats the pope to permit him to march on Constantinople. Nicholas III. refuses his consent, and retains the ambassadors until the following year. After their departure, he sends to Constantinople four Franciscans in the quality of legates. They are charged to request that the patriarch and the bishops shall make their profession of faith according to the formulary which is sent to them, that the symbol be sung among the Greeks as among the Latins, with the addition *And of the Son*, as also to agree to a truce during which they shall treat of peace for Michael Paleologos with Charles of Sicily and his son-in-law Philip, titular emperor of Constantinople since the death of his father Baldwin II. But Paleologos is no longer in a position to conclude anything. Discontent is universal. His subjects, even his relatives withstand him. Two sons of Michael direct an insurrection; another rising declares itself in Natolia. The Latins who occupy Thebes, Athens, Negropont, and the Morea send succours to the insurgents. At the arrival of the legates, Michael invites his clergy to employ consideration in regard to them, protesting, that, whatever happens, there shall be no change in the usages of the Greeks; nor addition to the symbol. The Greek clergy wrote to the pope in ambiguous and evasive terms; the emperor repeats in a letter his profession of faith and the oath made in his name in the general council, without saying anything of the new demands of the legates, which are not even mentioned (1279).

At last eyes open in Rome. It is understood that peace is a pure illusion, and that apart from the emperor, the patriarch, and some others, it is universally repelled. Thus the ambassadors whom Paleologos sends at the time of the promotion of Martin IV. are ill received. The new pope, at the solicitation of King Charles, chooses that moment to excommunicate the Emperor of Constantinople, as promoter of the schisms and heresies of the Greeks.

But in the year 1297 Michael entered into a conspiracy

plotted by John Procida, a Neapolitan lord, against the King of Sicily, whom the rigour of his government and the arrogance of the French had made generally odious. Procida put himself into relations with the Greek emperor, with the pope, Nicholas III., and with Peter III., King of Aragon, who put forward a claim to the throne of Sicily, as husband of Constance, sole daughter of Mainfroy. The pope approves the enterprise; Michael supplies money to arm a fleet; Peter of Aragon prepares it in Catalonia. The death of Nicholas does not put a stop to the conspiracy. It bursts out in Palermo, the 30th of March 1282, the day of the passover; the French are cut down. This massacre, called the *Sicilian Vespers*, spreads over all the island. Michael Paleologos dies in the month of December of the same year. He had succeeded, by an apparent zeal for the union, to turn aside the perils with which the power of Charles of Anjou threatened him; and when at last his policy is laid open, the rising in Sicily creates for Charles embarrassments which allow him to think of the conquest of Constantinople no longer. The new emperor, Andronicos, free to act according to his own pleasure, immediately renounces the pretended union. A strong reaction makes itself felt; the churches are purified; penance is imposed on the partizans of the pope; the patriarch Veccus is banished.

In Sicily, while Charles of Anjou besieges Messina, Peter III., King of Aragon, disembarks and receives the crown at Palermo (1282). He is excommunicated by the pope, who commands a crusade to be preached against him, and gives the kingdom of Aragon to one of the sons of Philip the Bold, King of France. A considerable reinforcement of French troops having arrived in Pouille, Peter III., to paralyse the effect of it, proposes a duel in the plains of Bordeaux to Charles of Anjou, who allows himself to be taken by it. While that prince foolishly goes to meet an adversary who takes care not to present himself, his son Charles is made prisoner in a naval combat and conducted into Catalonia. King Charles of Anjou dies overwhelmed with vexations (1285). He has for successor Charles II., his son, called the limping.

Philip the bold, accepting for his son the crown of Aragon, leads an army of crusaders to the conquest of the country. Maladies soon oblige him to retire; he dies at Perpignan (1285).

Peter of Aragon survives him by only six weeks. His Spanish states pass to Alphonso, his eldest son, and Sicily to James, his second son. Pope Honorius IV. (1285-87) excommunicates James and Constance, his mother, as accomplices in the revolt of the Sicilians. Charles II. of Anjou recovers his liberty in virtue of a treaty concluded with Alphonso of Aragon (1288). Nicholas IV. (1288-92) disapproves the conditions of that act, annuls it and excommunicates the two brothers Alphonso and James. He solemnly crowns at Rome Charles II., who does homage to him for the kingdom of Sicily. Finally peace is concluded between the houses of France and Aragon, in presence of the legates of the pope. The king of Rome gives up his right on Aragon, and Alphonso enters into an engagement to constrain his mother and his brother to renounce Sicily; but that prince dies some months afterwards. Despite the summonses, prohibitions, and excommunications of the pope, James leaves the government of Sicily to Frederic, his younger brother, and repairs to Saragossa, where he is crowned King of Aragon (1291).

At the same time, news is received in Italy of the capture of Acre, the last possession of the Christians in Palestine. Notwithstanding the efforts of Gregory X., no effective succours had been sent into that country. The levy of tithes had given occasion to great difficulties; what had been gathered was turned to another use (1282). Most of the princes had returned into Europe. The affair of Sicily occupied France and a good part of Italy and Spain. In the rest of the Italian peninsula, the Genoese were at war with the Pisans, and there reigned a spirit of independence difficult to restrain. Intestine dissensions distracted Castille. Rodolph, king of the Romans, took pains to confirm his power. Edward the first, king of England, was alone free in his actions; but he had already passed eighteen months in Palestine, and seemed little desirous to return to it.

The oriental Christians, left to themselves, had not known how to live under friendly relations. Everything was full of troubles in the countries of Antioch and Tripolis (1279). Henry II., king of Cyprus, had seized Acre, and had been crowned king of Jerusalem at Tyre (1286). After having made a truce with the Sultan of Egypt, who had just laid Tripolis in ruins, he returned to Cyprus, leaving the guarding of Acre to his brother (1288). At the solicitation of the king of Cyprus and Jerusalem, pope Nicholas IV. had a crusade preached with a crowd of exhortations and indulgences (1290). The king of England takes up the cross. But Philip the handsome, king of France, declines the proposal that he should guard the holy land until the general movement into it. The pope sends a troop of crusaders who break the truce with the Saracens. The Sultan of Egypt besieges the city of Acre, and carries it by assault (April 1291). All the inhabitants are killed or captured, the city is pillaged and destroyed. The king Henry had embarked during the night with his soldiers and three thousand other persons. The inhabitants of Tyre abandon their city and make their escape by sea. Berytus makes no resistance. The Latins retain nothing in the country. All who can flee repair to Cyprus. At the news of the catastrophe, Nicholas IV. attempts to reanimate the zeal of the princes. He tries to reconcile the Venetians and the Genoese. The prelates receive order to preach the crusade. Councils assemble. The pope addresses letters to Andronicus Paleologus, to the emperor of Trebisonde, to the kings of Armenia, Iberia, Georgia, and even to the Khan of the Tartars. Philip the handsome, solicited by ambassadors, cares little for Palestine. Edward, king of England, shows a more friendly disposition; but his zeal seems at bottom to be only a pretext in order to get the tithes. Rodolph of Hapsburg, in whom the pope had some hope, dies in the month of September 1291; his successor, Adolphus of Nassau, is neither rich nor powerful. Nicholas IV. himself dies the following year; and the division which arises among the cardinals leaves the see vacant two years and three months.

Every serious thought of another crusade seems to vanish. These enterprises, as foolishly conceived as imprudently conducted, entailed the loss of several millions of men, and swallowed up immense sums, which had been better thrown away. They broke into fragments and ruined the Greek empire, from that time an easy prey to the Ottomans. But the western churches and monasteries were enriched thereby. The popes had found in them means to satisfy their avarice and ambition. They had been enabled to obtain considerable imposts, to raise armies led by their legates, and, with the aid of indulgences, to impel innumerable multitudes, not into Palestine only, but also against the dissidents of Europe, against emperors, kings, and princes, who were declared heretics as soon as they gave umbrage to the Court of Rome, or refused to obey its absolute orders. Accordingly, the temporal authority of the holy see declined at the same time as the spirit for the crusades grew weak. The fall of the pontifical omnipotence will closely follow the abandonment of the holy land.

END OF VOLUME SECOND.

TURNBULL AND SPEARS, PRINTERS, EDINBURGH.

www.ingramcontent.com/pod-product-compliance
Lightning Source LLC
Chambersburg PA
CBHW021209230426
43667CB00006B/620